Organisation of Housekeeping Management

Dr. Raj Kumar Singh
D.H.C.T. Mangt. (W.B.)
P.G.D.B. Mangt. (U.P.)
C.F.N. (Delhi)
MHCIMA (London)
Ph.D. (Management)
Director
'SAMS' Institute of Hotel Management,
Varanasi

AMAN PUBLICATIONS
NEW DELHI

Published by :
Rajiv Jain for Aman Publications
LG-4A, Ganpati Bhawan, 4675-B/21, Ansari Road,
Darya Ganj, New Delhi-110002
Ph. : 23255012, 23282127
E-mail: sshjbs@yahoo.com

First Published 2005

ISBN–81–8204–006-X

Sole Distributor :
Jindal Book Services
LG-4A, Ganpati Bhawan,
4675-B/21, Ansari Road,
Darya Ganj, New Delhi-110002

Laser Typesetting by :
Deep Printers, New Delhi-110002

Printed by :
Tarun Offset, Delhi, India

Preface

A characteristic common to all hotels, regardless of size and category, is the need for housekeeping services, which can range from very sophisticated to a simple matter of "refreshing" rooms once a week. For instance, a luxury hotel, casino, or resort usually requires that the rooms be impeccably clean, that the bed linen is changed every time the bed is used, and that turndown service is provided daily. On the other hand, the service for a university residence room might consist in just providing the tenant with a fresh set of sheets every Monday morning.

Housekeeping is an important component of the lodging segment of the hospitality industry for which skill standards should be developed. The function of housekeeping is to create clean, safe and healthy environments in a variety of settings. Mid-range service hotels generally require that guestrooms are thoroughly cleaned daily, that bed and bathroom linen is changed every day, and that 24-hour housekeeping service is provided seven days a week. In any case, because housekeeping services must always be provided, the management of the housekeeping department in every lodging establishment is of critical importance to the success of the property. It is essential that future graduates of hospitality programs understand the options that the industry offers regarding housekeeping management positions.

The present volume is an essential practical introduction to the field of housekeeping management. With expanded attention to leadership and training, budgeting and cost control, and the increasingly vital responsibility for environmentally safe cleaning, it also includes the latest developments in the industry. For students in hotel and restaurant management and professionals seeking to enhance their management capacities, this book continues to be an indispensable resource for leading a winning housekeeping operation in any establishment, from the smallest bed-and-breakfast to the largest luxury hotels.

Contents

Preface

1. Organisation of Housekeeping Management 1
2. Staffing Patterns 48
3. Technical Skills 86
4. Human Resource Management 155
5. Maintenance of Culinary Services 200
6. Risk Management 255
7. Waste Management 277

Index 304

1

Organisation of Housekeeping Management

Hotels and other accommodations are as diverse as the many families and business travelers they accommodate. The industry includes all types of lodging, from upscale hotels to RV parks. Motels, resorts, casino hotels, bed-and-breakfast inns, and boarding houses also are included.

Establishments vary greatly in size and in the services they provide. Hotels and motels make up the majority of establishments and tend to provide more services than do other lodging places. There are five basic types of hotels—commercial, resort, residential, extended-stay, and casino. Most hotels and motels are commercial properties that cater mainly to business people, tourists, and other travelers who need accommodations for a brief stay. Commercial hotels and motels usually are located in cities or suburban areas and operate year round. Larger properties offer a variety of services for their guests, including coffee shops, restaurants, and cocktail lounges with live entertainment. Some even provide gift shops, newsstands, barber and beauty shops, laundry and valet services, theater and airline counters, swimming pools, and fitness centers and health spas.

Larger hotels and motels often have banquet rooms, exhibit halls, and spacious ballrooms to accommodate conventions, business meetings, wedding receptions, and other social gatherings. Conventions and business meetings are major sources of revenue for these hotels and motels. Some *commercial hotels* are known as conference hotels—fully self-contained entities specifically designed for meetings. They provide physical and recreational facilities for meetings, in addition to state-of-the-art audiovisual and technical equipment.

Resort hotels and motels offer luxurious surroundings with a variety of recreational facilities such as swimming pools, golf courses, tennis courts, gamerooms, and health spas, as well as planned social activities and entertainment. Resorts are located primarily in vacation destinations near mountains, the seashore, or other attractions. As a result, the business of many resorts fluctuates with the season. Some resort hotels and motels provide additional convention and conference facilities to encourage customers to combine business with pleasure. During their off season, these establishments solicit conventions, sales meetings, and incentive tours to fill their otherwise empty rooms.

Residential hotels provide living quarters for permanent and semipermanent residents. They combine the comfort of apartment living with the convenience of hotel services. Many have dining rooms and restaurants that also are open to the general public.

Extended-stay hotels combine features of a resort and a residential hotel. Typically, guests use these hotels for a minimum of 5 consecutive nights. These facilities usually provide rooms with fully equipped kitchens, entertainment systems, ironing boards and irons, office spaces with computer and telephone lines, access to fitness centers, and other amenities.

Casino hotels provide lodging in hotel facilities with a casino on the premises. The casino provides table wagering games and may include other gambling activities, such as slot machines and sports betting. Casino hotels generally offer a full range of services and amenities and may also contain conference and convention facilities.

In addition to hotels and motels, bed-and-breakfast inns, recreational vehicle (RV) parks, campgrounds, and rooming and boarding houses provide lodging for overnight guests. Bed-and-breakfast inns provide short-term lodging in private homes or small buildings converted for this purpose and are characterized by highly personalized service and inclusion of a full breakfast in the room rate. Their appeal is quaintness, with unusual service and decor.

RV parks and recreational camps cater to people who enjoy recreational camping at moderate prices. Some parks and campgrounds provide service stations, general stores, shower and toilet facilities, and coin-operated laundries. While some are designed for overnight travelers only, others are for vacationers who stay longer. Some camps provide accommodations, such as cabins and fixed campsites, and other amenities, such as food services, recreational facilities and equipment, and organized recreational activities. Examples of these overnight camps include, children's camps, family vacation camps, hunting and fishing camps, and outdoor adventure retreats that offer trail riding, white-water rafting, hiking, and similar activities.

Other short-term lodging facilities in this industry include guesthouses, or small cottages located on the same property as a main residence, and youth hostels—dormitory-style hotels with few frills, occupied mainly by students traveling on low budgets. Also included are rooming and boarding houses, such as fraternity houses, sorority houses, off-campus dormitories, and workers' camps. These establishments provide temporary or longer term accommodations that may serve as a principal residence for the period of occupancy. These establishments also may provide services such as housekeeping, meals, and laundry services.

In recent years, hotels, motels, camps, and recreational and RV parks affiliated with national chains have been growing rapidly. To the traveler, familiar chain establishments represent dependability and quality at predictable rates. National corporations own many chains, although several others are independently owned but affiliated with a chain through a franchise agreement.

Increases in competition and in the sophistication of travelers have induced the chains to provide lodging to serve a variety of customer budgets and accommodation preferences. In general, these lodging places may be grouped into properties that offer luxury, all-suite, moderately priced, and economy accommodations. The numbers of limited-service or economy chain properties—economy lodging without lobbies, restaurants, lounges, and meeting rooms—have been growing. These properties are not as costly to build and operate. They appeal to budget-conscious family vacationers and travelers who are willing to sacrifice amenities for lower room prices.

While economy chains have become more prevalent, the movement in the hotel and lodging industry is towards more extended-stay properties. In addition fully equipped kitchenettes and laundry services, the extended-stay market offers guest amenities such as in-room access to the Internet and grocery shopping. This segment of the hotels and other accommodations industry has eliminated traditional hotel lobbies and 24-hour personnel, and housekeeping is usually done only about once a week. This helps to keep costs to a minimum.

All-suite facilities, especially popular with business travelers, offer a living room and a bedroom. These accommodations are aimed at travelers who require lodging for extended stays, families traveling with children, and business people needing to conduct small meetings without the expense of renting an additional room.

Increased competition among establishments in this industry has spurred many independently owned and operated hotels and other lodging places to join national or international reservation systems, which allow travelers to make multiple reservations for lodging, airlines, and car rentals with one telephone call. Nearly all hotel chains operate online reservation systems through the Internet.

Lodging Management

To lodge means to furnish guests with room or quarters, generally on a temporary basis. This broad definition implies that the lodging industry is quite diverse, for the renting of living space can range from a simple room in a boarding house to a spacious suite in a luxury hotel or a bungalow in a lavish resort.

Since the beginning of recorded time, people have travelled and therefore have been in need of lodging. For instance, the excavated ruins of Pompeii in Italy include houses of rest and solace where, as long ago as 79 A.D., wayfarers and seamen of the time were able to relax and be entertained for a fee. Lodging facilities that were used for economic purposes were built along transportation routes where travelling parties found it convenient to make rest stops en route to their destinations.

In Marco Polo's time, rest areas were strategically placed at a distance of a day's ride by caravan. Polo was able to travel from Venice to the Mongol Empire of Kublai Khan in Central Asia by making scheduled stops along the way, where food and safe shelter were available. Chaucer's Canterbury Tales, written around 1390 in England, contains lively descriptions of inn-keeping practices of the time. In Don Quixote, many of Cervantes' ideals are put into practice at an inn in La Mancha, Spain. What we know today as inns had their origin in England some centuries ago, the term meaning "a public house that provides lodging for travellers and others." These taverns with rooms for rent were usually located along highways to provide a convenient overnight stay for those travelling by coach. The introduction of railways in the nineteenth century created the need for a large number of these hostelries along the numerous lines that crisscrossed the country. Today, the term inn implies a small hotel, although properties called "inns" often contain a large number of rooms; for example the Holiday Inn Crowne Plaza in New Orleans has 439 guestrooms. The term hotel derives from the French hostel. The modern French word hotel suggests "a more or less commodious establishment with up-to-date appointments," though this was not necessarily true one hundred years ago. Today, the term hotel defines a lodging establishment offering accommodation, food and beverage, and amenities to guests.

The New Orleans' Windsor Court Hotel, which consumers have rated as one of the best hotels in the United States, advertises meeting facilities, outdoor pool, health club, ballrooms, concierge services, five-diamond dining room, chamber music, and 24-hour suite service. Nightly rates at the Windsor Court range from $320 for regular guestrooms to $990 for two-bedroom suites. The first spas were operated in Europe and consisted of resorts located by mineral springs, which were believed to have curative powers. Today, spas offer a wide array of health-related services ranging from curative massage and mud baths to weightloss programs.

Besides hotels, motels and resorts the lodging industry today offers a variety of establishments aimed at fulfilling the needs of the current market. The most common are:

— Bed and Breakfast Inns

— Time-Share Condominiums

— Cruise Ships

— Institutional Lodging Establishments

— Casinos

Bed-and-breakfast inn

Bed-and-breakfast inns are usually small, privately owned establishments located in suburban and rural locations. They are often uniquely appointed converted private homes that cater to travellers seeking a homey, personal environment.

Bed-and-breakfast inn

Time-share condominiums are apartments, villas, or bungalows usually built near popular vacation spots that are sold to individual owners who use them or rent them out to transient guests. Time-share owners also have the option of trading with other owners of units located in different parts of the country or the world.

Cruise ships

Cruise ships can be described as floating luxury hotels/resorts that provide most of the same services and amenities as properties located on land. Having become quite popular in the vacation and convention markets, cruise ships are one of the fastest growing segments of the hospitality industry.

Institutional Lodging Establishments

Institutional lodging is provided by housing facilities that are integral parts of institutional organizations, such as hospitals, retirement homes, universities, and colleges. In some cases this type of lodging requires limited services, such as weekly cleaning or catered meals, which are provided by contracting companies. With the adoption of gaming by a large number of Native American tribes, casinos have grown in popularity in many states of the United States.

Casinos

Casinos are generally first-class hotels that provide elaborate facilities for gambling, ranging from the ubiquitous slot machine to the sophisticated baccarat or roulette tables. These highly profitable establishments often offer luxurious lodging and lavish entertainment at low cost to attract potential customers.

Lodging properties

Lodging properties can be independently owned, owned by a multi-unit chain, franchised, or managed by a management company. Properties that are independently owned are not affiliated with any multiple -property entity and are usually managed by their owners. This type of property still represents the largest segment of the lodging industry. A typical in dependently owned establishment is small in size and is located in a relatively small community.

There are advantages and disadvantages to independent operation: on the positive side, independent lodging establishments can provide guests with unique, personalized service while saving royalty and management fees that otherwise would have to be paid to franchisors and/or management companies. On the negative side, such properties may not have name recognition to travellers, they lack collective advertising power, and they are unable to benefit from a national/ international reservation system. Often, independently owned and managed properties join reservation referral systems and marketing associations, such as Best Western International, Leading Hotels and Resorts, or Utell International.

Chain properties operate under the direct control of the chain's headquarters. Establishments belonging to the same chain display the same logo and offer identical services by category. For instance, a Hilton four-star hotel must provide similar service and amenities whether it is located in Florida or in Oregon. This assures guests of consistency in price, room layout, menus, sports facilities, and so on. There exist a large number of chains in the world, such as Ritz Carlton and Loews in the United States, Four Seasons in Canada, and Grupo Sol Melia in Spain. An effective way for owners of lodging properties to take advantage of the marketing and central reservation power of chain systems is to contract the right to conduct business displaying the logo of the chain by franchising. However, once the franchise is granted, the franchisee must comply with the corporation's requirements regarding service and amenities to be provided to guests.

When hotel owners lack the operative expertise necessary to manage their properties efficiently, they may choose to contract with a management company. In this case, the owner signs a contract delegating the property's operations to such a company in exchange for either paying a basic fee or allowing the management company to retain an agreed-upon percentage of the revenue or income, or a combination of the two.

Classification of Lodging facilities

Accroding to their sizie the lodging facilities can be classified into:

— *Small*: up to 75 rooms
— *Medium*: from 75 to 200 rooms
— *Large*: from 200 to 500 rooms
— *Very large*: more than 500 rooms

The size of a property can be used to estimate the amount of work required of the housekeeping department on a daily basis to maintain the property.

Lodging properties can also be categorized by service. Economy or budget properties focus on meeting the basic needs of the travelling public-that is, clean, comfortable rooms that are not expensive. The market segments typically attracted to economy properties are guests travelling with children, bus tours, and budget-minded retirees. Many of these properties do not offer food and beverage services except for breakfast, although they all feature TV and some have a swimming pool, whirlpool, and tennis courts. Mid-market properties offer all the amenities expected in a "home -away-from -home setting." Restaurants, coffee shops, bars, luggage service, meeting rooms, health club, and room service are generally offered in such properties. The quality of bed linen, towels, room furniture, lobby decor, and customer service must be good or very good. Travellers who frequent properties of this type are business people, individual tourists, conventioneers, and guests wishing to receive a guaranteed level of excellent service.

Often, mid-market properties feature suites that consist of a bedroom, adjacent living room, and a kitchenette with refrigerator. Suites are very appealing to families with children or to two couples travelling together. Luxury properties offer world-class service, which includes any type of convenience that would be expected by any traveller in any country in the world. Committed to the ultimate in hospitality, luxury properties may feature extravagant amenities like Godiva or other imported chocolates, speciality toiletry items, slippers, silk robes, and special services like executive floors, concierge, foreign language translators, nanny, and private secretary.

The American Automobile Association (AAA) is the most common rater of lodging establishments in the United States. As a service to its members, this organization provides travel guides that are updated annually describing the properties and evaluating their services. The ratings are determined by field inspectors who base their decisions on thorough evaluations of the properties' design, decor, fittings, comfort, and of their levels of service, cleanliness and upkeep. In general, AAA awards three diamonds to economy establishments while mid-market properties are assigned four diamonds. Invariably, luxury hotels and resorts receive a rating of five diamonds. In some countries, an official branch of the government performs the classification of lodging properties to ensure that the quality of their lodging establishments is consistent.

Relations with other Departments

Relation with front desk

The communication between the housekeeping department and the front desk is greatly improved when the property uses a computerized system. For instance, when a guest checks out, the front desk clerk enters the departure in the computer and it appears instantly in the housekeeping monitor. When housekeeping has rooms ready to be sold, the information is entered in the system and it too shows up quickly in the front desk terminal.

Relation with maintenance department

The relationship between housekeeping and the maintenance department -must be as close as that with the front office. Every piece of equipment, fixtures, and furniture in the guestrooms, hallways, linen and laundry rooms, public areas, and employee locker rooms must be in perfect working order at all times. The number of items that may be in need of repairs in a single guestroom can be substantial: beds, chairs, desks, TVs, radios, lights, doors, toilets, faucets, walls, heating, air conditioning,

and so on. It is therefore imperative that good communication between the two departments exists at all times. For instance, if a guestroom lock is broken, maintenance must be notified, the room must be put out of order, the work performed, the area cleaned, and the room put back in vacant ready status.

There are two types of maintenance performed by the engineering department in hospitality properties. Regular maintenance is performed when an item is broken and needs to be repaired. In this case, a three-part work order form is filled out by a housekeeping employee who forwards two copies to engineering and keeps the duplicate filed until the work is completed.

When work is completed, one of the copies is returned to housekeeping for comparison, the work is inspected, and the area cleaned. When a problem is urgent and engineering does not promptly address it, housekeeping generates a second request work order to remind that department that the work must be completed. If the repair needs to be done in order to be able to sell the room that day, an urgent request is sent to engineering so that the work is given priority over other nonessential jobs.

The orderly flow of information between housekeeping and engineering about items or areas in need of attention is of critical importance. As the housekeeping department staff is directly involved in cleaning most sections of the property, they are in the best position to find areas in need of maintenance or repair. Preventive maintenance consists of inspecting guestrooms and other areas on a regular basis to identify repair and maintenance needs. In most hotels, the executive housekeeper and the chief engineer cooperate in combining room cleaning with preventive maintenance programs.

Relation with human resources departments

Communication between the housekeeping and human resources departments is necessary when considering personnel staffing. When an employee is needed in the housekeeping department, an employee requisition is filled out and sent to human resources to initiate the process. After receiving the request, human resources advertises for the position, pre-screens the candidates, conducts the first interview, and checks references. The final candidates are then sent to housekeeping for a second interview and hiring selection.

Human resources is usually also involved in the orientation of new housekeeping employees, at which time the company's philosophy, compensation package, pay schedule, and rules and regulations are explained in detail to the new worker. This department also ensures that the new employee fills out all necessary forms related to legal residency, income tax, and personal information. Good communication with human resources will result in hiring the right employees to fill housekeeping vacancies.

Relation with food and beverage department

Food and beverage is the second major revenue center in the property after the rooms division. The food and beverage division in large hotels comprises the property's kitchens, restaurants, coffee shops, cafeterias, bars, lounges, banquets, catering services, clubs, and room service. In large hotels, the housekeeping department should only be indirectly involved in the cleaning of food and beverage outlets. However, the communication between food and beverage and housekeeping is necessary in some specific areas.

There must be good cooperation regarding the pickup of room service material from guestroom areas. Housekeeping must see to it that hallways are free from trays and carts placed there by guests and section housekeepers; therefore, calls to room service must be regularly placed to remind this department to clear all areas.

The laundry room must provide the food and beverage department with clean napery on a daily basis. This often means that the laundry manager must request that the soiled linen be delivered to the laundry room on time, properly sorted out, and free from food scraps and table debris. Furnishing clean

uniforms to cooks, waiters, and bartenders is also usually the responsibility of the housekeeping department. As communication with food and beverage service personnel is traditionally difficult, efforts must be made to establish good relationships between departments.

The primary goal of the sales and marketing division is to sell the products and services offered by the property. Given that cleanliness is one of the most important reasons for guests to choose a particular lodging property, the onus of providing this critical service falls on the housekeeping department. There must be good communication between sales and housekeeping if customer satisfaction is to be achieved.

For instance, if sales and marketing has guaranteed late check-out to a large group of guests attending a convention without notifying housekeeping, some of the rooms might not be cleaned in time to be available for a tour group scheduled to check-in that same evening. If sales and marketing has promised that forty rooms will be available for early check-in to a company attending a conference at the property and housekeeping has not been notified, there might not be enough manpower that morning to clean the rooms on time. Communication between sales and housekeeping is also necessary when specific rooms or suites must be available for inspection to meeting planners who are considering the property for a possible convention.

Equipment Management

The housekeeping categories used by the housekeeping department usually include: housekeeping salaries and wages, payroll taxes and benefits, and other expenses. Salaries and wages include those of the entire housekeeping department; payroll taxes and benefits include the operator's share of additional costs related to payroll; the category of other expenses encompasses any other cost incurred by the housekeeping department that is not payroll-related.

The buying function in lodging chains is often centralised. Items like soap, linen, mattresses, pillows, furniture, and fixtures are procured by the company's purchasing department and shipped to the different units on request. Purchasing in large independent properties is done by the purchasing agent, who is a specialised buyer in charge of procuring products for all departments in the property. Smaller properties often allow the department heads to purchase goods for their respective areas of responsibility. In any case, it should be the job of the executive housekeeper to always pretest and approve all items used in the housekeeping department and decide the quantities and the specifications of the products to be bought. It should not be the job of the purchasing agent, or any other person for that matter, to purchase material and supplies without the consent of the executive housekeeper. It is also important to solicit the input of janitors, section housekeepers, housepersons, and laundry personnel on the appropriate characteristics of the items that in the end are to be used by them. All merchandise purchased should have precise specifications, which are descriptions of the products' quality and factors that should reflect precisely the performance needs for each particular institution. Specifications should be stated clearly, giving the information needed to assure proper identification. For instance, a luxury resort does probably require the best bed linen money can buy, while a small, inexpensive motel may just need bed linen of fair quality. Before buying a product, prices should be obtained from at least three different vendors.

Product price and vendor dependability and service should be reviewed once or twice every three months. Purchasing decisions should be made based not only on price but on quality, suitability, and storage availability as well. There may be three types of entities involved in the purchasing function: producers, middlemen, and consumers.

Producers manufacture the items to be sold and sometimes sell the products directly to the consumers. Middlemen may bring the different commodities to their own warehouses from which they distribute them to consumers or act as order takers

and have the goods shipped directly from the manufacturer. Middlemen always add a charge to the product's price.

Usually, the fewer middlemen through which a product passes, the lower the price. However, although purchasing directly from the manufacturer may be less expensive, very often lodging properties benefit from buying through brokers (middlemen) because these can provide better service and in some cases employee training at no cost. Another disadvantage from buying directly from manufacturers is that they often require the purchase of large quantities of goods. In this case, the money saved because of lower price is upset by the cost of having assets tied down for long periods of time.

There is great competition among purveyors of cleaning and guest supplies. Some will lower their prices initially to obtain the property's account. Others may offer prizes or kickbacks to get their foot in the door.Executive housekeepers should be aware of these often unethical tactics and decline any "free" personal gifts. If the executive housekeeper needs to order products directly from a manufacturer, filling out a formal purchase order may be necessary. The purchase order is, in essence, a sales contract stating the specifications of the product to be delivered and the conditions involving payment. When the merchandise has been previously bought by the property's buyer and stored in the main storeroom, the housekeeping department usually needs to fill out a requisition form before the products can be obtained. Executive housekeepers should always be on the lookout for new items on the market. Testing for new, better, or less expensive products often leads to improving the department's bottom line.

The range of inventory used in the rooms division of lodging operations is quite large, varying from textiles, guestroom furnishing and amenities to sophisticated department equipment and supplies. The executive housekeeper must control the function of purchasing by defining clearly what is to be procured, who will be in charge of the buying, what specifications are to be considered, and what quantities will be needed. The person in charge of purchasing must consistently provide the needed quantities of products in housekeeping inventories. Although in some cases purchasing is done by the corporate office or by the property's purchasing agent, the executive housekeeper is ultimately responsible for the cost and results of what is purchased. For some products, linen for instance, pars need to be established; for others, for example soaps and paper products, maximum and minimum quantities are set up. Pars can be defined as the number of required on-hand items to perform housekeeping operations. In the case of linens, for instance, the optimum number of pars is 4. This means that ideally the property should have on hand one set of sheets and pillowcases set up in the guestroom beds at any given time, another set being laundered, an additional set ready to go in floor closets and room attendant carts, and one final set on reserve.

For guest and cleaning supplies, the maximum quantity is the greatest number of units that should be in stock at any given time, while the minimum quantity refers to the fewest number of units. For example, the maximum and minimum number of cases of soap could be 35 and 25 respectively. That means that if at any given time the soap inventory is above 35, the product is overstocked. On the other hand, if the number of cases falls below 25, additional supplies must be ordered. This system eliminates the risk of overstocking or of running out of products. The receiving function of goods ordered must also be controlled.

Unless adequate inspection and receiving procedures are used, the best purchasing system may fail because it is at this point that determination must be made of whether or not the products meet the specifications and quantities of the order previously placed. Failing to inspect the merchandise adequately may result in higher costs, lower quality, theft, and fraud. On receiving a shipment, the goods should be compared with those listed on the receiving sheet or purchase order to verify the correctness of the delivery. If the goods meet the prearranged requirements, they are accepted by signing the invoice or delivery memo. If the products do not meet inspection requirements, they should be refused and a notation indicating the reasons for refusing the delivery made. The function of storing merchandise must also be controlled adequately.

Access to storerooms must be limited to authorised personnel only. The storeroom should be locked off -hours and a record should be kept of the person entering it and of the merchandise taken. Valuable items like towels and some guest supplies should be stored in an area that remains locked at all times. The storage area should be designed to hold the specific products stored in it; bottom shelving levels should be at least 10 inches off the floor to ensure adequate ventilation and to allow for cleaning underneath.

A rotation system should be established by which oldest stock is placed in front and issued first. In large properties, housekeeping items may be stored in the main storeroom. In this case, the housekeeping department will need to fill a requisition form to request products. Every requisition should bear the signature of a person designated by the executive housekeeper to sign it. Nothing should be requested without an approved signature.

When products are stored in the housekeeping department, issuing controls must also be established so that the merchandise is handed out to authorised personnel only. Floor closet storage should also be locked at all times and access limited to the section housekeepers, housepersons, or supervisors in charge of the area. To account for the cost of housekeeping operating assets used, physical inventories are conducted regularly, in most cases monthly. Linens, uniforms, and cleaning and guest supplies inventories are taken by counting all items on hand and listing them on a physical inventory form.

Laundry chemicals may be included in the cleaning supplies category or counted separately for better control. The purpose of taking physical inventories is to find out what amount of items for each category is on hand and to work out its current market value. Once the value of items used is ascertained, the costs are expensed against the revenue produced for the same period and the percentages obtained compared to the amounts budgeted for the different categories.

The cost of items used is determined by adding the total purchases during the month to the opening inventory and subtracting the merchandise on hand as per the physical inventory for every category. Physical inventories are difficult to conduct as all items that need to be accounted for must be counted one by one. In the case of linens, for instance, linens are found in guestrooms, laundry room, linen room, floor closets, room attendant carts, etc. To keep tight control on valuable items, for example imported chocolates for special guests, a perpetual inventory system may be implemented.

Executive housekeepers must administer and maintain their proprieties' fixed assets classified as Furniture, Fixtures and Equipment (FF&E), Software, and Department Equipment. Although new establishments are usually handed over to the management team equipped with allitems needed for operation, the executive housekeeper is directly involved in the replacement, refurbishing, and upkeep of most fixed asset items in the property. For this reason, executive housekeepers must have appropriate knowledge of the assets that are under their control.

Regardless of their type of service, lodging properties must maintain interior design consistency standards throughout the building. Whether a property has been classified as economy, mid-market, or luxury, its guestroom and public area design, colour patterns, fabric and upholstery quality, and overall appearance must befit the category they represent. Doing piecemeal refurbishing or renovating must always be avoided. Colours, for instance, must be complementary. In general, blue is a complement of orange, green of red, and yellow of violet. Using several light tints and shades of the same colour makes rooms seem larger, while full-intensity hues tend to make the room seem compact. Adjoining walls should be painted the same colour to provide a sense of continuity.

When covering-walls, smaller prints should be used in small rooms and in all cases, colour patterns should be complementary in fabrics, wall coverings, and carpets. Earth tone colours which often used in *art deco* design, such as ocher, mauve, and burgundy, are quite popular in guestroom and lobby outlines. These soothing colours, when combined with terracotta vases, lamp bases, and statuettes, are often found in classic settings and are generally pleasing to most guests.Surfaces look better and last longer when finished with durable materials like marble, granite, and corian. Public areas should be attractively decorated and furnished with special touches to please guests. For instance, lobbies may be fitted with fireplaces, bookcases, and live plants to make them seem more homey and inviting to travellers.

Executive housekeepers are generally responsible for the refurbishing and upkeep of the furniture in guestroom, public, and employee areas. Furniture should be solidly built, easy to maintain, functional, and attractive. It is not advisable to purchase pieces of furniture directly from a catalogue; instead, the executive housekeeper should carefully examine samples to ensure that the products have been built to withstand repeated rough use.

All furniture tops should be plastic-laminated or finished with water-repellent polyurethane to avoid scratches, rings, and stains caused by abusive treatment and spilled liquids. Desk chairs should have padded backs to provide comfort to guests and prevent wood from hitting desktops. Furniture dotted with glides or casters will prevent carpet damage when pushed or pulled around the room.

Luggage racks are better if built-in and fitted with wall-protecting panels, as there is a greater likelihood that the luggage will bump against and deteriorate walls when detached racks are used. Desks should be large enough to accommodate a desktop computer and a fax machine. TV/VCR units should be an actual piece of furniture, rather than simply a conventional metal stand, and should be fitted with 180-degree swivels so that guests can see the screen from anywhere in the room.

Case furniture such as chests of drawers, credenzas, armoires, desks, and bureaus also should be purchased with durability in mind. Drawers should be equipped with nylon ball bearings and slide glides so that they don't jam when opening and closing. In general, guestrooms should provide a warm residential look; for instance, love seats and armchairs can replace the standard chairs so often found in hotel rooms.

Upholstery fibers may be natural, synthetic, or plastic. Natural fabrics, such as cotton, linen, silk, and wool, are rich looking and long wearing but expensive and delicate to maintain because they stain easily. Synthetic fibers are less expensive and easy to clean but they are less elegant and more likely to generate static electricity. Often, upholstered materials are a blend of natural and synthetic fabrics. The greatest advantage of upholstery plastic materials such as vinyl is that they can be easily cleaned by just wiping with a soapy cloth; however, they generally have a duller appearance than natural or blended materials. Upholstery fabrics should be strong enough to withstand repeated shampooing. Treating fabrics With soil-retardant sprays can decrease the need for dry-cleaning the material. It is also important that upholstery fabrics be treated with flame-retardant finishes.

Before putting upholstered furniture fabrics into use, they should be pretested to ascertain the best way to clean the pieces without causing shrinkage or discoloration. Some fabrics can be cleaned with solvent, others can be cleaned with water and detergent, and some only allow for vacuuming. In general, synthetic fabrics such as nylon and plastics such as vinyl are the most stain-resistant and easy-to-clean upholstery materials.

Beds are the central attraction in guestrooms and often a big selling point for travellers when choosing a lodging property. When asked to pay an average of $70.00 per night per room, guests expect to receive a clean, well-maintained sleeping area and a comfortable bed. In commercial operations, beds consist of a frame to support the springs and mattresses and unattached headboards. Bed frames usually consist of metal bars with legs attached to each corner or of a metal or wood platform.

The main advantage of platform frames is that room attendants don't have to vacuum underneath the box frame, thus saving time when cleaning the room. Headboards are mounted on the wall and should match the general design of the room's furniture. It is important to know the composition of the bed structure of each property in order to figure out the maximum member of people that the property can house. Knowing the different types of beds and how many guests can stay in the rooms will help executive housekeepers plan for bed and bathroom linen and supplies.

Another type of sleeping equipment is the mobile bed. Families on vacation and travelling high school or college groups often require additional sleeping accommodations in guestrooms. The rollaway, or bed on wheels, consists of a folding frame with an attached bed spring body. The mattress in rollaways must be made of latex foam or have very light, flexible innersprings so that they too can fold with the frame.

Because rollaways are unable to provide a comfortable surface to hold the weight of an adult person, they should be recommended only for children or young people to avoid legitimate complaints about the property's not providing adequate acco-mmodation. Cribs are also essential to have in order to accommodate infants or young children. While cribs should be collapsible to save storage space, their extension mechanisms should be kept in good working order to prevent the crib from collapsing when being used.

Dual-purpose sleeping equipment is common in guestrooms. These pieces of furniture provide both seating space and extra sleeping capacity, eliminating the need to roll in a mobile bed on short notice. Sofas, couches, chair-beds, and in-wall beds are the most common dual-purpose pieces of furniture found in lodging properties.

Sofas, couches and chair-beds convert into beds by removing the cushions and pulling out the folding frame and mattress or by dropping the back to the level of the seat. In-wall beds, also called Murphy beds, are concealed in the wall behind a panel, giving the room the appearance of a studio or parlour rather than a bedroom. The wall is balanced in such a way that it can be swung open with a gentle pull on a handle.

The main purpose of bed box springs is to act as shock absorbers between the mattress and the bed frame itself. Box spring coils are more rigid than those of mattresses to provide a firm base for the mattress to rest on. Besides cushioning the mattress, box springs increase the height of beds, giving them a more elegant look. Surveys of favourite guest amenities conducted regularly by hospitality magazines consistently show that guests put comfortable mattresses at the top of the list, second only to cleanliness.

Most mattresses used in lodging operations are of the innerspring type; they have metal coils that support the weight of the sleepers while conforming to their body contours. The strength and number of coils determine the mattress firmness, which may range from medium to super firm.

Heavy-gauge steel wire coils are best, allowing for weights to flex down a specific area without disturbing the space surrounding the pressure points. This allows for two persons of different weights to lie side by side and each get different levels of buoyancy. The firmness of the mattress is determined by the gauge of steel used, the number of turns of each coil, and the way the coils are attached to the mattress frame.

Preferably, the springs should be encased in fabric pockets to provide independent coil action, rather than being attached to each other with wire or hooks. Good mattresses have sufficient padding to cushion the springs beneath and provide a smooth surface.

The padding should be nonallergenic and comply with the government flame-spread regulation, which states that a lighted cigarette should not be able to ignite the insulation. The recommended way to purchase mattresses is to inspect a cutaway section to make sure that the padding is sufficiently dense, that the coils are of fine quality and closely spaced, and that the covering fabric is well attached to the main body.

Lodging properties may also use foam mattresses, especially for their rollaway beds. The synthetic material used in this type of mattress is usually latex foam or urethane. Although less expensive, rubber mattresses do not provide the adequate firmness expected by an adult guest, nor do they last nearly as long as those built with innersprings. Water-filled

mattresses (waterbeds) became quite popular with the public when they were first used in the 1960s, but they soon proved to be inconvenient with lodging operators because they often leaked and because the water had to be heated, which became costly.

Although today's waterbeds are efficiently built with individually filled cells that do not need to be heated because of an insulating foam layer, there doesn't seem to be a great demand for them from lodging guests. Lodging properties, however, should have a few waterbeds to fulfil the request of interested travellers.

Guestrooms and lodging property lobbies are also furnished with accessories such as mirrors, decorations, pictures, and lights, to complement the furniture. The colour and style of fixtures should be balanced with the overall room decor; a vermilion vase, for instance, will probably not match a surrounding of pale yellow hues.

The amount, style, and quality of furnishings will dramatically affect the appearance of rooms. For instance, strategically placed mirrors can give small rooms an illusion of depth; serene motifs in paintings will provide a feeling of tranquillity; triple magnification make-up mirrors and wall-mounted hair dryers in bathrooms are a welcome amenity; a well-stocked mahogany bookcase in the lobby will provide a homey feeling to guests who enjoy reading.

Beautiful carpeting can enhance the appearance of lodging properties and make a lasting impression on guests. On the other hand, discoloured, worn, or dirty carpets are usually sources of guest complaints. The first step in selecting the right carpet is to match its colour, texture, and pattern with the design of the area where it is to be installed. Then, other factors need to be considered, such as determining the anticipated level of wear and tear caused by the intensity of traffic, the location of the carpet, and the budget allocated for it.

When heavy traffic is expected, carpets should feature strong resistance to abrasion, as well as texture retention and anti-soiling and staining characteristics. The location of the carpet should determine specifications such as enhanced colourfastness, antimicrobial protection, resistance to snags, and resilience under rolling loads. Besides durability and stain resistance, carpets in lodging properties should be capable of withstanding repeated cleaning treatment.

Before purchasing carpet, be sure you fully understand the warranty coverage offered by the manufacturer or installer. Warranties for commercial carpets should include protection for wear and tear, colourfastness (fading from sunlight and atmospheric contaminants), tuft bind deterioration, static charges, backing strength, ravelling of seams and edges, and any other manufacturing defects. Carpets must be professionally installed in order to comply with the manufacturer's instructions. If carpeting is not installed properly, it will buckle and wear out fast.

One important component of the installation process is to use a quality carpet cushion or pad that will prolong the life of the carpet. In general, denser, thicker pads yield better results than thinner, softer ones by holding their shapes longer and being more resistant to dirt and stains. In back-of-the-house areas that are subject to traffic of heavy carts and where an impression of luxury and coziness is not necessary, carpets may be glued directly to the floor.

Carpets should be dense to the point of not showing the backing when bending a piece with both hands with the pile facing up. In woven carpets the density of the pile is measured by the number of lengthwise yarns in a 27-inch width of carpet.

Executive housekeepers should have sufficient knowledge of carpet construction to ensure that the right carpet is selected for each area in the property. There are three main elements in the composition of carpets: the pile, or face; the backing, or material to which the pile is secured; and the padding, or cushion on which the carpet rests. Most commercial carpets are tufted, that is, the yam is threaded through the backing material to form loops.

The backing material usually is woven jute or polypropylene with a layer of adhesive latex extended over the material to anchor the tufts. Knitted carpets are made by interlacing together the pile yam and the backing. The process of embedding the pile fibers electrostatically into a layer of adhesive material applied to the backing is called flocking. Weaving is the old-fashioned way of making carpets using conventional looms. The yarns are interlaced together to form the pile and the backing.

As with linen, the yarns woven lengthwise are called the warp and the yarns going across are the wefts. The process of making carpets by compacting the fibers and the backing by mechanically punching them together is called needle punching.

Improper lighting in rooms may discourage guests from staying in a particular establishment. Guests, particularly business travellers, expect to find adequate lighting to be able to work over flat surfaces such as tables and desks, or to read in bed or sitting on a couch or armchair.

Lights of adjustable intensity should be placed strategically so that guests can arrange their preferences to suit their needs; for example, subdued lighting for relaxation or bright lighting for working or entertaining friends. Having three-way lamps or lights activated by rheostats give guests the option to set the mood of the room to their liking.

Floor lamps are not recommended in guestrooms because they can be easily knocked over and they create tripping hazards. Desk lamps should have the on-off switches at the base to reduce the risk of guests burning their fingers on the light bulb or upsetting the shade's balance when reaching around to locate the switch. Lampshades should be made of plastic rather than paper or fabric for longer life.

When choosing fluorescent lighting, warm rather than cool light-giving units should be installed to avoid harsh tones of light. Pink incandescent light bulbs provide tones that enhance the appearance of guests when they look at themselves in the mirror. One advantage of fluorescent lights is that they use less energy and last longer than regular bulbs. In all cases, sufficient wattage must be provided in lamps that guests will use for reading or working purposes.

Long gone are the days when hoteliers could sell rooms equipped with a minimum of basic features. Today's business traveller is putting a new spin on the concept of guestroom equipment. Lodging chains that cater to corporate clientele offer in-room or satellite office support services including computers and fax and copy machines.

Guestrooms are often equipped with multi-line telephones complete with voice mail and PC compatibility; some hotels even provide cellular phones and 24-hour access to translators and information in other languages. Office centers are fitted with hightech office support equipment, such as computers with desktop publishing, video room, and drafting center.

Most hotels today offer TV in-room movie channels, and several chains have added VCRs in the rooms, together with video tape movie vending machines located in the lobby that guests can operate with their credit cards. Refrigerators and microwave ovens are quite common in suite hotels, and coffee-makers, together with selections of coffee and tea blends, are now available in the rooms of most properties.

Wide-screen television sets and high-quality clock radios are a must in four- and five-diamond properties, as are in-room safes. In-room strongboxes are seen as a last-ditch defence for the guests' personal belongings, including items as large as lap-top computers. The locking systems of in-room safes range from ordinary keys to programmable push-buttons, magnetic-lock devices, and the guest's credit card.

Some microprocessor safes automatically lock for 30 minutes after four false attempts to open them. Besides being a great convenience for guests who don't want to line up for safety deposit boxes, in-room safes are effective against thieves and even employees who may use stolen keys to burglarize rooms. Valuables can be stored by guests themselves and remain secure during trips to the pool, jogging around the block, or going out to dinner. Some safes have built-in memory, which enables the front office personnel to read the date and time of the most recent safe openings and closings. This can provide convincing evidence in case of a loss claim against the property.

Some up-scale lodging properties, particularly resorts and first class hotels, offer minibars in their guestrooms and suites. Stocked with beverages and snacks, minibars can be profitable because guests are often tempted to have a last drink before going to bed or first thing in the morning. Fully automated minibars can electronically sense when an item is removed, sending the corresponding charge to the guest's room account. Non-automated units must rely on the honesty of the guest to notify the front desk just before checking out if goods have been consumed.

Depreciable fixed assets that are not furniture or equipment, such as bedspreads, mattress covers, blankets, pillows, and window coverings may be categorized under the classification of software. As with mattresses, bedspreads should be purchased with the qualities of durability, comfort, maintenance, and fire safety in mind. Bedspreads are an important component in the decor of guestrooms and should complement the motif, colour, and design of the room. Fabrics made of 100 percent polyester offer excellent resistance to fading, staining, shrinking, and wrinkling.

Woven fabrics perform better than knitted ones, which can make pattern colours appear faded if the knit loosens. Polycottons, a blend of polyester cotton, are less expensive than fabrics made of 100 percent polyester, but their life span is shorter, they have fewer fire-retardant qualities, and they fade more easily. While the normal recycling life span of a good bedspread should be at least 5 years, polycotton bedspreads only last from 2 to 3 years.

Other factors to consider when specifying bedspreads are their fill and seaming. Fill is one of the key elements that determines the appearance of bedspreads. The number of ounces of fill per square yard should be 7 or more. Non-compressed fills are better than mechanically packed fills because of their ability to spring back to its original 'loft is greater.

Wide, seamless bedspreads are preferred to those constructed with seams because they don't come apart as easily. Bedspreads can be large enough to reach to the floor or just to cover the mattress. In this case a pleated cloth skirting called a dust ruffle may be placed between the mattress and the box spring to extend around the sides and foot of the bed. Washable bedspreads should be purchased with the guarantee that they will not shrink, fade, or wrinkle. Par levels for bedspreads should be one plus 10 percent to allow for washing and replacement.

The purpose of blankets is to act as insulators. A heavy blanket does not necessarily keep the warmth of the body from escaping through it. On the other hand, a material (even if it is light) that is tightly woven will retain body heat. However, all blankets should be porous enough to allow any moisture buildup under them to escape to the surrounding air. Wool is a delicate natural fiber that is very warm but that requires extreme care when laundered.

Cotton, on the other hand, washes easily but it is a poor insulator and shrinks up to 15 percent if not purchased preshrunk. Synthetic fibers such as acrylics and polyester, if properly constructed, are suitable to commercial operations. Acrylic fibers are warmer than polyester but not as strong. Because guests may fall asleep while smoking in bed, blankets should be fire retardant. The size of the blanket should be large enough to cover the length and width of the mattress and have some additional inches for tucking.

All mattresses should be fitted with moisture-proof covers at all times to prevent staining. Vinyl plastic covers are impermeable and can be washed like any other fabric. Their use is recommended for cribs or small cots for young children and hospital beds. Felt pads made of moisture-proof, flame-retardant, 100 per cent polyester resist shrinkage and are quite durable. Quilted all-cotton pads are very comfortable but have a tendency to shrink and pucker after a few washings.

Comfortable pillows are a necessary complement to comfortable mattresses. It is advisable to provide two pillows per person for most guests like to prop them up high to watch television in bed. Most commercial pillows axe filled with synthetic fiber, mainly polyester. Synthetic pillows are quite common in commercial properties because they are inexpensive, easy to launder, and nonallergenic. When purchasing pillows, it is important to make sure that the fill is of good quality so that it springs back into shape easily; lumpy, heavier fills are an indication of inferior grade. The synthetic covering of the pillow must be fire retardant and stain proof and able to withstand frequent washings. Pillows with natural fills such as down and feathers are very expensive, particularly goose down. Lodging properties should stock a few natural-fill pillows to meet the occasional request for them.

Because of the price, down and feather pillows should be provided to guests on a loan basis, that is, a record should be kept in the housekeeping department of the room number where the pillows were delivered and then should be recovered after the guest's checkout. The first consideration for selecting wall coverings is that they match the general decor of the room; the second, and just as important, consideration is their durability and ease of maintenance. The two most common forms of wall coverings are paint and vinyl.

The paint used to finish walls should be easy to wash with soapy water and of very good quality so that the surface doesn't require repainting after a short period of time. Vinyl wall coverings are available in several thicknesses to suit the area to be covered; for instance, walls covered with thin layers are vulnerable to bumps from baggage and carts and should be used only to cover no-traffic areas. Heavier vinyl can withstand heavy impacts and can be used over surfaces susceptible to abrasion. Although far more expensive than paint, vinyl wall coverings generally pay for themselves because they require very little maintenance. Vinyl coverings are made by laminating the material to cotton or polycotton backings and are glued to walls using an adhesive paste. To prevent mildew from loosening the vinyl from the adhesive, the glue should contain a mildewcide. Fabric wall coverings can provide rooms and hallways with a luxurious, elegant look but they should be avoided in commercial operations because of the difficulty of cleaning or replacing them when soiled. Wallpaper should be used only if it is stain and water-resistant and allows for damp cleaning with soap and sponge.

Service areas, busy hallways, and elevators where carts and dollies may gouge the wall's should be protected with rubber or heavy vinyl cove base and wall guards. Corner salients should be reinforced with thick plastic corner guards.

Most windows in guestrooms are covered with curtains and sheers. Windows in offices, lobbies, and employee areas are usually fitted with vinyl blinds. Because of their susceptibility to fading, fabrics used for curtains must be resistant to direct sunlight. As curtains attract dust and odours, they require frequent washings and dry cleaning; for this reason, it is advisable to purchase good-quality, vinyl-coated fabrics that can retain their shape and colour for long periods of time. Curtains should be flame retardant to comply with local fire departments specifications. Drapery can be simple or quite ornate. Valances, and shirred or pinch-pleated fabrics, can add elegance and warmth to rooms, although they will require more cleaning time to keep them dust free. In all cases, the curtain rods and cords must be sturdy to avoid damage; having batons instead of cords may reduce the chance of breakage.

The housekeeping department needs major pieces of equipment to clean guest, public, and employee areas and to transport clean and soiled linen, trash, and supplies. In all cases, the department equipment used in housekeeping should be of heavy-duty quality, able to withstand rough and continuous use. Often, purveyors of chemical supplies also carry a complete line of equipment. In some cases, manufacturers have their own representatives who will describe the machines and demonstrate their performance. Perhaps the most significant piece of housekeeping equipment is the housekeeping cart. Usually, one cart is assigned to the cleaner of each section of guestrooms and one to each janitor. The cart should be large enough and have enough shelves to carry a full complement of supplies needed in each working shift in order to avoid unnecessary trips to the linen room for additional supplies.

Although sturdy, the cart must be light and maneuverable enough to be pushed by one person from door to door and from floor to floor, including pushing it into and out of service elevators. The cart should be contoured with rubber bumpers to protect walls and wall corners and have casters with brakes of superior quality. Some carts can be purchased with side panels that can be locked in order to prevent linen and guest amenities from being exposed to whomever walks past them, thus eliminating theft. If fitted with laundry and trash bags, these should be made of heavy-duty material to withstand hard use. Plastic baskets or caddies containing guest amenities and cleaning supplies are generally placed on the top shelf of carts.

Several types of vacuum cleaners are used by housekeeping. One requirement common to all of them is that they be heavy-duty and powerful enough to provide efficient, one-pass cleaning. The typical vacuum cleaner used in guestroom carpet cleaning is upright, with one or two motors. The dual-motor type has one motor to drive the beater brush and another to provide the suction.

Some useful characteristics of commercial vacuums are as follows: having collector cups or zipper receptacles instead of paper bags (some models can be messy and difficult to empty, in which case it is better to use disposable bags), long electric cable, wraparound bumpers, secondary filters to protect the vacuum motor, adjustable brush settings, three-position handles, and self-lubricating brushes. Some vacuums are incorporated into the housekeeping cart. This arrangement, however, may cause some difficulties. Because the hoses must be long enough to reach all corners of the room, suction power may be reduced. And since the vacuum must be operated in hallways, the noise permeates throughout the area. Also, because the machine is attached to the cart, repairs and maintenance are more difficult to perform on site than in the engineering shop. Large-area vacuums are used in hallways and lobbies that contain extensive areas of carpeting. In very large ballrooms and meeting rooms, vacuums with 30-inch brushes should be used.

Wet/dry vacuums are designed for wet pickup on any type of hard flooring surface. Equipped with a wide squeegee, they can be used to remove liquids when hard floor& are stripped or for any kind of liquid absorption. Back vacuums worn by the housekeeper, are convenient for dusting and cleaning vertical or high surfaces and fixtures, especially curtains, drapes, and wall coverings. Back vacuums are light, quiet machines equipped with adjustable straps and hoses that can be expanded to three times their normal length.

Floor machines are designed to mechanically polish, buff, strip, scrub, grind, sand, burnish, and shampoo surfaces. Usually one multipurpose machine can be used for several tasks by changing the pad as needed to accomplish the task at hand. Burnishers are used when the property has large areas of terrazzo or tile floor. These machines are capable of burnishing up to 30,000 square feet per hour. Polishers are heavily weighted machines used to grind, sand, and polish marble and other stone floors.

Scrubbers are used to automatically scrub hard or resilient surfaces by applying a stripping solution and recovering the liquid as the machine is pushed along the surface. Large scrubbers feature 40-gallon stripping solution and recovery tanks, a 34-inch self-propelled scrubber, 37-inch squeegee assembly, and can service 44,000 square feet per hour. Extractors are used to clean carpets and rugs. The simplest and least expensive consists of a machine with two tanks-one that holds the cleaning solution and one that collects the suctioned liquid. A better version has a beater brush attached to the wand to deepen the penetration of the cleaning solution into the carpet fabric.

Self-contained extractors are very convenient to operate as they don't require a wand or hoses. The best models have four-phase cleaning action (spray, scrub, rinse, and extract in one pass) with a spray power of 100 PSI. Self-contained carpet extractors are also available with dry foam instead of liquid solution.

When large lodging properties use drinking glasses made of glass (rather than plastic), glass washers are necessary. The practice of washing housekeeping glasses in the kitchen's dishwashers is not an effective one as it is usually seen as an "encroachment" by the food and beverage department personnel.

When operating a glass washer, the right type of detergent and the correct water temperature as determined by the local health department must be provided. Rather than transporting trash, soiled linen, and supplies in plastic bags, lodging properties should use light trucks or hoppers. This is preferable to hauling material in bags carried over the shoulder, especially along public hallways.

Cleaning supplies are categorised under operating assets and are included in the property's operating budget. Cleaning supplies comprise the chemicals necessary to perform the myriad cleaning jobs throughout the property and the nonchemical utensils needed to apply, scrub, rub, cleanse, wipe, etc. The chemicals onto all types of surfaces. There are several hundred manufacturers of cleaning chemicals, each of which markets and sells countless products. The responsibility of selecting and using the right chemicals rests with the executive housekeeper.

In large properties, the purchasing function, including housekeeping products, is performed by the purchasing agent. However, it should be up to the executive housekeeper to determine what products to use in the department, and to inform the purchasing agent of the specifications and characteristics required for the supplies to be bought.

Because marked differences exist among products, before choosing cleaning supplies they should be tested by the employees who will use them regularly. Janitors, housepersons, and section housekeepers must agree that the products chosen will be effective. An agreement should be made between the department and the vendor to train workers, at no cost, on how to use the cleaning supplies properly.

As with many other products, price should be only one of the factors regarding the purchasing decision, the others being availability, service, and quality. For instance, if a product is difficult to obtain, if the purveyor doesn't provide training and technical support, and if much larger quantities than a more expensive one have to be used, you might not obtain the expected value from it. Shopping for cleaning supplies must be done competitively; that is, trying to obtain the best price for the same or comparable product. When asking for a product quotation, the executive housekeeper must be very specific regarding its packaging, composition, and concentration. It is important to designate specific days and time to receive sales people. Placing orders by phone can help save time, although direct contact with vendors is essential as they generally are specialists in their fields and therefore are able to suggest the solution to severe cleaning problems. Periodic shipments of supplies may be arranged for those products used in large quantities; however, in no case should vendors be allowed to place an order without the direct approval of the person in charge of purchasing.

Because the cleaning supplies market is quite competitive, it is common for vendors to offer free items and personal prizes to the person in charge of buying. It is only ethical to assume that any discount or give-away should benefit the property and not the buying individual. Accepting gifts or kickbacks should be prohibited, so for example if a vendor gives the purchasing agent tickets for an upcoming football game, the tickets should be rejected or, if accepted, raffled off among all employees.

Bulk purchasing of chemicals generally allows for great savings in price to the housekeeping department. There are, however, serious disadvantages with buying chemicals in large quantities. For instance, over-buying products may mean having to store them for long periods of time, tying up resources and space. Chemicals may also deteriorate while in storage and actually be more labour intensive. For example, decanting a liquid from a 55-gallon drum into smaller containers may take a considerable amount of time.

Although pre-measured chemicals are ready to be used as purchased, thus not requiring much handling, their higher cost is a disadvantage. The fact that they generate a lot of trash as they are used is also an inconvenience. In-house chemical dispensers or mixing stations can be a good alternative to both bulk and pre-measured products. The dispensers, plumbed to hot or cold water, can automatically mix bulk chemicals, eliminating human error and labour cost from the process. The three major purposes of chemicals used in the housekeeping department are to remove dirt, to destroy harmful microorganisms, and to preserve and beautify furniture, fixtures, and surfaces.

Chemical cleaners are manufactured to remove soils from surfaces through chemical action. The stronger the chemical is, the better effect it will have on getting the job done. The strength of cleaning chemicals is measured on the pH scale. pH is the symbol for the logarithm of the reciprocal of hydrogen ion concentration in gram atoms per liter. Cleaning chemicals that have been enhanced with alkalis or acids to strengthen their cleaning powers can be dangerous to humans and often cannot be used on certain surfaces. A neutral cleaner can be used for all types of jobs but its cleaning power is limited.

The executive housekeeper should have adequate knowledge of the department's needs to select cleaning chemicals appropriate for each type of cleaning job to be performed regularly in the housekeeping department. Generally speaking, high-alkaline cleaners are effective degreasers while acidic cleaners are good for fighting lime and rust, which are always found in urinals and toilets. Another name for cleaners is detergents. Detergents act chemically to emulsify dirt, holding it in suspension so it can be removed away from the surface. Synthetic detergents are easy to rinse off and often have excellent cleaning, deodorizing, and germicidal characteristics.

Most cleaning detergents are made from mineral oils. All-purpose cleaners have neutral pH-balanced formulas for general-purpose cleaning jobs. They usually are synthetic detergents, often vegetable oil based, of which pine oil is very popular because of its pleasant scent and strong deodorizing power.

All-purpose cleaners may have corrosion inhibitors to protect metal surfaces. Single-purpose cleaners are heavy-duty cleaners used for specific cleaning jobs. Abrasive cleaners are cleaning powders or pastes combined with silica for tough cleaning jobs. These cleaners will scratch soft surfaces like fiberglass or porcelain. Gentler cleansers made with nonscratching calcite instead of silica greatly reduce their abrasive action.

Degreasers are highly effective cleaners, often biodegradable, that remove grease, tar, ink, food deposits, smoke film, fats and other grimy soils. Degreasers can be highly effective on concrete floors. It is important to remember that some products advertised as degreasers may be toxic and therefore not suitable for use on kitchen surfaces. Although most all-purpose cleaners can be used as deodorizers, stronger chemicals are needed to counteract stale odours.

Deodorizers can be purchased as mists, wall and urinal blocks, cup and wick, and aerosols. Glass cleaners are ammonia- and alcohol-based products that clean and provide a protective coating to glass surfaces. Glass treated with good-quality glass cleaners resist fogging caused by moisture and temperature changes and in some manner repel dust, dirt, fingerprints, and smudges.

Most glass cleaners can also be used as multipurpose cleaners on chrome, stainless steel, enamel, formica, ceramic tile, and other washable surfaces. Metal cleaners are nonscratching products that remove rust, tarnish, corrosion, and grime from metal surfaces and fixtures. These products can be used on brass, stainless steel, copper, chrome, and aluminium materials. Metal cleaners, can be purchased as liquids, aerosols, pastes, and cotton wadding.

Another purpose of housekeeping supplies is to beautify surfaces and fixtures. Furniture polishes are liquid waxes or oils or silicone-based sprays designed to protect and give shine to wood, leather, vinyl, metal, and plastic surfaces. When pigments are added to liquid furniture polish, the product helps cover nicks and scratches in wood furniture, panelling, and floors.

Most metal surfaces can be dusted, cleaned, and polished with metal polishes. Strong liquid metal polishes can remove rust, corrosion, tarnish, and grime from brass, stainless steel, copper, chrome, and aluminium. Cream polishes are quite effective in cleaning sterling silver, silver-plated utensils, nickel, and pewter.Strong acidic cleaners are needed to clean away lime and rust deposits in restroom and bathroom fixtures. Bowl cleaners may contain hydrochloric or phosphoric acid to cut scale and calcium deposits with little or no scrubbing. Milder bowl cleaners are nonacid and nonabrasive, designed not to etch or pit porcelain fixtures, but their cleaning power is lower. Most toilet cleaners kill bacteria and viruses, including the HIV-I virus, on contact.

Janitors and section housekeepers should be trained well in how to handle these powerful products. Acidic bowl cleaners, for example, should not come in contact with metal attachments, stone, or tile surfaces. Public and employee urinals are usually deodorized and disinfected with paradichlorobenzene blocks that neutralize offensive odours. Graffiti removers consist of a gel formula that effectively effaces ink, crayon, lipstick, some spray paints, magic marker, and bumper stickers from most hard surfaces. These powerful products should not be used, however, on rubber, vinyl, plastic, or painted surfaces.

Besides cleaning, housekeeping chemicals can be used to control and kill pathogenic bacteria by sanitizing and disinfecting surfaces and utensils. Disinfectants are germicidal chemicals that kill microorganisms and prevent them from multiplying. Often, germicides are combined with chlorinated liquid detergents to act both as germ killer and cleanser, making them effective against many forms of microorganisms, including salmonella, fungi, and a broad range of viruses. Aerosol disinfectants are generally much stronger as they are able to eliminate most bacteria and viruses such as herpes simplex, influenza, and HIV-I. Hand soaps are also important in fighting contagious diseases.

Liquid soaps used by employees in back-of -the -house areas should be antimicrobial and capable of reducing nosocomial infections caused by the fungal organism candida albicans. Guest liquid soaps should be formulated with emollients to soften the skin, have a pleasant fragrance, and produce a rich lather.Hard and resilient floor cleaners must be pH neutral, that is, mild enough to clean dirt from surfaces without affecting polymer finishes, sealers, and shines. Floor cleaners are water- or vegetable oil-based and can be applied to synthetic surfaces, marble, terrazzo, and other washable floors. Stronger solvent-based cleaners, capable of erasing heel marks, rubber burns, tar, and grease from concrete and hard wood surfaces are very effective but will affect the floor finish when applied.

Strippers are chemicals used to remove and clean old floor finishes prior to rewaxing, resealing, or refinishing them. These products penetrate and emulsify worn wax buildup, polymer and acrylic finishes, and surface dirt deposits. After the floor has been stripped, the alkaline residue should be neutralized with a neutralizer rinse prior to applying a new finish.

Floor sealers are used to protect porous surfaces such as concrete, terrazzo, wood, and marble from staining. Stronger sealers have a substantial amount of solids and are formulated to fill scratches and provide a base for floor finishes. Some sealers can coat and polish surfaces at the same time. Resilient floor finishes usually contain detergent-resistant acrylic polymers. Good products are burnishable and resistant to scuffing and black marks, acting both as sealers and finishes.

Carpet shampoo is marketed under many commercial brands, and its composition can be different as well. Some shampoos are water-based and are a blend of polymers, biodegradable surfactants, and solvents. Soil-retarding carpet shampoos provide a fluorochemical barrier to protect against dirt, dust, spills, and stains.

Defoamers are silicone foam suppressors used to eliminate foam from the recovery system of steam cleaners. Antistatic sprays are designed to eliminate static electricity buildup on wool and synthetic carpets caused by foot traffic or low humidity. Spot removers are concentrated formulas used to pre-spray carpets before shampooing to remove tar, grease, lipstick, graffiti, and food or beverage stains.

The number of nonchemical cleaning supplies in the housekeeping inventory can be substantial, ranging from broom to wringer. Upright brooms are sold under several denominations, such as janitor, warehouse, household, lobby, porter, and whisk brooms. In all cases, upright brooms should be heavy duty and have wire bands to help retain their shape. Push brooms usually consist of a combination of horse hair and synthetic fibers. For durability, the broom block should be attached to the handle by a sturdy metal brace. Wet mops also come in a variety of forms: four-ply cotton-synthetic fiber blend mops have good absorption; mops with looped ends are more durable than cut-ended. Some brands feature mildew- and bacteria -resistant mops with scrubber headbands and double banding. Tight twisted, string-style eight-ply mops are specially designed for floor finishing applications. Mop buckets /wringers come in different shapes and forms as well.

Dual bucket systems consist of two overlapping buckets mounted on a mobile platform with casters; one bucket holds the cleaning solution and the other carries the rinse water for better sanitation. Heavy-duty plastic buckets are preferable to zinc ones as they are quieter, have no corrosion, and will not dent.

Hazardous materials are dangerous as they can harm both workers and property. Knowing how to safely handle, mix, and store them can protect employees, guests, and the company from explosions, fires, environmental contamination, higher insurance premiums, and costly litigation. Besides being dangerous, chemicals are expensive and strict guidelines should be followed to hold employees accountable for their proper dilution and use.In order to protect workers from unsafe working conditions, the Occupational Safety and Health Administration (OSHA) requires that employees handling chemicals are informed of the risks that these chemicals pose and that the employer provides appropriate training on how to use them safely. Failure to comply with OSHA's HazComm regulations may result in fines if inspections of the property indicate that the directions have not been followed. HazComm requires that a list of all hazardous chemicals used in the housekeeping department be compiled and kept updated.

The executive housekeeper must then develop a program to let all employees be aware of, and alert to the hazardous materials they will come in contact with, teaching them about their specific characteristics and dangers. The program may include lectures provided by distributors of chemical products, videos, discussions, and hands-on demonstrations. Other important steps include ensuring that all containers of chemicals are properly labelled and that workers follow approved disposal procedures. The label must state the name of the chemical, hazard warnings, and the manufacturer's name and address. Because people who work in housekeeping maybe unable to understand English, labels with colour codes or signs are strongly recommended.

Workers should wear the right personal protective equipment when handling certain chemicals-mainly gloves, face masks, and goggles. Mixing or combining hazardous materials must be done strictly following the manufacturer's guidelines. Acids and caustics, for instance, can cause violent reactions when combined. Transferring liquids from one container to another can produce flammable vapours that can ignite easily.

Worker exposure to hazardous materials may cause allergies, such as eye, nose, and throat irritation, skin rashes, anxiety, and nausea. In severe cases, chemicals may cause dizziness, vomiting, blindness, and even death. Besides complying with OSHA's regulations, the housekeeping department must display a list of all the chemicals used, specifying information about the manufacturer, the product's hazardous ingredients, its physical and chemical characteristics, flammability, recommended handling, health hazards, and what to do in case of ingestion, fire, or explosion.

This information is obtained from the manufacturers' material safety data sheets (MSDT) provided when the product is purchased. Employees working with chemicals should be required to read and understand product warning labels. The list must be updated and made available to employees at all times. Chemicals should never be stored near food products but in separate storage, preferably under lock and key. Flammable liquids and sprays should be stored in a cool, dry place away from heat and sunlight. Enclosing them in metal lockers is best, in order to avoid possible fires from spreading.

Lodging companies provide their guests with guestroom items intended to make their stay as convenient and comfortable as possible. These items also raise the guests' perceived value for the rate paid when occupying a room or rooms. Upscale lodging establishments outdo each other by offering a vast range of amenities aimed at pampering their guests while they relax in their rooms. Today's hoteliers view personal-care amenities as a positioning tool for their lodging properties, in that the more plentiful and novel they are, the higher value for the rate paid is perceived by guests.

Coffee makers, together with several blends of gourmet and decaffeinated coffee and a variety of teas, are common. Besides the typical candy placed on the pillow at turndown-service time, companies are adding speciality confections, such as Belgian and Italian chocolates or fancy fortune mints described as "rectangles attractively wrapped with witty fortunes and/or proverbs inside the wrappers."Chocolate chip and oatmeal cookies, cosmetics, and safe -for-all-fabric stain removers are just a few of the $300million-a-year products that the industry invests in indulging guests.

Depending also on the quality of lodging establishments reusable supplies can range from the barely essential items offered by economy properties to the highly sophisticated, state-of-the-art technology found in first-class establish-ments. Supplies provided by most lodging properties are coat hangers, ice buckets, waste-baskets, ashtrays, Bible, and, recently, electronic equipment. Coat hangers should be made of wood or hard plastic instead of flexible wire. Hangers with ball tops rather than hooks are usually not taken by guests, although some travellers find it difficult to fasten them to the lip on the closet rod.

Women's hangers with skirt clips are designed for garments that hang better clipped than on a bar. Hangers are also available with clamping trouser bars to assure guests that the clothing will stay in place. Ice buckets are preferable if they are insulated with polyethylene liners and have a lid; stainless steel buckets are very durable and have a stylish look. Providing tongs with the ice bucket is a nice touch. Rather than plain-looking rectangular rubber waste-baskets, oval fireproof ones made of metal with simulated grain leather are more elegant. For smoking rooms, heavy crystal ashtrays with bevelled edges are best.

Classical Lodging Establishment: Example of Hilton Hotels

Hilton Hotels Corporation is recognized around the world as a preeminent lodging hospitality company, offering guests and customers the finest accommodations, services, amenities and value for business or leisure. Through ownership of some of the most recognized hotels in the world and the newly enhanced brand portfolio, Hilton is now able to offer guests the widest possible variety of hotel experiences, including four-star city center hotels, convention properties, all-suite hotels, extended stay, mid-priced focused service, destination resorts, vacation ownership, airport hotels and conference centers. Today's Hilton can be viewed as a major industry competitor in a number of areas:

— *Owning hotels*: Hilton owns such unique, irreplaceable hotel assets as New York's Waldorf=Astoria, The Hilton Hawaiian Village Beach Resort and Spa. on Waikiki Beach, the Hilton Waikoloa Village and Chicago's Palmer House Hilton and the Hilton San Francisco on Union Square. These large-scale properties occupy the best locations in the nation's best markets.

— *Managing/franchising hotels*: The company is a prominent franchisor of hotels across its entire brand family, with income from management or franchise fees accounting for some 30 percent of Hilton's total cash flow.

— *Vacation ownership*: Hilton Grand Vacations Club, the company's vacation ownership business, operates properties across the country including such desirable locales as Las Vegas, Orlando, Miami, New York and Honolulu.

— *International*: A global strategic alliance with Hilton International, the London-based company which owns the rights to the Hilton brand outside of the U.S., brings to customers a single, seamless Hilton system of 2,000 hotels in more than 50 countries throughout the world. Additionally, Conrad Hotels offers five-star luxury hotels in New York, England, Ireland, Belgium, Hong Kong, Singapore, Turkey and Egypt. The following pages outline how Hilton has become an industry success through a vision of aggressive expansion efforts and cutting-edge innovation.

Business Travel Programs

— Since 1919, Hilton Hotels has led the way with innovations for executives on the road. Recent innovations include:

— Hilton Hotels designed a program of special services with the business traveler in mind. Executive Floors is available at most Hilton and Hilton International properties. Separate check-in, complimentary continental breakfast, evening hors d'oeuvres and in-room fax machines are just some of the amenities available with most Executive Floors guestrooms.

— Our fully-staffed business centers help business travelers with many office tasks such as graphic presentations, faxing, copying and word processing.

— In September 1995, Hilton Hotels Corporation was the first hotel company to team up with American Express to offer a no-fee co-branded credit card that features what many frequent travelers value most. The Hilton Credit Card from American Express offers card members one of the richest rewards structure of any leading travel rewards card program, no annual fee and a low introductory interest rate.

In recent years, Hilton Hotels has taken an aggressive stand to upgrade its national network of hotels and ensure consistent delivery on the Hilton promise. Recent initiatives include:

— *Strategic Performance Management System.* The Hilton Balanced Scorecard tracks financial and competitive performance along with internal and external customer satisfaction/loyalty measures in order to align the efforts of team members system-wide. Since 1997 the scorecard has provided managers with actionable information by utilizing hotel-specific priority reports based on customerdriven needs and a continuous improvement process to implement operational service and product improvement. This approach also encourages an innovative entrepreneurial spirit focused on all of Hilton's constituents by linking results to a variety of reward and recognition initiatives. The Hilton Balanced Scorecard was featured in the August 1999 edition of the Cornell University Hotel and Restaurant Administration Quarterly in an article entitled "Hilton Hotels: A Comprehensive Approach to Delivering Value for All Stakeholders."

— *Upgrading hotels.* The company has spent more than $1 billion renovating flagship properties such as The Waldorf=Astoria., the Hilton Hawaiian Village Beach Resort & Spa., the Hilton Chicago O'Hare Airport and Hilton New York. Renovations are ongoing throughout the system, in order to maintain excellence in appearance and accommodations.

— *Hilton Quality Service Institute (HQSI).* In 1992, Hilton Hotels established this institute at its world headquarters in Beverly Hills, California. The HQSI provides an intensive series of workshops that educate all Hilton property managers regarding Hilton Hotels' corporate programs and service philosophy. The end result is greater consistency and quality among individual properties.

— *Franchise review.* Hilton Hotels has undertaken a vigorous franchise review process, eliminating those hotels that do not meet the company's standards.

— *Satisfaction Guarantee.* The 100% Satisfaction Guarantee is an operating culture and philosophy that focuses each team member and owner on complete guest satisfaction.

Marketing Programs

This drive for quality has worked hand-in-hand with a series of national marketing programs that appeal to Hilton's key target audiences. These programs include the following:

— *Guest Reward program.* Hilton's acclaimed guest reward program, Hilton HHonors® Worldwide was expanded April 3, 2000 and now includes Doubletree, Embassy Suites Hotels, Hampton Inn, Hampton Inn & Suites, and Homewood Suites by Hilton hotels, along with Hilton and Conrad.. Only Hilton HHonors. now offers members the ability to earn both Points & Miles. for stays at nearly any rate, at more than 2000 hotels around the globe.

— *Family vacations.* Hilton Vacation Station is a program of special family services and amenities designed to help families traveling with children maximize their leisure time together. The program is available at more than twice as many U.S. locations as its primary competitors and located in the most popular vacation destinations across North & South America.

— *Mature travelers.* Among the first businesses to recognize the importance of travelers over age 60, the company has created Hilton Senior HHonors® Worldwide, one of the hotel industry's only membership-based travel programs for mature travelers.

Hilton's marketing programs, renovations and aggressive expansion all underscore a continued commitment to those principles that have made the Hilton name synonymous with first-class hospitality. Hilton has been on the forefront of hotel innovation since its inception. Hilton's firsts include:

— First hotel company to list on the New York Stock Exchange - June 23, 1946.

— First company to operate a hotel gift shop. Called the Hilton Country Store, the gift shop reflected Conrad Hilton's determination to maximize every square foot of hotel space and serve the hotel guest.

— In 1997, Hilton Hotels Corporation (HHC) and British company Hilton Group plc, formalized a global marketing alliance to reunite the Hilton name worldwide for the first time in over 30 years. Hilton International (now a wholly owned subsidiary of Hilton Group) was spun off from HHC in 1964. Hilton Hotels Corporation continued to operate hotels separately in the U.S. and Conrad International Hotels Corporation, a subsidiary of Hilton Hotels Corporation, operates hotels outside the U.S. There are more than 2000 Hilton, Conrad International, and Vista hotels in 50 countries, and the reunification of the brand further enhances Hilton's leadership position in one of the world's fastest growing industries.

— With customer service as a Hilton hallmark, the company was the first brand to offer amenities such as air conditioning and direct-dial telephones as standard features in guestrooms.

— Pioneered concept of airport hotels with the opening of the San Francisco Airport Hilton in 1959.

The company now boasts 40 airport properties located strategically in major markets in the U.S.

— First upscale lodging company to develop the concept of franchising hotels, 1966. Formed Hilton Inns, Inc. to create a network of franchise hotels bearing the Hilton name. This practice is now an industry standard. Hilton has approximately 1,352 properties under franchise agreements.

— Another breakthrough in customer service was the development of centralized reservation services, HILTRON, uniting all Hilton Hotels, in 1973. Today, HILTRON has a 99 percent up-time that remains unrivaled in the industry. In 1999, Hilton announced the successful launch of its new $30 million state of the art central reservation system (CRS) called HILSTAR, creating a network of more than 500 hotels worldwide.

— In what may be the most aggressive travel-related sleep experiment to date, Hilton Hotels, in cooperation with the

National Sleep Foundation (NSF) and an array of sleep-product manufacturers, introduced 25 Sleep-Tight Rooms. in October, 1996. The rooms are part of a nationwide program to determine how to increase sleepability among travelers. Hilton Hotels and NSF began their relationship in 1994 by establishing the "Sleep and the Traveler" cooperative research effort, which led to the development of these special guestrooms.

— Hilton Hotels Corporation and Hilton Grand Vacation Company introduce the Urban Vacation Ownership Product and announce The Hilton Club - New York, located on two designated floors of the Hilton New York, as the flagship property in the new Hilton Club Collection.. The Hilton Club concept establishes a distinctive new niche in the vacation ownership industry by incorporating a spectacular urban setting and a collection of high-end services and exclusive travel privileges tailored for Members Only.

2

Staffing Patterns

A characteristic common to all hotels, regardless of size and category, is the need for housekeeping services, which can range from very sophisticated to a simple matter of "refreshing" rooms once a week. For instance, a luxury hotel, casino, or resort usually requires that the rooms be impeccably clean, that the bed linen is changed every time the bed is used, and that turndown service is provided daily. On the other hand, the service for a university residence room might consist in just providing the tenant with a fresh set of sheets every Monday morning.

Mid-range service hotels generally require that guestrooms are thoroughly cleaned daily, that bed and bathroom linen is changed every day, and that 24-hour housekeeping service is provided seven days a week. In any case, because housekeeping services must always be provided, the management of the housekeeping department in every lodging establishment is of critical importance to the success of the property.

It is essential that future graduates of hospitality programs understand the options that the industry offers regarding housekeeping management positions. Graduates wishing to achieve the position of executive housekeeper in a relatively short period of time should keep in mind that a small or medium-sized property does generally offer the best opton for candidates to reach their goal.

In large or very large establishments, where housekeeping operations are quite complex, it will take longer for candidates to become managers of the department. In any case, the position of executive housekeeper will always be a challenging and rewarding one as well as an adequate springboard from which to work toward the goal of becoming the property's general manager.

When looking for their first job, hospitality graduates should understand the difference between working for properties that are independently or chain-owned, franchised, or run by management companies. An independently owned establishment might not offer substantial opportunities for advancement, as the owners do not usually have any other properties. In this case, the waiting period for reaching an executive position can be a long one.

On the other hand, chains offer limitless job opportunities, as these corporations generally expand nationally and internationally by building new places or merging with other companies. If a management company manages a large number of properties, the possibilities for advancing could be as large as those offered by chains. However, it is not unusual for these companies to be rather small, in which case not many openings will occur regularly.

Often, independent operators own franchised properties. In this case working for a "Marriott" or "Sheraton" hotel doesn't mean that you will be working for these corporations, as the owners have merely contracted with the chains the right to display their commercial names.

Lodging is an integral part of the hospitality industry. Hospitality involves the reception of guests and the provision of services to them with liberality and kindness. The task of providing hospitality and services to guests in a friendly and efficient manner falls mainly on the property's rooms division. The overall success of an operation depends on the profitability of the rooms division, which generally accounts for a large share of a hotel's sales while generating a gross profit percentage from 70 to 80 per cent of the revenue.

Besides providing lodging, and professional services such as check in, luggage handling, and room upkeep, rooms division personnel must provide the "home-away from-home" feeling so cherished by travellers who are temporarily separated from their families. Offering tastefully decorated guestrooms and public areas and impeccable cleanliness in a subdued, relaxing atmosphere is also of the utmost importance.

Large properties are divided into operational units called divisions. Two of these divisions-Rooms, and Food and Beverage are revenue-generating centers, while the others are considered to be support centers. The executive in charge of the rooms division is the Rooms Division Director, who in some properties may be called resident manager, executive manager, or senior assistant manager. The rooms division director reports directly to the property's general manager.

As a member of the executive committee, the rooms division director takes an active part in policy-making decisions related to operations. Other members of this committee generally include: the Food and Beverage Director, in charge of the food and beverage division; the Sales Director, who deals with sales, marketing, and public relations; the Controller or chief financial officer; the Human Resources Director, in charge of personnel matters; and the Plant Manager, responsible for the engineering and maintenance needs of the property. Of the rooms division, which is divided into departments, the front office and housekeeping departments are of critical importance to the property.

The Executive Housekeeper is the head of housekeeping and is therefore directly responsible for managing what is in most cases the largest department of the establishment. The position of executive housekeeper in the organizational chart is that of department head, equal in rank to the front office manager, the security manager, and the remaining managers in charge of departments in other divisions.

In smaller properties, the division directors do not exist; instead, department heads manage the different units and report directly to the general manager. The housekeeping department is an integral part of all the areas into which a lodging operation is divided. Although housekeeping's primary communication takes place with the front office and engineering departments, a strong relationship must exist with an the other units of the property as well. For instance, room service, a department in the food and beverage division that delivers food to guestrooms, must be in direct contact with housekeeping for the removal of trays and carts. The sales department, which often must have access to ready rooms to be shown to meeting planners or tour operator representatives, must communicate this need to the housekeeping department.

Guestrooms in lodging properties are sold by the front office. The front desk must know at every given moment what rooms have been cleaned and are available for occupancy. Housekeeping must provide the front desk with a listing of rooms that are ready for occupancy so guests can be checked in. If the communication between the two departments is poor or breaks down, delays in guest checking will occur or people will be checked into rooms that are thought to be ready but that in fact are occupied or not ready. If this happens often, the property's reputation will suffer. The cycle of communication begins early each day, when the front desk provides the housekeeping department with a written (or computer-generated) report called the night clerk's room report.

The housekeeping employee in charge of opening the house transfers the information received from the front desk into forms to be distributed to the housekeeping supervisors who, in turn, will notify the room attendants before they begin to work in their respective sections. As guests check in and out of the hotel throughout the day, the front desk notifies housekeeping. When discrepancies are found between the status of rooms received from the night clerk and the physical inspection of the rooms, the front desk is immediately notified. For instance, if the front desk reports that a certain room is vacant and housekeeping finds it occupied, a discrepancy exists and the front desk should be notified.

There are several reasons why discrepancies may occur. The most common are:

— A guest switches from one room to another and the front desk neglects to change its records.

— An error is made by the night clerk when filling out the night clerk's report.

— A guest is given the wrong room key by mistake.

— The room is used by an unauthorized employee.

— The room is sold by the front desk without being recorded, and the money is pocketed by the clerk.

— A guest checks in or out between the time the report is made and the check is conducted.

FUNCTIONS OF HOUSEKEEPING MANAGER

The hotel industry is having generally long working hours and a shift in housekeeping could start as early as 5.30am. The working week will not always be Monday to Friday as often the weekends are a hotel's busiest times. The work can also be physically difficult - carrying heavy cleaning equipment, moving furniture, constantly on one's feet. The job may involve meeting a variety of people and dealing with guests on a one to one level so the development of good interpersonal skills will be an advantage.

The housekeeper will usually develop good managerial skills in order to deal with other staff members and customers in a range of situations. Depending on the seniority of the position the housekeeper may have to manage budgets so a degree of numeracy and accounting ability in this regard will be developed. The major concern of direction and management of housekeeping programs is the maintenance of environmental sanitation within acceptable levels of bacteriological, as well as visual, cleanliness.

Accordingly, housekeeping supervisory positions whose paramount requirement is trade, craft, or laboring experience and knowledge are exempt from the General Schedule and excluded from this series. Such supervisory positions are excluded even though they may operate through subordinate supervisors. In contrast, housekeeping positions whose paramount requirement is knowledge of housekeeping techniques and management procedure, techniques, methods, and practices needed to effectively plan, organize, conduct, and manage a housekeeping program are covered by the General Schedule and included in this series.

Housekeeping management and supervisory positions that are under the General Schedule because of a paramount requirement for knowledges and experience related to "management" rather than to trades and crafts may, nevertheless, include a secondary requirement for such trades, craft or laboring experience and knowledge. Conversely, supervisory housekeeping positions which are exempt from the General Schedule because of a paramount requirement for trades, craft, and manual laboring experience and knowledge, may include a secondary requirement for managerial skills similar to those of managers and supervisors under the General Schedule.

Determination of the pay category of housekeeping position therefore must be based on a careful assessment of the paramount requirement of the position, i.e., does the position primarily require managerial knowledges and skills, or are trade, craft, or manual laboring experience and knowledge the paramount requirement for supervising or directing the involved housekeeping work operations.For example, fully operational Housekeeping Officer positions which have the full range of managerial responsibility.

Assistant Housekeeping Officers reporting to Housekeeping Officers with full managerial responsibility are also covered by the General Schedule when they share in these managerial responsibilities to such an extent that they are the basis for the paramount requirement of the position.

On the other hand, supervisory positions reporting directly to Housekeeping Officers are exempt from the General Schedule when the performance of supervisory duties, such as planning, scheduling, assigning, coordinating, directing, or reviewing work activities, is primarily based on the application of trade, craft, or manual laboring experience and knowledge rather than on management experience and knowledge of management methods and techniques.

Usually, a careful assessment of the paramount requirement of a position will be sufficient to determine its pay category. Only after such a careful assessment has been inconclusive, may a position be considered to be borderline with respect to pay category. However, in borderline situations, the total working environment of the position, such as the nature of the work organization, working and pay relationships, normal career progression, and management intent must be considered.

The Housekeeping Officer is fully responsible for planning, organizing, staffing, directing, controlling and evaluating the program at their specific health care facility. They coordinate housekeeping activities with other programs and activities in the ; initiate, shape and set policy, procedures, standards and goals; develop and apply an internal program of management review, appraisal and improvement; establish the balance between quality and quantity in light of budget and ceiling constraints; provide for formal and on-the-job training and instruction; and, assume an active role in the overall management responsibility for a health care facility through participation and service in the committee structure.

Housekeeping Officers formulate, implement, coordinate and control comprehensive environmental sanitation programs. They respond to the myriad components of the health care environment and have the administrative authority to use discretion in effecting needed change for the benefit of guests, staff and visitors.

The technical aspects of the Housekeeping Officer position revolve around the development and maintenance of standards for cleanliness and sanitation. These standards encompass such areas as the frequency of cleaning; the methods, procedures and safety precautions to be followed; the selection, measurement and proper use of housekeeping and cleaning supplies; and the use and maintenance of housekeeping equipment.

In developing standards to meet the unique requirements of a particular, the Housekeeping Officer must take into consideration both the unique physical characteristics of the local and the functions of various specialized departments and medical programs. Maintaining these standards involves such activities as continuing inspections by the Housekeeping Officer and subordinate supervisors; a bacteriological monitoring program including the systematic collection, incubation and analysis of sample micro-organism cultures; and an aggressive program to test and perfect housekeeping techniques, procedures and products.

Housekeeping Officer positions require both technical expertise in housekeeping operations and program management ability. A number of these qualification requirements are mentioned or implied in the preceding occupational information section and the remainder of this standard.

The following is not all inclusive, but it does summarize the more important knowledges, skills and abilities required for housekeeping management positions:

— ability to develop procedures which mesh the specific goals of the housekeeping department with the broad overall goals of the , and ability to work with other managers to coordinate respective programs;

— ability to delegate authority;

— ability to analyze problems and make decisions taking into full consideration a wide range of factors and requiremens;

— ability to communicate effectively with a wide variety of people, e.g., justifying program goals and plans to top managers and motivating housekeeping employees;

— familiarity with government-wide, agency, and rules and regulations in areas such as budget, personnel and labor relations, and ability to develop operating procedures for implementing these requirements in the local housekeeping program;

— practical working knowledge of some of the basic principles of chemistry, biology and bacteriology as applied to environmental sanitation, infection control, and choice and use of cleaning agents and equipment, and as gained by on-the-job training supplemented by related experience, education or special outside courses;

- knowledge of housekeeping methods and techniques; of various floor, wall, and ceiling covering materials and their properties; and of current developments concerning new cleaning agents, techniques and equipment.

These and related qualification requirements have been taken into consideration in establishing the grade structure and are reflected in the grade-level criteria. Trainees receive systematic classroom and on-the-job training in all major facets of the housekeeping program. Instruction and assignments provide a basic familiarity with objectives and procedures, departmental relationships, and especially with housekeeping objectives, practices, and procedures.

The training typically provides indoctrination in management philosophy and supervisory techniques, as well as actual experience in supervising workers, assigning work, establishing schedules, establishing performance standards, and conducting studies to determine whether changes in procedures should be made. Trainees gain experience in specific techniques for such things as various types of cleaning, linen control and management, laundry operation, interior decoration, testing new products or equipment, and monitoring the level of a bacteriological cleanliness by coordinating or performing culture sampling.

All work is performed under close supervision, with detailed instructions provided for specific assignments, and additional guidance given during the course of assignments as necessary. Work is evaluated both for technical accuracy and as an indicator of ability to grasp and successfully apply basic housekeeping principles and practices, ability to exercise initiative and assume responsibility, and potential for successfully performing more responsible housekeeping management work.

With general instructions as to objectives, priorities and deadlines, the Housekeeping Assistant uses initiative in planning and carrying out assignments which are covered by instructions, policies, previous training or accepted pracork is reviewed in terms of the adequacy of methods, procedures, recommendations and results; and as an indicator of ability to grasp and solve new and changing problems, effectively deal with housekeeping employees, coordinate housekeeping activities with other departments and potential for successfully performing more responsible housekeeping work.

The housekeeping officer is fully responsible and accountable for planning, directing and monitoring all aspects of the housekeeping program. This includes responsibility for performing the full range of the following duties and responsibilities:

— Determining long-range, intermediate, and short-range program goals and policies independently or jointly with higher management and/or the appropriate committee(s);

— Developing and implementing organizational structures and operating plans and procedures to achieve program goals, monitoring effectiveness and efficiency of operations within the established framework, and making adjustments as necessary;

— Determining need for and allocation of resources, and accounting for their effective use;

— Coordinating program efforts with other internal activities, and, as necessary, program management officials at the headquarters level;

— Understanding agency and local policies and priorities and communicating them throughout the housekeeping department; and communicating the goals of the housekeeping program to other departments;

— Establishing personnel management policies for the housekeeping department which are in line with the general personnel policies of the agency and the local ; dealing with personnel actions affecting key employees and with other actions with possible serious repercussions; and

— Delegating authority to subordinate supervisors and holding them responsible for the performance of their respective organizational units.

In determining whether the Housekeeping Officer position is to be evaluated at this level, the emphasis must be on the impact the additional functional areas actually have on the position. Positions which involve marginal responsibility for potentially substantive functional areas should not be assigned to this level. The following examples illustrate the degree of responsibility the Housekeeping Officer must exercise over various substantive functional areas to receive credit at this level. Other functional areas may also be credited if they demand comparable specialized technical knowledge and management skills.

— *Interior Decoration*: Responsibility for interior decoration involves a major role for developing a hotel-wide decorating plan that is both conducive to guest well-being and pleasing to visitors and employees. In developing the plan, the durability, clean ability, suitability, expense and aesthetic value of various types of fabrics and furniture must be fully considered. While the preferences of hotel staff are considered in making decorating decisions, the Hotel Housekeeping Officer exercises final authority for selections, subject only to adjustment by top hotel management and/or the hotel's interior decoration committee.

— *Laundry:* Responsibility involves active participation (together with the laundry plant manager who is responsible for day-to-day laundry operation) in managing the technical operations of the laundry. This includes such activities as the selection and use of equipment, establishment of work standards, and development and revision of work flow procedures.

— *Control of Linen Management*: The Housekeeping Officer is responsible for the full cycle of linen management. This includes determination of the type of linen to be purchased, the quantity necessary to be kept in stock, establishment of quotas for each ward and other using points within the hotel, establishment of transportation methods and systems for both clean and soiled linen, and arrangement for laundering, repair and replacement of linens.

The areas of responsibility of the housekeeping department will be different depending on the size of the property. In small lodging operations the executive housekeeper is usually in charge of the cleaning and upkeep of most areas. In this particular case, very close cooperation between housekeeping and other departments is necessary to have the job done efficiently. For instance, if housekeeping is in charge of cleaning the banquet rooms, the manager needs to know the type and time of functions in order to provide the necessary service. In some cases, because the preparation and service of food begins very early in the morning and ends quite late in the evening, the cleaning function in food and beverage areas must be provided late at night. In large properties, the division of work by area is spread out among the different operating departments.

Often some of the cleaning functions-such as cleaning the kitchen, restaurant, and grounds-are contracted out to outside companies. Before contracting out cleaning tasks, it is important to obtain cost estimates from two or three different sources based on the size of the areas and the type and frequency of the cleaning desired. Once the contract has been signed, it is essential to check the quality of the work performed by the contractor. In no case should the cost of the services contracted be substantially higher than the cost of the same services performed by in-house personnel.

An ideal division of work in large properties would keep the housekeeping department from having to clean areas that are operated by the food and beverage or engineering divisions. There are several reasons for this: the housekeeping department usually does not have the necessary technical resources, the time, nor the expertise to clean ovens, walk-in refrigerators, kitchen hoods, and swimming pools or to prune palm trees and trim rose bushes.

Once the cleaning and maintenance responsibilities for all the areas of the property have been established, the respective department heads must plan the activities necessary for the upkeep of their areas, secure sufficient resources, and provide personnel to service them effectively.

The first step in planning the upkeep of the different areas assigned to the housekeeping department is to establish a list of the items that need to be regularly cleaned and maintained. A cleaning inventory list for guestrooms, for instance, will include all items that need to be cleaned, checked, and maintained in each room. The list should follow the sequence that section housekeepers keep when servicing guestrooms, for example, beginning with the entrance door to the rooms, standing lamps, window sills, furniture, and so on and ending with vacuuming the carpet. Another example of cleaning inventory would be that drawn for the lobby of the hotel, which might include not only furniture and fixtures but a water fountain, plants, bookcase, chandelier and so on. Area cleaning inventories can be combined with cleaning frequency schedules, including what needs to be cleaned and how often the items must be cleaned in one single document.Once the area cleaning inventory lists have been prepared, the frequency for cleaning and maintenance of each item should be established. Generally items need to be cleaned daily, biweekly, weekly, monthly, and so on. Examples of daily service in the lobby area would be the windowsills; plants could be dusted twice a week, the water fountain polished once a week, the air vents on the wall once a month, and so forth.

Besides cleaning items on a regular basis, most areas are deep cleaned once or twice a year. In this case, the cleaning crews scrape and scrub every nook and cranny until all surfaces are spotless. Deep cleaning projects generally coincide with low occupancy periods and are coordinated with repairs being done in the area by the engineering department. After compiling cleaning inventories and frequency schedules, performance standards must be established. Performance standards are used to inform subordinates of the equipment and supplies they must use to clean an item, of the method or way of doing the job, and of the expected cleaning outcomes. It is not good enough to tell section housekeepers and janitors to "clean well." "Cleaning well may mean different levels of cleanliness to different people. An example of performance standard to clean a vanity top could be. Spray all-purpose cleaner on the vanity top and wipe the surface clean with a sanitized rag, wiping it dry until no spots, marks, or specks remain." The development of cleaning performance standards should be established keeping in mind the direct input of the workers who are assigned to do the cleaning.

The written cleaning standards should be a part of the department's standard operating procedures (SOPs) and strictly observed during the training period of new employees. Properties that have written cleaning standards in place are able to measure employee performance by comparing the worker cleaning outcomes with the established standards.The assignment of guestrooms for daily cleaning is usually done randomly in small hotels. That is, the section housekeepers and gathered at the beginning of the shift and giver, a number of rooms to service on an individual basis. In large hotels, however, house keeping teams should be formed to which the same sections of rooms are consistently assigned.

There are several advantages to allotting the guestrooms to teams. Individual housekeepers take ownership of the rooms they clean day in and day out, showing pride for the work they perform, which increases their morale. Teams create a sense of unity, of common interests and responsibilities (esprit de corps) by which room attendants are less likely to let their partners down by calling in sick, thus improving attendance. A team may consist of four or five section housekeepers, a team supervisor, and a houseperson. The section housekeeper cleans guestrooms while the supervisor coordinates the work of the teams and inspects rooms. The housepersons assist in the work by providing the team with supplies, hauling the trash, vacuuming the hallways, moving heavy objects around, and so on. Guestrooms are divided by creating a pictorial representation of all rooms and allocating a certain number of them to every section housekeeper of each team. The criteria for guestroom cleaning workload vary from hotel to hotel depending on the size of the rooms, the number of furniture and fixture pieces to be cleaned, and the level of quality that management wishes to provide. As the workers need to be given two days off per week to avoid overtime, the department will need a larger number of workers to substitute for those who are off. The problem becomes more complicated if the property operates an on-premise laundry. Let us suppose that this is the case and that the laundry is operated by one fun team consisting of five section housekeepers, one supervisor, and one houseperson.

The internal organization of the housekeeping department follows the same pattern as that of the property as a whole. The chain of command begins with the executive housekeeper and goes on to encompass all employees in the department. Besides the section housekeepers, supervisors, and housepersons needed to clean the guestrooms, and the laundry room workers, the housekeeping department needs additional personnel to service other areas of the property, such as offices, public and back-of the-house sections, and linen room.

The employees in the department's work force can be classified into management, fixed, evening, laundry, and guestroom cleaning teams. The executive housekeeper, housekeeping manager, and laundry manager fall under management. These employees are salaried and are required to work a minimum of 40 hours each week. The housekeeping fixed employees are the janitors and the linen room attendants. These workers are usually hourly employees who are guaranteed 5 days' work regardless of guestroom occupancy.

The reason for guaranteeing fixed work is that whether or not the guestrooms have been sold out, lobbies, offices and other front and back-of -the-house public areas must be serviced on a daily basis. The evening team takes over the duties of the department at the end of the morning shift when all regular teams clock off. The jobs generally assigned to the evening shift are cleaning late checkout and day-rate guestrooms, providing turndown service, counting soiled linen, servicing public and back-of-the-house areas, preparing carts for the morning shift, washing guestroom glasses, and filling out guest requests as the evening progresses. As with the janitors, the evening team is composed of hourly employees who are guaranteed 5 days of work regardless of occupancy. The guestroom cleaning and laundry teams are also composed of hourly employees, but the number of hours they are scheduled to work depends on the number of guestrooms sold daily. For instance, if the hotel is full all section housekeepers who are not off duty that day will be needed to clean all guestrooms, but if the occupancy drops to 80 per cent, only enough section housekeepers to clean 80 per cent of the guestrooms with be called to work.

Facilities in all parts of young America were commensurate with the demand of the travelling public, and early records indicate that a choice was usually available at many trading centers and crossroads. The decision as to where to stay was as it is today, based on where you might find a location providing the best food, overnight protection, and clean facilities. Even though the inns were crude, they were gathering places where you could learn the news of the day, socialise, find out the business of the community, and rest.

With the growth of transportation-roadways, river travel, railroads, and air travel-Americans became even more mobile. Inns, hotels, motor hotels, resorts, and the like have kept pace, fallen by the wayside, overbuilt, or refurbished to meet quality demands. Just as the traveller of earlier times had a choice, there is a wide choice for travellers today. We therefore have to consider seriously why one specific hotel or inn might be selected over another. In each of the areas we mentioned-food, clean room, sociable atmosphere, meeting space, and security-there has been a need to remain competitive. Priorities in regard to these need areas, however, have remained in the sphere of an individual property's management philosophy.

In addition to the areas of hospitality we discussed, professional housekeeping requires a staff with a sense of pride. Housekeeping staffs must show concern for guests, which will make the guests want to return-the basic ingredient for growth in occupancy and success in the hotel business. Such pride is best measured by the degree to which the individual maids say to guests through their attitude, concern, and demeanour, "Welcome, we are glad you chose to stay with us. We care about you and want your visit to be a memorable occasion. If anything is not quite right, please let us know in order that we might take care of the problem immediately." A prime responsibility of the executive housekeeper is to develop this concern in the staff; it is just as important as the other functions of cleaning bathrooms, making beds, and making rooms ready for occupancy.

According to Mackenzie, the elements that today's managers work with are ideas, things, and people. These are the main components of an organisation and are in the center of the figure. The manager's task that is related to ideas is to think conceptually about matters that need to be resolved. The task related to things is to administer or manage the details of executive affairs. The task related to people is to exercise leadership and influence people so that they accomplish desired goals The functions of a manager can be thought of as continuous functions and sequential functions. Many times a question may be asked: "But what does the manager do?" The manager should be seen to do several continuous functions, as well as several sequential functions.

The continuous functions relating to ideas and conceptual thinking are to *analyse problems.* Those related to things and administration are to *make decisions,* and those related to people and leadership are to *communicate* successfully. Problems are analysed, facts gathered, causes learned, alternative solutions developed, decisions made, conclusions drawn, communications generated, and understanding assured. The sequential functions of management are more recognisable as a part of the classical definition of management. They involve the planning, organising, staffing, directing, and controlling of ideas, things, and people.

Mackenzie sets forth various activities in each of these sequential functions that should be studied and recalled whenever necessary. According to him , a manager's sequential functions are divided into five areas—planning, organising, staffing, directing, and controlling. The management plan involves seven basic activities:

I. *Forecasting*—Establishing where present courses will lead
2. *Setting objectives*—Determining desired results
3. *Developing strategies*—Deciding how and when to achieve goals
4. *Programming*—Establishing priorities, sequence, and timing of steps
5. *Budgeting*—Allocating resources
6. *Setting procedures*—Standardising methods
7. *Developing policies*—Making standing decisions on important recurring matters

Getting organised involves arranging and relating work for the effective accomplishment of an objective. Managers organise by making administrative or operational decisions. The four activities involved in getting organised are as follows:

1. *Establishing an organisational structure:* Drawing up an organisational chart
2. *Delineating relationships:* Defining liaison lines to facilitate coordination
3. *Creating position descriptions:* Defining the scope, relationship, responsibilities, and authority of each member of the organisation
4. *Establishing position qualifications:* Defining the qualifications for people in each position

The third sequential function, staffing, involves people. Leadership now comes into play and communication is established to ensure that understanding takes place. There are four activities:

1. *Selecting employees:* Recruiting qualified people for each position
2. *Orienting employees:* Familiarising new people with their environment

3. *Training:* Making people proficient by instruction and practice
4. *Developing.* Improving knowledge, attitude, and skills

The first three sequential functions of management—planning, organising, and staffing—might be performed before an operation gets under way. The last two sequential functions—directing and controlling—are carried out after the operation has begun or is in process. As with other managerial relationships involving people, leadership is accomplished through communication. In the directing of operations, there are five basic activities:

1. *Delegating:* Assigning responsibility and exacting accountability for results
2. *Motivating:* Persuading and inspiring people to take a desired action
3. *Coordinating:* Relating efforts in the most efficient combination
4. *Managing differences:* Encouraging independent thought and resolving conflict
5. *Managing change:* Stimulating creativity and innovation in achieving goals

The final sequential function of management is to control organisations and activities to ensure the desired progress toward objectives. There are five basic activities in the controlling of operations:

1. *Establishing a reporting system:* Determining what critical data arc needed
2. *Developing performance standards:* Setting conditions that will exist when key duties are well done
3. *Measuring results:* Ascertaining the extent of deviation from goals and standards
4. *Taking corrective action:* Adjusting plans, counselling to attain standards, replanning and repeating the several sequential functions as necessary

5. *Rewarding:* Praising, remunerating, or administering discipline.

The following employee characteristics are commonly found in man in housekeeping departments.

— Cultural diversity abounds in most housekeeping departments. Racial minorities, particularly black and Hispanic employees, are to be found in numbers that are disproportionate to their representation in the general population.

— The reason for this situation is obvious; the doors of opportunity have been closed to these Americans for generations (many of these doors are not yet fully open). Consequently, these Americans have gravitated to those few areas of employment left open to them.

— In many parts of the country, particularly the Southwest, Florida, New York, and many major urban centers, English is not the predominant language spoken in the housekeeping department. In fact, in many housekeeping departments many workers can neither speak nor write in English.

— Housekeeping often attracts individuals with little formal education. Many workers are functionally illiterate, and others can be classified as being "math illiterate." This can have a particularly telling effect upon departmental efficiency and communications.

— Many of the employees come from lower socioeconomic backgrounds. These environments can often be a major factor in the formation of employee attitudes and behaviours that are not compatible with traditional corporate values. For instance, these individuals tend to have a work ethic that is far different from that of middle America. These employees often need to be taught such fundamentals as the need for punctuality, personal hygiene, and how to communicate with the guest.

— A worker may often have emotional or economic problems, or may even have a dependency problem. It is not

> suggested that the executive housekeeper is the only manager within the hotel who faces these problems, but many would argue that the frequency of these problems is higher in housekeeping than in other areas. Housekeeping often attracts displaced housewives, single parents, and former welfare recipients who have a higher incidence of these problems.

Although there may be numerous properties throughout the United States where these traits and characteristics are not found in the employees of the housekeeping department, they do appear frequently enough to require the astute housekeeping manager to prepare for such eventualities. The motivation of employees is accomplished by the manager having created an environment in which employees can motivate themselves. Managers cannot hope to directly motivate other human beings; however, they can provide a climate where self-motivation will take place.

As most housekeeping administrators know, a formal training program is an indispensable element in achieving productivity goals. There are, however, certain training approaches and concerns that are not being addressed by all housekeeping administrators. These concerns include the educational background of the staff. Many housekeeping workers may be illiterate or may not be able to communicate in English. Written training materials, such as manuals, posters, and written tests, are quite useless when the staff cannot read, write, or speak the English language.

Special audio/visual training materials are often required in housekeeping departments, and the written training materials must often be made available to the workers in Spanish or other languages. The introduction of these materials does not rectify the problem, however. Consequently, many housekeeping departments have initiated remedial educational programs so that employees can not only learn to read and write in English; but can also earn their high school diplomas.

The executive housekeeper does not have to implement these remedial programs from scratch; he or she can turn to a number of sources of assistance found in most communities, such as the public school or the community college system. These sources can often provide qualified bilingual adult instruction at little or no cost to the company.

Another tactic is to reimburse employee tuition if remedial classes are completed at the local community college. The payoff to the housekeeping department is twofold. First, productivity benefits because the level of communication has increased. Second, the esteem level of the employees should certainly increase when they begin to achieve their personal educational goals, and a self-assured workforce will ultimately become a more competent and productive workforce.

Delegation is one of five activities of direction. Others view delegation as the most valuable activity. The other activities—motivation, coordination, managing differences, and managing change—can be seen as stemming from a manager's ability to delegate properly. Too often we hear the phrase, "delegation of responsibilities and authority." In fact, it is impossible to delegate a responsibility. To delegate actually means to pass authority to someone who will act in behalf of the delegator. The passing of such authority does not relieve the delegator of the responsibility for action or results, although there is an implied accountability of the person to whom power has been delegated to the person having that power.

The responsibility of a manager for the acts or actions of his or her subordinates is therefore absolute and may not be passed to anyone else. When an executive housekeeper is assigned overall responsibility for directing the activities of a housekeeping department, carrying out this responsibility may require the completion of thousands of tasks, very few of which may actually be performed by the executive housekeeper. It is therefore a responsibility of management to identify these tasks and create responsibilities for subordinates to carry them out.

A good operational definition of delegation is the creation of a responsibility for, or the assignment of a task to, a subordinate, providing that person with the necessary authority (power) to carry out the task and exacting an accountability for the results of the subordinate's efforts. The lack of any one of the three elements of this definition creates a situation whereby the manager abdicates the responsibility to manage. Thorough and complete delegation, where possible, will free the manager from tasks that can be performed by subordinates, allowing the manager time to manage the operation.

FUNCTIONS OF CLEANING WORKERS

Building cleaning workers—including janitors, maids, housekeeping cleaners, window washers, and rug shampooers—keep hotel buildings in good condition. Some only do cleaning, while others have a wide range of duties.

Janitors and cleaners perform a variety of heavy cleaning duties, such as cleaning floors, shampooing rugs, washing walls and glass, and removing rubbish. They may fix leaky faucets, empty trash cans, do painting and carpentry, replenish bathroom supplies, mow lawns, and see that heating and air-conditioning equipment works properly. On a typical day, janitors may wet- or dry-mop floors, clean bathrooms, vacuum carpets, dust furniture, make minor repairs, and exterminate insects and rodents. They also clean snow or debris from sidewalks in front of buildings and notify management of the need for major repairs. While janitors typically perform most of the duties mentioned, cleaners tend to work for companies that specialize in one type of cleaning activity, such as washing windows.

Maids and housekeeping cleaners perform any combination of light cleaning duties to maintain private households or commercial establishments, such as hotels and restaurants. In hotels, aside from cleaning and maintaining the premises, maids and housekeeping cleaners may deliver ironing boards, cribs, and rollaway beds to guests' rooms. They also may wash bedframes, brush mattresses, make beds, and disinfect and sterilize equipment and supplies with germicides and sterilizing equipment.

Janitors, maids, and cleaners use various equipment, tools, and cleaning materials. For one job they may need a mop and bucket, for another an electric polishing machine and a special cleaning solution. Improved building materials, chemical cleaners, and power equipment have made many tasks easier and less time consuming, but cleaning workers must learn the proper use of equipment and cleaners to avoid harming floors, fixtures, and themselves.

Cleaning supervisors coordinate, schedule, and supervise the activities of janitors and cleaners. They assign tasks and inspect building areas to see that work has been done properly, issue supplies and equipment, and inventory stocks to ensure that an adequate amount of supplies is present. They also screen and hire job applicants, train new and experienced employees, and recommend promotions, transfers, or dismissals. Supervisors may prepare reports concerning the occupancy of rooms, hours worked, and department expenses. Some also perform cleaning duties.

Cleaners and servants in private households dust and polish furniture; sweep, mop, and wax floors; vacuum; and clean ovens, refrigerators, and bathrooms. They also may wash dishes, polish silver, and change and make beds. Some wash, fold, and iron clothes; a few wash windows. General houseworkers also may take clothes and laundry to the cleaners, buy groceries, and perform many other errands.

Building cleaning workers in large hotles often work in teams consisting of workers who specialize in vacuuming, picking up trash, and cleaning rest rooms, among other things. Supervisors conduct inspections to ensure that the building is cleaned properly and the team is functioning efficiently.

Building cleaning workers usually work inside heated, well-lighted buildings. However, they sometimes work outdoors, sweeping walkways, mowing lawns, or shoveling snow. Working with machines can be noisy, and some tasks, such as cleaning bathrooms and trash rooms, can be dirty and unpleasant. Janitors may suffer cuts, bruises, and burns from machines, handtools, and chemicals. They spend most of their time on their feet, sometimes lifting or pushing heavy furniture or equipment. Many tasks, such as dusting or sweeping, require constant bending, stooping, and stretching. As a result, janitors also may suffer back injuries and sprains.

A recent survey conducted in USA reports that building cleaning workers held nearly 4 million jobs in 2002 in the country. More than 6 percent were self-employed. Janitors and cleaners work in nearly every type of establishment and held about 2.3 million jobs. They accounted for about 57 percent of all building cleaning workers. About 28 percent worked for firms supplying building maintenance services on a contract basis, 21 percent were employed in educational institutions, and 2 percent worked in hotels.

First-line supervisors of housekeeping and janitorial workers held about 230,000 jobs. Approximately 22 percent worked in firms supplying building maintenance services on a contract basis, 14 percent were employed in hotels, 7 percent held jobs in nursing and other residential care facilities, and 5 percent worked in hospitals. Other employers included educational institutions and amusement and recreation facilities.

Maids and housekeepers held about 1.5 million jobs. Hotels, motels, and other traveler accommodations employed the most maids and housekeepers—27 percent—while private households employed the second most: 25 percent. Eight percent were employed in hospitals; and, a similar percentage worked in nursing and other residential care facilities. Although cleaning jobs can be found in all cities and towns, most are located in highly populated areas where there are many office buildings, schools, apartment houses, nursing homes, and hospitals.

No special education is required for most janitorial or cleaning jobs, but beginners should know simple arithmetic and be able to follow instructions. High school shop courses are helpful for jobs involving repair work.

Most building cleaners learn their skills on the job. Usually, beginners work with an experienced cleaner, doing routine cleaning. As they gain more experience, they are assigned more complicated tasks.

In some cities, programs run by unions, government agencies, or employers teach janitorial skills. Students learn how to clean buildings thoroughly and efficiently, how to select and safely use various cleansing agents, and how to operate and maintain machines, such as wet and dry vacuums, buffers, and polishers. Students learn to plan their work, to follow safety and health regulations, to interact positively with people in the buildings they clean, and to work without supervision. Instruction in minor electrical, plumbing, and other repairs also may be given. Those who come in contact with the public should have good communication skills. Employers usually look for dependable, hard-working individuals who are in good health, follow directions well, and get along with other people.

Building cleaners usually find work by answering newspaper advertisements, applying directly to organizations where they would like to work, contacting local labor unions, or contacting State employment service offices.

Advancement opportunities for workers usually are limited in organizations where they are the only maintenance worker. Where there is a large maintenance staff, however, cleaning workers can be promoted to supervisor and to area supervisor or manager. A high school diploma improves the chances for advancement. Some janitors set up their own maintenance or cleaning businesses.

Supervisors usually move up through the ranks. In many establishments, they are required to take some inservice training to improve their housekeeping techniques and procedures and to enhance their supervisory skills.

A small number of cleaning supervisors and managers are members of the International Executive Housekeepers Association, which offers two kinds of certification programs to cleaning supervisors and managers: Certified Executive Housekeeper (CEH) and Registered Executive Housekeeper (REH). The CEH designation is offered to those with a high school education, while the REH designation is offered to those who have a 4-year college degree. Both designations are earned by attending courses and passing exams, and both must be renewed every 2 years to ensure that workers keep abreast of new cleaning methods. Those with the REH designation usually oversee the cleaning services of hotels, hospitals, casinos, and other large institutions that rely on well-trained experts for their cleaning needs.

Overall employment of building cleaning workers is expected to grow about as fast as the average for all occupations through 2012, as more office complexes, apartment houses, schools, factories, hospitals, and other buildings requiring cleaning are built to accommodate a growing population and economy. As many firms reduce costs by contracting out the cleaning and maintenance of buildings, businesses providing janitorial and cleaning services on a contract basis are expected to be one of the faster growing employers of these workers. Although there have been some improvements in productivity in the way buildings are cleaned and maintained—using teams of cleaners, for example, and better cleaning supplies—it is still very much a labor-intensive job.

Average growth is expected among janitors and cleaners and among cleaning supervisors, but less-than-average growth is projected for maids and housekeeping cleaners. In addition to job openings arising due to growth, numerous openings should result from the need to replace those who leave this very large occupation each year. Limited formal education and training requirements, low pay, and numerous part-time and temporary jobs induce many to leave the occupation, thereby contributing to the number of job openings and the need to replace these workers.

Much of the growth in these occupations will come from cleaning residential properties. As families become more pressed for time, they increasingly are hiring cleaning and handyman services to perform a variety of tasks in their homes. Also, as the population ages, older people will need to hire cleaners to help maintain their houses. In addition, housekeeping cleaners will be needed to clean the growing number of residential care facilities for the elderly. These facilities, including assisted-living arrangements, generally provide housekeeping services as part of the rent.

JOB AND WORKFORCE QUALITY

To those who care about the health and vitality of the U.S. economy, the hotel industry is more than just another industry. The industry itself builds cities, drives economic development, and provides a diverse set of jobs, including entry-level jobs that can be a launching pad into the American labor market. It is a key sector with a broad set of stakeholders: not only hotel owners, managers, and workers, but also local elected officials seeking to develop their cities, planners and developers who make urban development deals, and community-based organizations, including the many that represent recent immigrants and work to connect their members and clients to jobs in the industry.

Hotels have always played and continue to play a vital role in our communities. Key challenges will define the hospitality industry in the 21st century. And success in meeting these challenges hinges on the ability of the industry's stakeholders to come together and solve their common problems.

Currently employing 1.8 million workers nationwide, the hospitality industry has been among the nation's fastest growing industries over the past 30 years. It is particularly important in large metropolitan areas, which account for about two-thirds of the rooms in the industry. As the industry has grown, shifting ownership and growing competition have increased pressures on managers to turn quarterly profits and shed units that are outside the firms' "core" competencies.

In recent decades, the industry has undergone widespread consolidation and a shift from private to public ownership. Both trends signal a much more intense competitive environment. Large corporate chains, each owning a range of brandname chains targeted at different segments of the market, now dominate an industry once populated by small family-owned hotels. From 1990 to 2000, the market share of chains increased significantly from 46 to 60 percent, while the share of independent hotels decreased dramatically, from 54 to 40 percent. The pace of mergers is expected by many industry insiders to speed up in the next few years to the extent that, as many analysts predict, "eventually five mega-hotel companies will control the worldwide hotel business".

As a result, competition in the industry has grown ever more intense, and pressures to cut costs have mounted dramatically. Now more than ever, managers of each department are responsible for making their unit a "profit center." Over and over again, hotel executives and managers told us: "You're only as good as your last quarter." Hotels' increasing need to contain costs is clearly revealed in the growth of subcontracting, particularly of restaurant outlets. No longer are food and beverage outlets allowed to be "necessary evils," moneylosing amenities that the hotel simply has to provide.

Instead, hotel restaurants are now required to be money makers, which has led many hotels to seek outside companies to take over their food and beverage operations. Tight labor markets have also challenged the industry. Low unemployment rates through the year 2000 made recruitment and retention of frontline workers a central problem in the industry. Though the recent economic slowdown hit the industry with exceptional force (especially after 9/11), there are already signs of recovery in the sector. Given the relatively low wages that frontline jobs offer, the problems of recruitment and retention are likely to grow again as the economy expands.

The vast majority of hotel workers are in entry-level positions in the housekeeping and food and beverage departments. Wages for these jobs are generally quite low, and are substantially lower than those of the average U.S. worker. There has been a significant demographic shift in the race and ethnicity of entry-level hotel workers over time. Whereas African-American workers once dominated "back of the house" hotel jobs, now, in most metropolitan areas, recent immigrants do. The number of Hispanic workers in the hotel industry, in particular, has grown rapidly in the past few decades.

Seen through the eyes of the industry's frontline workforce, hotel employment often offers low wages, irregular hours, little training, and almost no hope of advancement into familysupporting jobs. The result is that workers often feel little loyalty to employers and frequently simply leave the job for a similar one earning just a dime or two more per hour. Seen through the eyes of many frontline managers, high turnover is evidence of an unreliable workforce, and training is therefore too risky an investment.

The result is that employers under-invest in workers, pursue technologies that require little training, and re-create the low job quality that pushes the workers to leave in the first place. Thus, a low-wage and low-investment equilibrium appears to dominate much of the industry. But there are important exceptions. Some hotels have pursued higher wage strategies, and are rewarded with more loyalty from the workforce and higher quality service - for which customers will often pay a premium.

Housekeepers often face a quota of 16 rooms to be cleaned each day. That's two rooms an hour. Imagine increasing the cost of all rooms by $1 per night (a tiny price change when rooms are over $100) and delivering all of the increased revenues to the housekeepers. The housekeepers could bring home an extra $2 per hour, a significant increase that is very likely to improve retention and employee loyalty. In addition, one might consider taking a portion of that rate increase and putting it toward a pooled training fund for entry-level workers. Now, in the real world the situation is clearly more complex, but the thought experiment does illustrate that, especially in markets where room rates are $100-$200 per night, there is the potential for a strategy focused on quality service, training, and good jobs. But to say that such a strategy can be competitive does not ensure that it will be pursued.

Challenges in Recruitment

Recruiting and retaining good workers is clearly one of the biggest problems in the hotel industry. While the recent economic downturn moved this problem off the screen temporarily, the brief recovery is already bringing it back. Every hotel had a hard time finding workers and holding onto them, and they all expected to face this challenge in the future. Managers identified changing worker demographics, increasing competition from jobs with higher wages, and the widespread negative perceptions of hotel jobs as all working against recruitment and retention in the industry. There are three main responses to the challenges of recruitment and retention that continue to plague this otherwise booming industry:

1.Standard Response: Watching the Revolving Door Spin...

The most common response to the recruitment and retention problem is essentially no response. Even if they recognize the problem, many managers do not have the resources to deal with it and simply accept that their entry-level jobs are going to be high-turnover. Part of the dynamic here is the constant pressure on managers to reduce costs. The motto among most managers was: "Do more with less."

In hotels across the country, the amount of work has substantially increased; room quotas are rising for housekeepers, kitchens have fewer workers. But greater workloads lead to higher rates of injury; for example, in 2001 over three-quarters of Las Vegas hotel housekeepers reported experiencing work-related pain severe enough to see a doctor and take time off from work, while 83 percent reported taking medication within the last month for work-related pain. This means fewer workers on staff at any given time (and, therefore, almost no one able to move up or laterally into other positions) and, in the end, lower quality service, which eventually but inevitably hurts the bottom line.

Moreover, when workload increases, so does turnover. As a consequence, hotel managers are continually struggling to recruit workers for a never-ending chain of job openings, all the while watching helplessly as newly hired and trained workers walk out the revolving door. At one hotel, the wages for housekeepers and laundry workers have remained unchanged for several years, even though the cost of living in the city has been rising. The Director of Hotel Operations has been unable to convince the hotel to raise wages and has watched his workers leave for better jobs outside the hotel industry. He has had to rely more and more on the few remaining housekeepers to work overtime, which only further decreases job satisfaction and increases the speed of the revolving door.

Understaffing has led many hotels to increase their use of shortsighted cross-training. "Shortsighted" because cross-training is not inherently a bad strategy as long as it creates opportunities for training and upward or lateral mobility, and as long as employees get paid according to the job they are performing. But many hotels that use as few employees for as many different job categories as possible, while paying them the least amount possible. As a cook at one hotel observed: "There's not really a choice whether or not to work other stations.

Many hotels have also turned to subcontracting some of their operations in order to cut costs and avoid having to deal with recruitment and turnover - effectively offloading these problems onto someone else. But there is a growing recognition in the industry that there is a downside to this practice: loss of control over quality, loss of control over staff, and loss of potentially significant profits.

As one hospitality consultant points out: "It is extremely important to consider the relationship between the hotel operator and the food and beverage operator... Who controls the space, who gets priority on meeting space and operating contracts set forth to allow the restaurant and the hotel to maximize revenues." Furthermore, according to the consultant, "the perception for the guest should be seamless, the restaurant and hotel must work together on all aspects to succeed".

2.Getting to the problem

Other hotel managers have been more proactive in dealing with recruitment and retention problems - using employee recognition programs, referral bonuses, and connections with community-based organizations. But while these strategies are a step in the right direction, in the end they are only partial solutions. This is because they are often implemented in a piecemeal, short-term fashion, rather than being part of a long-term, full-scale investment in solving the recruitment and turnover problems.

Additionally, when managers focus specifically on recruitment, they can develop programs and benefits for new employees that leave their long-term staff feeling disrespected and overlooked. For example, offering a raise only in the rate paid to new hires or giving signing bonuses to new employees can lead to friction and resentment within the workforce. As a result, these strategies have had only limited success. In some hotels have employee recognition programs in order to boost employee morale and job satisfaction, with the hope that productivity will increase and turnover decrease. For example, one hotel recently created a "Housekeeping Team Player" program and hosted a luncheon for the housekeepers in thanks for the hotel's consistently high ratings for cleanliness. Yet many workers complained that this program really didn't improve their morale.

A number of hotels have also gotten more sophisticated about their reliance on employee referrals. For example, in one hotel, recently increased the employee bonus from $50 to $200 if the referral stayed on the job nine months. Manager at this hotel believes that employee referrals have decreased turnover rates so much that she relies exclusively on them for recruitment and no longer uses local newspapers and other traditional recruitment venues. Some hotels have also tried to establish connections with community-based organizations, which can provide English as a Second Language (ESL) and other skills classes and help to recruit workers.

The Human Resources (HR) Director at one hotel, for example, has long been struggling to fill her entry-level positions. She decided to become an active member of the Chamber of Commerce, and every week also sends a list of job openings to all local community organizations and colleges. But unfortunately, very few job candidates come from these sources because her hotel's wages simply cannot compete with other entry-level jobs in the city. There is also the problem that community outreach takes a significant amount of effort and time, which the HR Director simply does not have. Moreover, as a single hotel, it is hard to establish and maintain relationships with all the various local groups.

3. Building the High Road

Although there are many difficulties in implementing an all-out, longterm battle against the challenges of recruitment and retention, the evidence of several hotels doing just that. The primary elements of these "high-road strategies" include: increasing wages and benefits, making job openings available to all workers (including those traditionally not considered appropriate for the job), offering ongoing training programs in ESL, safety, and managerial preparation, and implementing farsighted cross-training. Most often, underlying these high-road strategies are strong partnerships between a group of hotels, community colleges, and local unions in order to alleviate the costs and risks of such programs for individual hotels.

The most fundamental way to improve recruitment and retention is to enhance job quality. And the primary way to do so is to increase wages and benefits. As an Assistant Front Desk Manager pointed out: "You get what you pay for. There is a real difference in the quality of higher versus lower paid employees. When GRAs [guest room attendants] are paid more, they do a much, much better job than those that are paid less. When they're paid poorly, they simply don't take ownership of their job." Training is another critical component. Although the training programs are being cut back or eliminated in many hotels, long-term and company-paid training in ESL, safety, and managerial preparation is an essential element to building the high road in the hotel industry.

In study after study, emphasis on continuous training programs has been found to reduce turnover, improve customer service, and increase profit. One oft-cited hotel, which recently won a National Training Award, has reaped enormous benefits from its new training program. In the first year, staff turnover plummeted to 11 percent and customer complaints dropped to virtually nil, while net profit was up 276 percent. Expanding the recruitment pool to nontraditional workers can benefit both hotels and their employees. A small number of hotels have implemented cross-training in such a way that is beneficial to both management and employees - what we term farsighted cross-training. Hotel managers get increased productivity and adequate staffing levels; employees get increased job security, decreased job tedium, higher wages, and real opportunities for upward and lateral mobility.

Challenges and Solutions

There is no better way to attract and keep workers than to offer them real chances for growth and advancement. In fact, the hotel industry is one of the very few sectors that already has a well-established career ladder for workers without a college education. The significance of this fact cannot be understated. In many workplaces, it is virtually unheard of for an employee with little more than a high school degree to start at the bottom and eventually move into the upper ranks of management. Yet in the hotel industry, entrylevel workers do just that. In the front desk department, career ladders have been an excellent way to find good workers, train them, and develop a strong core of upper-level managers who know the industry inside and out.

The problem is that this career ladder doesn't yet extend to the majority of workers, and in the housekeeping and food and beverage departments, such ladders are unattainable. Most people continue to regard the hotel industry as one of "burger flippers and bed makers," not one in which they can develop a career. Dishwashers, low-level cooks, and housekeepers may occasionally become supervisors in their departments, but they almost never move across job categories into better jobs (such as the front desk) or up into the ranks of management.

Additionally, even lateral movement between "back of the house" positions is stunted. The departments rarely look to other divisions inside the hotel to those workers who would appreciate the variety, new skills, and other attributes offered by lateral moves. At best, this lack of mobility - across and within key departments, as well as from the "back of the house" to the "front of the house" - represents the loss of a potentially valuable opportunity for hotels. At worst, it is a real drag on long-term productivity. As Peter Drucker argued in a recent Harvard Business Review article, "The attenuation of the relationship between people and the organizations they work for represents a grave danger to business. ... If by off-loading employee relations, organizations also lose their capacity to develop people, they will have made a devil's bargain indeed". There are three main responses to the issue of mobility for frontline workers in the hospitality industry:

1. Inhibiting the Creation of Career Ladders

Many hotel managers understand that there is a mobility problem, but feel that they have neither the time nor the money to address it. They may not be aware, however, that they are pursuing strategies that actually inhibit the creation of career ladders - for example, cutting training programs, subcontracting departments, and eliminating midlevel jobs to streamline costs and bureaucracy. Because many front-line workers are recent immigrants with limited English-speaking skills, and because few have any experience in customer service and managerial skills, the obvious first step in boosting worker mobility is extensive training in ESL and managerial skills. This is easier said than done, however.

Because of growing pressure on hotels to increase profits, as well as the difficulties of scheduling classes for employees who work around the clock, we can found that while many hotels had tried at some point to offer such training programs, these training programs have been drastically reduced or cut altogether. Subcontracting clearly inhibits the creation of career ladders in hotels, though it is rarely intended to do so. For example, subcontracting a hotel's restaurants means that housekeepers won't have the opportunity to move laterally into food and beverage work, which can be less back-breaking and, in some cases, more lucrative.

Subcontracting out valet jobs means fewer higher level positions for doormen and room attendants to move into. Perhaps the greatest barrier to worker mobility is the extraordinary flatness of the job hierarchy in hotels, with a large number of entry-level workers at the bottom, very few managers at the top, and almost no positions in between. This polarization has increased significantly in recent years, as hotels have sought to downsize and streamline bureaucracy by eliminating many of the middle positions that, in the past, may have allowed for upward advancement.

2.Doing Nothing at All

While some hotels do not use strategies such as subcontracting that negatively affect opportunities for advancement, they also do not make a concerted effort to encourage job mobility for all entry-level workers. Many hotel managers believed that entry-level workers did not want to move up or try other jobs in the hotel. As one HR Director maintained, dishwashers have a "labor, blue-collar mindset; they get satisfaction out of cleaning up after the tornado has hit." This opinion was not uncommon.

In some cases the housekeepers and dishwashers are "happy working a full shift and then going home, without the added responsibility of being a manager." And, in some cases, this may be true. However, assuming this is true for all entry-level workers will undoubtedly create an environment that makes it nearly impossible for any housekeepers or dishwashers to move out of their jobs. Another common belief is that entry-level employees do not (and never will) have the managerial skills necessary to move up in the industry.

As one hotel manager noted: "Some people just have managerial potential, others don't. Some managers are trained, but they still don't get it. Managing takes special skills and common sense." By assuming that managerial skilis are wholly innate and un-teachable, and by assuming that housekeepers, for example, do not have these innate skills, hotel managers create a self-fulfilling prophecy.

3.Building the High Road

Although few hotels have strong internal advancement procedures. Well-developed training programs are an important component, as are strong internal promotion policies and partnerships with other hotels, community colleges, and/or unions that facilitate information-sharing and alleviate costs. Strong internal promotion policies are the most important component, and they can extend far beyond simply trying to increase promotion within any one particular department. Hotel managers can also think creatively about increasing mobility between departments and even between hotels owned by the same corporation. For example, cross-department mobility might mean using housekeepers as banquet servers during the winter season, when rooms are empty and the banquet halls are overflowing. In some hotels, this practice alleviated the hotel's critical labor crunch for banquet servers while solving the problem of slack work for housekeepers during the off-season. Moreover, this strategy benefited workers by providing a variety of work tasks, training in a new job, and increased job security.

Cross-hotel mobility is also an important component in facilitating job mobility and advancement in the industry. Currently, the careers of most hotel managers extend well beyond the boundaries of one or even two hotels. In fact, if a manager stays more than five years in any given position, she is considered stagnant and not interested in moving up. Although this emphasis on cross-hotel mobility does not yet apply to entry-level workers, it would be extremely beneficial. Because the majority of hotels are currently owned by large corporations that own a wide variety of hotel chains, being able to move between properties would open up many more job opportunities for workers at all levels. The best training programs in the industry invest in a range of real skill development programs and focus on training that benefits both workers and firms. Training must be valued by both parties; otherwise, classes won't fill up and workers won't advance. And successful advancement training programs focus not only on technical skills but also on leadership, problem-solving, and teamwork skills.

3

Technical Skills

Housekeeping is an important component of the lodging segment of the hospitality industry for which skill standards should be developed. The function of housekeeping is to create clean, safe and healthy environments in a variety of settings. The primary facilities that have housekeepers on staff include hotels and motels, healthcare facilities, nursing homes/retirement centres, airports and public buildings.

Occupational Definitions

Housekeeper

Housekeeper is the entry-level position. Housekeepers do the primary cleaning in guestrooms, public areas, offices and back of the house. The housekeeper reports to the assistant director or the director of housekeeping.

Supervisor

Supervisors monitor the work of housekeepers to ensure quality standards and expected performance levels for productivity are maintained. The supervisor reports to the assistant director or the director of housekeeping.

Assistant director of housekeeping

The assistant director of housekeeping assists the director of housekeeping with the supervision of housekeeping employees, report problems to the director, provides feedback to the director for employee evaluations, trains the housekeepers, and performs other tasks as designated by the director of housekeeping. The assistant director may perform primary cleaning tasks as needed within the facility. The assistant director reports directly to the director of housekeeping.

Director of Housekeeping

The director of housekeeping is responsible for ensuring guestrooms, meeting and banquet rooms, and public areas are clean, orderly, and well maintained. The director supervises all housekeeping employees, has the authority to hire or discharge employees, plans and assigns work assignments, inform new employees of property regulations, inspects housekeeping personnel work assignments and requisitions supplies. The director is also responsible for drafting and maintaining the housekeeping department's operational budget. The director reports to the rooms division manager/director of facility operations.

Rooms Division Manager/Director of Facility Operations

Management of the housekeeping department is an important function of the rooms division manager/director of facility operations. Management functions include: developing and maintaining the housekeeping operational and capital improvement budgets; developing departmental policies and procedures; and maintaining, training and supervising staff.

Employment Opportunities

A strong career ladder exists between entry-level housekeeping positions and rooms division manager/director of facility operations. Many of the major chains require their general managers to have held one of the two senior positions in housekeeping before moving up the ladder to rooms division manager. This requirement is in place because the housekeeping department usually has the largest labour force, budget, and scope of operation within the lodging property. Ocupations in all four components of the lodging standards cluster are significant and growing at or above the statewide average rate. Occupancy rates and property expansion will continue to rise over the next 15 years. The career track is vertical and horizontal. By virtue of training and experience, employees are able to assume more complex and responsible positions. Employees also have the opportunity to move geographically and to work in different types of properties. The career ladder as reflected on the housekeeping standards matrix shows the potential for upward mobility in the lodging industry.

Performace Skills Needed in Houskeeping Operations

Safety of Guests

Conditions of Performance

Given the following:

- Safety equipment and systems
- Safety materials and training
- Safety checklists with standard operating procedures
- Material Safety Data Sheets (MSDS)
- Chemical storage and labeling procedures
- Safety signage
- Safety log
- In-house property forms (e.g., safety status checklist, safety violation, work order, etc.)
- First aid kit
- Disaster drill policy and procedures
- Emergency evacuation plans
- Local, state and federal regulations
- Property policy and procedures
- Environmental Protection Agency (EPA) regulations/ guidelines

Work to be Performed

— Maximize guest and property safety.

Performance Criteria

— All safety hazards that can cause falls, burns, cuts, poisoning or other accidents are eliminated. All safety violations are reported to designated staff. All safety violation documentation is completed.

— All breaches of safety are reported immediately. Identification of potential safety risks is ongoing.

— Skill is performed without error.

Performance Elements

1. Remove all electrical cords, objects or spills located where they could cause injury or damage.
2. Clean up or temporarily cover all spills on floors and work surfaces.
3. Replace frayed electrical cords.
4. Maintain appropriate fire extinguishers and fire protection equipment
5. Store combustible materials away from ignition sources according to property policy and procedures.
6. Store caustic or poisonous substances away from food preparation or serving areas according to property policy and procedures.
7. Ensure required MSDSs are updated and easily accessible.
8. Post evacuation plans for all stairwells and elevators.
9. Ensure all exit signs and warning indicators are in working order.
10. Maintain evacuation equipment
11. Maintain first aid equipment, supplies, kits and systems.
12. Report all safety violations to designated staff.

13. Ensure exterior seasonal maintenance of walkways and parking areas is performed.
14. Ensure preventive measures are taken to prevent accidents during inclement weather.
15. Ensure maintenance of elevators and escalators is performed.

Performance Assessment Criteria

All local, state and federal regulations are followed.

Product

- — All safety hazards are identified and reported to maintenance and/or eliminated.
- — All safety violations are logged and reported to designated staff.
- — All appropriate procedures for extreme weather conditions are followed.

Process

— All performance elements are critical for maximizing guest and property safety.

Maximize Guest and Property Security

Conditions of Performance:

Given the following:

— Key control procedures

— Loss prevention and asset protection procedures

— Lost and found procedures

— Property policy and procedures

Work to be Performed

— Maximize guest and property security.

Performance Criteria

— All security procedures related to specific risks and breaches are followed. All suspected and actual security risks and breaches are reported to designated staff. All confidential guest information is protected according to property policy and procedures.

— All breaches of security are reported immediately.

— Identification of potential security risks is ongoing.

— Skill is performed without error.

Performance Elements:

1. Ensure key control.
2. Protect/verify guest identity.
3. Screen phone calls according to property policy and procedures.
4. Set/reset alarm systems.
5. Maintain security signage.
6. Protect property and guests' portable assets (e.g., computers, audiovisual equipment, televisions, linens, lost and found items, etc.).
7. Perform asset protection procedures.

Performance Assessment Criteria

— All appropriate staff hold licenses/certifications required by local ordinances.

— All local, state and federal regulations are followed.

— *Product* : All security related property policy and procedures are followed. All security violations are logged and reported to designated staff.

— *Process*: All performance elements are critical for maximizing guest and property security.

Accident/Incident Response

Conditions of Performance

Given the following:

— Property accident/incident response procedures

— Accident/incident-specific checklists

— First aid kit

— Accident report and log

— Incident report and log

— Disaster procedures

— *Emergency call lists for:*

- medical services
- police department
- fire department
- ambulance services
- general manager or manager on duty
- executive committee
- emergency response team
- electrician
- plumber

— *Emergency procedures for:*

- medical situations
- bomb threats
- robbery/theft
- civil disturbances
- fire
- natural disasters

Work to be Performed

— Follow accident/incident response procedures.

Performance Criteria

— All established procedures for handling accidents/incidents are followed. All accidents/incidents are reported to designated staff. The details of all accidents/incidents are logged and documented.

— Time to complete skill varies depending on information required for documentation and type of accident/incident.
— Skill is performed without error.

Performance Elements

1. Assess accident/incident situation.
2. Determine seriousness of accident/incident.
3. Inform facility emergency personnel.
4. Assist individual by most appropriate means.
5. Establish guest communication checkpoints as required.
6. Direct guest to temporary waiting areas as required.
7. Report accident/incident to designated staff or entity (e.g., worker's compensation office, insurance company, etc.).
8. Complete accident/incident documentation.

Performance Assessment Criteria

— All insurance, local, state and federal regulations are followed.
— *Product*: Facility emergency personnel are contacted. Accident/incident reports and logs are completed and reported to designated staff or entity.
— *Process*: All performance elements are critical for following accident/incident response procedures.

Developing Chemical Hazard Communication Program

Conditions of Performance

Given the following:

— Property policy and procedures
— Training manual
— Occupational Safety and Health Administration (OSHA) Hazard Communication Standard

— Material Safety Data Sheets (MSDS)
— Personal Protective Equipment (PPE)
— Environmental Protection Agency (EPA) standards/regulations

Work to be Performed

— Develop written chemical hazard communication program and plan for training employees.

Performance Criteria

— Written chemical hazard communication program for selected cleaning supplies is developed.
— Chemical hazard communication program is written according to OSHA Hazard Communication Standard.
— Program is concise and developed for standard employee training in use of chemicals used in Housekeeping.
— Time required to complete skill varies depending on number of chemicals being used, size of property, and scope of responsibility. Program is updated regularly.

Performance Elements

1. Select appropriate cleaning products.
2. Identify and list all chemicals used in housekeeping.
3. Obtain MSDSs and labels for each chemical.
4. Develop written chemical hazard communication program, including labels, MSDSs, and employee training, for list of chemicals, MSDSs and label information and proper usage.
5. Develop plan for implementation of chemical hazard training for employees.
6. Communicate hazard information to employees through labels, MSDSs, and formal training program. Employee training program must consist of

a. Direction for implementation in workplace,

b. Direction for reading, interpreting and maintaining information on labels and MSDSs, and where employees can obtain and use available hazard information,

c. Discussion of hazards of chemicals in work area by individual chemical or by hazard categories such as flammability,

d. Measures employees can take to protect themselves from hazards,

e. Specific procedures put into effect by employer to provide protection such as engineering controls, work practices, and use of PPE, and

f. Methods and observations-such as visual appearance or smell-workers can use to detect presence of hazardous chemicals to which they may be exposed.

Performance Assessment Criteria

— OSHA Hazard Communication Standard is followed.

— EPA Standards/regulations are followed.

— *Product*: Chemical hazard communication program is developed to ensure employers and employees know about chemical hazards in the workplace and how to protect themselves and others.

— *Process*: Under provisions of the OSHA Hazard Communication Standard, employers are responsible for informing employees of hazards and identities of workplace chemicals to which they are exposed.

Communicating with Guests

Conditions of Performance

Given the following:

— Property policy and procedures

— Room assignment sheet

Work to be Performed

— Communicate courteously with guests while providing assistance.

Performance Criteria

— Requests and services are provided to meet guest expectations.

— Accommodation requests of guests are provided. Time required to complete skill varies depending on request of guest, but is handled promptly.

Performance Elements

1. Establish eye contact with a smile.
2. Greet guests courteously and briefly when encountered.
3. Respond to guest questions and requests or consult appropriate staff or department if beyond scope of housekeeping.
4. Document and follow through with requests, comments and/or complaints.

Performance Assessment Criteria

— *Product*: Customer satisfaction is maintained.

— *Process*: All performance elements are critical for maintaining good guest relations and are numbered to show an appropriate sequence.

Enter Room for Service

Conditions of Performance

Given the following:

— Property policy and procedures

— Room assignment sheet

— Appropriate keys
— Do Not Disturb (DND) signage

Work to be Performed

— Enter room for service.

Performance Criteria

— Housekeeper is cognizant of room status.
— Room entry is made according to property procedures.

Performance Elements

1. Check room assignment sheet and room status.
2. Approach guestroom and observe if a DND sign is on knob and/or check that door is not double locked.
3. Knock on door and announce "Housekeeping." Wait 10 seconds for a response.

   Knock on door and announce "Housekeeping" a second time. If there is no response, open door slightly and repeat "Housekeeping." If no response, enter room and begin service.
4. Excuse yourself, leave quietly and close door if guest is found sleeping or in the bathroom.

   If guest is awake, excuse yourself and say you will return later.

   Discreetly close door and proceed to next room.
5. Report it to the supervisor if the room cannot be entered during the work shift.

Performance Assessment Criteria

— *Product:* Room to be serviced is entered without disturbing guests.

— *Process*: All performance elements are critical for completing the skill. Performance elements are completed in the order given.

Follow Do Not Disturb (DND) Procedures

Conditions of Performance

Given the following:

— Departmental policy and procedures

— Do Not Disturb (DND) signage

— Room assignment sheet

— Log book

Work to be Performed

— Check all occupied guestrooms on a daily basis with respect to guest privacy and safety following DND procedures.

Performance Criteria

— Housekeeping department employees must enter every occupied guestroom each day to check safety and security of guests.

— Skill is performed in 3-5 minutes. Guestroom with a DND sign is monitored throughout day.

Performance Elements

1. Monitor guestrooms with DND signs throughout morning.
2. Confirm status of guestroom with supervisor if room is indicated as vacant/dirty on assignment list.
3. Follow procedure for entering guestroom displaying DND signage.
   a. At 12:00 p.m., contact supervisor to determine if guest has requested a "late checkout." If so, indicate time of checkout on assignment sheet.

b. Determine, by checking computer for guestroom status, if guest has checked out and failed to remove signage

c. If room is vacant, remove DND sign and clean room.

d. If guest is still registered, have supervisor check room to determine if room is vacant or occupied. If vacant, clean room.

e. If room is occupied, have supervisor confirm guest's checkout time.

4. Follow procedure for stay-over/occupied guestroom displaying DND signage.

   a. At 2:00 p.m., contact supervisor to determine if guest has refused service. If no indication is given that guest has refused service, have supervisor contact guest.

   b. First, call the guestroom. If guest answers, apologize for disturbing them and determine if there will be a convenient time for guest to have room cleaned.

   c. If guest does not answer, proceed to room and attempt to enter.

   d. If room is unoccupied, do not refresh room. Leave a message for guest to contact housekeeping department upon their return to room to determine convenient time to have their room cleaned.

Performance Assessment Criteria

— *Product:* All occupied guestrooms are checked, following DND procedures, on a daily basis with respect to guest privacy and safety.

— *Process*: All "do not disturb" signs are observed. All policies and procedures are adhered to without fail.

Handle Guest's Property

Conditions of Performance

Given the following:

— Property policy and procedures

— Room assignment sheet
— Guest's property

Work to be Performed

— Handle guest's property in guestroom.

Performance Criteria

— Guestroom appears neat and personal items are organized with care.

Performance Elements

1. Arrange newspapers, magazines and books in a neat stack.
2. Discard only items in wastebaskets.
3. Organize personal items with care.
4. Report items found or damaged to supervisor (e.g., earring left on floor or perfume bottle that is broken).
5. Remove personal items from bed and lay aside prior to making bed. If items are of high value, document and notify supervisor before moving them.

Performance Assessment Criteria

— *Product*: Guest's property is handled with care.
— *Process*: All performance elements are critical for handling personal items in the guestroom. The steps are numbered to show an appropriate sequence for completing the skill; however, a different sequence may be used.

Maintain Department Inventory of Amenities and Supplies

Conditions of Performance

Given the following:

— Property policy and procedures
— Inventory control list

— Established minimum and maximum inventory
— Established reorder points
— Requisition form
— Computerized equipment with appropriate software

Work to be Performed

— Maintain department inventory of amenities and supplies.

Performance Criteria

— Requisition form is completed to replenish supplies necessary for occupancy level. Requisition form is completed legibly in 15 minutes with 100% accuracy. Time to complete skill may vary depending on size and type of facility.

Performance Elements

1. Obtain inventory control list.
2. Record supplies that need to be replenished.
3. Complete requisition form by listing supplies and quantities needed.
4. Distribute requisition form to appropriate staff person for approval.
5. File copy of form according to property policy and procedures.

Performance Assessment Criteria

— *Product*: Department inventory of amenities and supplies are maintained to meet occupancy levels.
— *Process:* All performance elements are critical for completing the skill. The steps are numbered to show an appropriate sequence for completing the skill.

Maintain Daily Inventory of Linens

Conditions of Performance

Given the following:

— Property policy and procedures

— Established linen par levels

— Linen requisition form

— Occupancy level forecast

Work to be Performed

— Maintain adequate supply of linens for occupancy level.

Performance Criteria

— Linen requisition is completed to assure par levels are maintained.

— Requisition form is completed legibly in 15 minutes with 100% accuracy.

Performance Elements

1. Identify par levels based on occupancy.
2. Communicate with laundry department if additional linen is needed.
3. Give linen requisition to appropriate staff person.
4. File copy in appropriate location.

Performance Assessment Criteria

— *Product*: Adequate supply of linens for occupancy level is maintained.

— *Process*: All performance elements are critical for maintaining an adequate linen supply. The steps are numbered to show an appropriate sequence for completing the skill.

Maintain Equipment Inventory

Conditions of Performance

Given the following:

— Property policy and procedures
— Established Preventative Maintenance (PM) program
— Reports of malfunctioning or broken equipment
— Requisition form.

Work to be Performed

— Maintain inventory of functioning equipment by: adhering to established PM program, initiating a work request to repair equipment, and/or completing requisition to purchase new or replacement equipment.

Performance Criteria

— Requisition/work order form is completed legibly in 15 minutes with 100% accuracy.

Performance Elements

1. Adhere to established PM program.
2. Obtain reports of malfunctioning equipment (e.g., vacuum cleaners, floor scrubbers, floor polishers, etc.).
3. Initiate work request for equipment repair.
4. Complete requisition for equipment purchase.
5. Give requisition to appropriate staff for approval.
6. File copy in appropriate location.

Performance Assessment Criteria

— *Product*: Inventory of functioning equipment is maintained.
— *Process*: All performance elements are critical for

maintaining functioning housekeeping equipment. The steps are numbered to show an appropriate sequence for completing the skill; however, a different sequence may be used.

Stock Housekeeping Cart

Conditions of Performance

Given the following:

— Housekeeping cart

— Room assignment sheet

— Access to linen room and supplies

— Supply list for housekeeping cart

Work to be Performed

— Stock housekeeping cart to par.

Performance Criteria

— Skill is completed in 15 minutes with 100% accuracy.

Performance Elements

1. Identify cleaning task to be completed.
2. Select cleaning product appropriate for surface to be cleaned.
3. Select equipment and cleaning supplies (e.g., broom, rags, wipes, dustpan, etc.) for task.
4. Check items on cart to determine the quantity of each item.
5. Stock/restock housekeeping cart to par.
6. Observe safety procedures when handling cleaning product and/or equipment.

Performance Assessment Criteria

— *Product:* Housekeeping cart is stocked to par.

— *Process:* All performance elements are critical for completing the stocking/restocking of the housekeeping cart. The steps are numbered to show an appropriate sequence for completion.

Cleaning Rooms

Conditions of Performance

Given the following:

— Property policy and procedures

— Room status report

— Room assignment sheet

Work to be Performed

— Determine order for rooms to be cleaned.

Performance Criteria

— Consideration of guest is high priority.

— Skill is completed in two minutes.

Performance Elements

1. Scan room status report.
2. Prioritize workday using assignment sheet. Clean guestrooms in the following order:
   a. Guest requests and VIP guestrooms
   b. Checkout rooms along with rooms needing early makeup
   c. Stay-over rooms
   d. Due-out rooms (These are cleaned last to avoid double cleaning.)

3. Report to supervisor, according to property policy and procedures, when there is a service refusal or a DND sign still on room door.
4. Obtain approval from supervisor for room to remain unserviced for more than two days.

Performance Assessment Criteria

— *Product*: An order or sequence for cleaning rooms is established for workday.

— *Process*: All performance elements are critical for completing the skill. The steps are numbered to show an appropriate sequence for completing the skill.

Perform Initial Cleaning Tasks

Conditions of Performance

Given the following:

— Property policy and procedures

— Stocked housekeeping cart

— Room assignment sheet

Work to be Performed

Perform initial cleaning tasks for each room.

Performance Criteria

Time to complete skill is five minutes per room.

Performance Elements

1. Position cart in front of door with open side facing guestroom door.
2. Enter room with cleaning supplies, amenities and cleaning cloths. Place cleaning supplies and cleaning clothes in bathroom. Place amenities in entryway.

3. Turn on all lights to check for bulbs that need to be replaced and assure that bulbs are replaced.
4. Open draperies and sheers and check hardware.
5. Open windows according to property policy and procedures.
6. Check Heating Ventilation and Air Conditioning (HVAC) to assure they are properly functioning.
7. Check condition of room by making note of any damage or missing items and notifying supervisor if anything of value is gone, something is in need of repair, or carpet needs to be cleaned.
8. Remove ashtrays, ice buckets, coffee carafe, and glasses and replenish.
9. Empty any beverages, cover room service food trays, set tray in hallway, and arrange for pick up following property policy and procedures.
10. Collect trash for proper disposal.
11. Empty and sanitize wastebasket and replace liners.

Performance Assessment Criteria

— *Product:* Initial cleaning tasks are performed for each room.
— *Process*: All performance elements are critical for completing the skill. Performance elements are completed in the order given.

Guestroom Cleaning Make Beds

Conditions of Performance

Given the following:
— Property policy and procedures
— Stocked housekeeping cart
— Room assignment sheet

Work to be Performed

— Make bed(s) with fresh linens.

Performance Criteria

— Bed is neatly made with clean bedding. Pillows are fluffed and tucked into case, sheets and blanket corners are mitered, and top sheet folded down. Bed spread is straight and smoothly placed on top of bed.

— Time to complete skill is 3-5 minutes per bed.

Performance Elements

1. Remove any personal items from bed.
2. Remove and check blanket and bedspread and if soiled or damaged, replace it.

Place bedspread, blanket and pillows on chair.

3. Strip bed(s); collect soiled linen from bathroom and place on cart.
4. Check mattress pad and mattress, making a note to inform supervisor if mattress is stained, has burn marks or other damage.
5. Check between mattress and box springs for any damage or guest property.
6. Return with clean linen for bed and bathroom.
7. Change mattress pad if necessary. Spread pad evenly over center of bed smoothing out wrinkles.
8. Make bed completely on one side before beginning on other side. Place bottom sheet on mattress, mitering corners.
9. Place top sheet on bed, smoothing it out with hand. Work clockwise around bed.
10. Place blanket on top of sheet also smoothing it out with hand.

11. Place third sheet over blanket when applicable.
12. Miter corners of top sheet and blanket along sides and at foot of bed.
13. Center bedspread evenly over bed and fold bedspread down from head of bed leaving enough room to cover pillows.
14. Fluff pillows and put on pillowcases working pillow down into case so no pillow ticking is showing. Tuck loose ends into the pillowcase. For sanitary reasons, do not hold pillow under chin or with teeth.
15. Position pillows at head of bed with tucked ends facing the center.
16. Pull bedspread up over pillow and tuck under pillow. Avoid hand contact with pillowcases after they are on pillows.
17. Step away and survey bed for smoothness.
18. Smooth out any wrinkles.

Performance Assessment Criteria

— *Product*: Bed(s) are properly made according to property policy and procedures.

— Process: All performance elements are critical for completion of the bed making skill. The steps are numbered to show an appropriate sequence for completing the skill; however, a different sequence may be used.

Clean Bathroom

Conditions of Performance

Given the following:

— Property policy and procedures

— Stocked housekeeping cart

— Person Protective Equipment (PPE)

Work to be Performed

— Clean bathroom according to property policy and procedures.

Performance Criteria

— Bathroom is cleaned and sanitized and clean linens are in place.

— Skill is completed in 5-10 minutes.

Performance Elements

1. Put on PPE.
2. Apply appropriate chemical to all fixtures and surfaces before attending to other tasks. When applying cleaner to toilet, flush toilet to remove any residue and apply cleaner around and beneath lip of bowl.
3. Clean shower area.
   a. Begin cleaning tub and shower area. Ensure proper working safety. Do not climb on or into tub for cleaning.
   b. Check drain.
   c. Clean shower curtain or door making sure to clean any accumulated mildew from the bottom. Change/replace shower curtain according to property policy and procedures.
   d. After cleaning tub, clean showerhead and tub fixtures leaving showerhead aimed in correct position.
   e. Immediately wipe and polish fixtures with dry cloth.
   f. Reposition door or curtain when finished cleaning.
4. Clean mirror.
5. Clean vanity and sink.
   a. Begin by cleaning countertop and basin, removing any hair from sink and drain.

b. Move guest property while cleaning and return when cleaning is completed.

c. Rinse and polish chrome fixtures so they shine.

6. Clean toilet.

   a. Begin cleaning exterior of toilet working down to toilet base.

   b. Scrub inside of toilet and under lip with brush, then flush again.

   c. Use damp cloth with cleaning solution to clean top of seat, lid, and sides of tank.

7. Clean walls, doors and fixtures.

   a. Spot-clean for fingerprints and obvious smudges on walls, especially around light switches and electrical outlets.

   b. Wipe down walls and clean both sides of bathroom door.

8. Tuck under corners of tissue and toilet paper and replace towels, washcloths, bath mats, toilet and facial tissue, and guest amenities according to property policy and procedures.

9. Clean floor including corners, under vanity, baseboards and behind door. Begin with far corner of bathroom and work toward door, mopping or wiping floor as you go.

10. Gather caddy and give bathroom final check.

11. Exit bathroom, turning out lights.

Performance Assessment Criteria Product

— Bathroom is properly cleaned and sanitized with clean linens, replenished tissues, and guest property and amenities in place.

Process

— All performance elements are critical for completion of the bathroom cleaning skill.

— The steps are numbered to show an appropriate sequence for completing the skill.

Miscellaneous Cleaning Tasks

Conditions of Performance

Given the following:

— Property policy and procedures

— Stocked housekeeping cart

Work to be Performed

— Dust and clean all furniture, lamps and other items in guestroom. Replenish collateral (e.g., paper, pens, etc.).

Performance Criteria

— Room furniture and other surfaces are free of dust.

— TV screen, mirrors, windows and other glass surfaces are clean and free of smudges.

— All walls are clean and free of spots or marks.

— Collateral is replenished.

— Skill is performed in five minutes.

Performance Elements

1. Apply dusting solution to dust cloth, not to surface to be dusted.
2. Dust items starting at door and work clockwise around room. High dust especially in corners.
3. Clean all mirrors and glass surfaces including television screen. Use disinfectant for cleaning telephone surfaces.
4. Dust and/or polish the following: picture frames, mirrors, headboards, lamps, shades and light bulbs; bedside tables, telephone, windowsills, window and sliding glass door tracks (when applicable); dresser including inside drawers;

television and stand or cabinet; chairs, closet shelves, hooks and clothes rod; top, knobs and sides of doors; air conditioning and heating units, fans or vents.

5. Replenish collateral according to property's policy and procedures.
6. Check walls for spots, marks or smudges and clean with damp cloth and all purpose cleaning solution.

Performance Assessment Criteria

— *Product*: Furniture, lamps and other items in room are properly cleaned and collateral is replenished.

— *Process*:All performance elements are critical for completion of the skill. The steps are numbered to show an appropriate sequence for completing the skill.

Vacuum Room

Conditions of Performance

Given the following:

— Property policy and procedures

— Vacuum cleaner

— Stocked housekeeping cart

Work to be Performed

— Vacuum carpeted areas within room.

Performance Criteria

— Carpet is clean and free of lint, dust, dirt, etc.

— Skill is completed in 2-3 minutes. Time to complete skill may vary depending on size of room.

Performance Elements

1. Check under beds and furniture and remove any guest property or debris.
2. Vacuum all exposed carpet, reaching under tables, chairs and raised furniture.

   Move minor pieces of furniture. (It is not necessary to move heavy furniture. These areas will be cleaned on a special project basis.)
3. Start at farthest end of room and vacuum toward entry. Close windows and position window treatment as you work past them to avoid backtracking across newly vacuumed carpet.
4. Remove vacuum cleaner from room, wrap cord, and place onto cart before proceeding to next room.

Performance Assessment Criteria

— *Product*: Room is properly vacuumed.

— *Process*: All performance elements are critical completion of the skill of vacuuming. The steps are numbered to show an appropriate sequence for completing the skill.

Complete Final Room Check

Conditions of Performance

Given the following:

— Property policy and procedures

— Housekeeping assignment sheet

— Stocked housekeeping cart

Work to be Performed

— Complete final check and complete housekeeping assignment form after cleaning room.

Performance Criteria

— Housekeeping assignment form, noting condition and status of room, is completed.

— Skill is completed in 1-2 minutes.

Performance Elements

1. Scan room carefully in circular fashion from one corner to next visually inspecting room.
2. Check to make sure all furnishings are in proper places and check for crooked lampshades.
3. Report unusual odours and spray air freshener according to property policy and procedures.
4. Note condition and status of room according to property policy and procedures.
5. Turn off light, close door and check to see that it is locked.

Performance Assessment Criteria

— *Product*: Final room check is completed according to property policy and procedures.

— *Process*: All performance elements are critical for the completion of the final room check.

Complete Guestroom Inspection

Conditions of Performance

Given the following:

— Property policy and procedures

— Room assignment sheet

— Room inspection forms

— Maintenance request forms

Work to be Performed

— Complete room inspection after attendants have completed work.

Performance Criteria

— Maintenance requests are completed immediately following inspection.

— Inspection is conducted randomly or every room may be checked daily depending on property's policy and procedures.

— Problems that may have been overlooked during cleaning are identified.

Performance Elements

1. Conduct room inspections to recognize quality cleaning jobs and to identify areas where improvement or additional training of staff is needed.
2. Inspect checkout rooms soon after room attendant reports they have been cleaned.

   Occupied rooms are inspected on varying schedule. Those rooms refusing service or displaying do not disturb sign are inspected according to property policy and procedures.
3. Inspect room in systematic manner (clockwise/counter clockwise) while completing room inspection form.
4. Complete work orders and/or maintenance requests when needed.

Performance Assessment Criteria

— *Product*: Room inspection is completed according to property policy and procedures.

— *Process*: All performance elements are critical for the completion of inspecting the guestroom. The steps are numbered to show an appropriate sequence for completing the skill.

Perform Guestroom Turndown Service

Conditions of Performance

Given the following:

— Departmental policy and procedures

— Stocked turndown cart

— Room assignment sheet

Work to be Performed

— Perform turndown service for each assigned guestroom.

Performance Criteria

— All turndown service tasks are completed in 5-7 minutes per guestroom.

Performance Elements

1. Position stocked cart in front of door with open side facing door.
2. Knock on door with "Turndown service" phrase. Knock again.
3. Document any refused turndown service with "R/S" (Refused Service) on assignment sheet and offer ice and appropriate amenity.
4. Turn on lights in entry way.
5. Check bathroom.
   a. Refresh towels (damp or soiled).
   b. Wipe out sinks.
   c. Empty trash.
   d. Wipe mirror.
   e. Straighten amenities.
   f. Point toilet paper and tissue.

6. Check bedroom.
    a. Turn down bedspread.
    b. Turn down top sheet.
    c. Turn down blanket and second sheet.
    d. Stand pillows at an angle.
    e. Place appropriate menu or note on pillow or sheet.
    f. Place appropriate amenity on pillow or sheet according to property policy and procedures.
    g. Place television remote control on night stand.
    h. Close drapes, fill ice container and empty trash.
7. Turn on radio to specified station.
8. Leave light on in bedroom.
9. Straighten clothes and shoes according to property policy and procedures.

Performance Assessment Criteria

— *Product:* Turndown services are performed for each assigned guestroom.

— *Process*: All performance elements are critical for the completing the skill. Performance elements are completed in the order given. This particular skill may be modified, depending on the property, to create a specific or custom effect.

Clean Hallways and Stairs

Conditions of Performance

Given the following:

— Property policy and procedures

— Stocked housekeeping cart

— Vacuum cleaner with attachments

Work to be Performed

— Clean hallways and stairways.

Performance Criterial

— Hallways and stairways are cleaned daily.

— Deep cleaning tasks (e.g., cleaning carpets, etc.) are performed on scheduled basis.

— Skill is completed in one hour or more depending on size of facility and areas to be cleaned.

Performance Elements

1. High dust (e.g., ceiling, walls, door vents, etc.) on regular basis according to property policy and procedures.
2. Dust all horizontal surfaces.
3. Dust all light fixtures and replace or report burned out lights.
4. Clean and empty ashtrays and ash urns.
5. Pick up trash and empty trash cans.
6. Sanitize telephones.
7. Clean (e.g., vacuum, dust mop, damp mop, etc.) floor.
8. Perform required floor maintenance on scheduled basis.
9. Clean baseboards beginning at one point in hallway and work down one side of hallway and back to starting point.
10. Wipe away smudges and marks on walls and doors.
11. Note conditions of emergency exit lights and report any damage or problems to supervisor.
12. Clean front and back of exit door and check to see that it properly opens and closes.
13. Clean fire extinguisher cabinets and other fixtures.
14. Report any damage to supervisor
15. Spot clean carpets as needed.

Performance Assessment Criteria

— *Product*: Hallways and stairs are cleaned according to property policy and procedures.

— *Process*: All performance elements are critical for the cleaning hallways and stairs. The steps are numbered to show an appropriate sequence for completing the skill; however, a different sequence may be used.

Clean Public Restrooms

Conditions of Performance

Given the following:

— Property policy and procedures

— Stocked housekeeping cart

— Sanitizing solutions

— Bucket, mop and floor-cleaning chemicals

— Personal Protective Equipment (PPE)

— Proper signage

Work to be Performed

— Clean and maintain sanitary, safe and attractive public restrooms.

Performance Criteria

— Public restrooms are cleaned twice daily, once in morning and once in evening. Frequency of cleaning may vary depending on customer usage and property policy and procedures.

— Time to complete skill is 3-4 minutes per fixture. Time may vary depending on size of room.

Performance Elements

1. Check to see that bathroom is vacant. Knock on door first and announce "Housekeeping," and wait for response. After three announcements, it is assumed safe to enter.
2. Prop door open when entering, and place an approved floor sign at entrance.
3. Flush toilets and urinals and apply appropriate cleaner/ sanitizer before attending to other tasks.
4. Empty trash containers, sanitize and reline with new bags.
5. Wipe down mirrors with cleaning solution leaving mirror free of streaks.
6. Empty and clean out ashtrays, urns and individual stall units.
7. Clean basins, checking drain traps for hair and debris.
8. Clean counter tops, checking for stains and damage.
9. Wipe fixtures with cleaning/sanitizing solution and damp rag and then polish bright work.
10. Wipe dry sinks and surrounding countertops and then polish.
11. Clean toilets and urinals using bowl brush and clean rag for each fixture.
12. Wipe and polish handles on toilets and urinals.
13. Clean partitions using spray bottle containing cleaning/ sanitizing solution and a damp cloth or sponge.
14. Wipe down wall with appropriate cleaning solutions depending on type of surface. Remove any graffiti.
15. Restock dispensers for toilet seat covers, toilet paper, tissue, paper towels, and soap.
16. Wipe and polish dispensers to remove any surface marks or smudges.
17. Sweep all exposed floor areas and baseboards.
18. Reassemble all cleaning supplies and return to cart.

19. Mop floor using clean warm water and an appropriate amount of cleaning/sanitizing solution.
20. Rinse floor, wringing out mop frequently.
21. Give one final visual check before leaving.
22. Move floor warning sign when floor is dry.
23. Report to maintenance any conditions that need attention.

Performance Assessment Criteria

— *Product:* Public restrooms are clean, sanitary, safe, odorless and attractive.

— *Process*: The performance elements are critical for cleaning and sanitizing public restrooms. Performance elements 19 and 20 may/may not be performed by the housekeeper depending on the property's policy and procedures. The steps are numbered to show an appropriate sequence for completing the skill; however, a different sequence may be used.

Clean Fornt Office and Lobby Areas

Conditions of Performance

Given the following:

— Property policy and procedures

— Stocked housekeeping cart

— Vacuum cleaner with crevice tools/detailing attachments

— Preventative Maintenance (PM) program

— Proper signage

Work to be Performed

— Clean front office and lobby areas.

Performance Criteria

— Front office and lobby are cleaned daily.

— Deep cleaning tasks (e.g., carpet shampooing, tile care, stone surface maintenance, etc.) are performed on scheduled basis.

— Time to complete the skill is 45-60 or more minutes depending on size of area.

Performance Elements

1. Complete high, middle and lower dusting requirements.
2. Clean and empty ashtrays and ash urns.
3. Pick up trash and empty and sanitize trash cans.
4. Clean and sanitize telephones.
5. Clean and polish water fountains.
6. Vacuum carpets and spot-clean.
7. Vacuum upholstered furniture.
8. Clean/sanitize handrails.
9. Set up wet floor signs prior to mopping floors.
10. Dust mop/damp mop hard surface floors.
11. Clean hard surface floors. Refinish floors on regular basis according to PM schedule.
12. Clean mirrors and glass table tops.
13. Spot clean carpets and upholstered furniture as needed.
14. Step out of way if guests approach; greet guests.

Performance Assessment Criteria

— *Product*: Front office and lobby areas are clean, neat and ready for business.

— *Process*: All performance elements are critical for the cleaning the front office and lobby areas. The steps are numbered to show an appropriate sequence for completing the skill.

Clean Elevators and Escalators

Conditions of Performance

Given the following:

— Property policy and procedures
— Stocked housekeeping cart Skill Standard
— Elevator/escalator key
— Vacuum cleaner with attachments
— Small brush or broom
— Proper signage

Work to be Performed

— Clean elevators and escalators.

Performance Criteria

— Elevators are cleaned daily and monitored throughout day for debris, etc.
— Time to complete skill is 15 minutes per elevator.

Performance Elements

1. Take elevator/escalator out of service and set up signage.
2. Clean elevator.
   a. Dust ceiling and lights. Note burned-out light bulbs.
   b. Dust all surfaces with dust cloth or damp cloth followed by clean, dry cloth. Work from top to bottom.
   c. Clean insides of elevator doors.
   d. Remove gum and tar from elevator floor, and remove spots from carpet.

e. Vacuum carpeted elevators.

f. Clean floors in elevators using dust mop, vacuum and/or attachments and damp mop.

g. Clean door tracks with vacuum crevice tools or small toy broom. Polish periodically with steel wool.

3. Clean escalator.

a. Dust all surfaces, including sides, with dust cloth or damp cloth followed by clean, dry cloth.

b. Remove gum and tar from escalator.

c. Wipe handrails of escalator with wet sterilized cloth.

d. Use special equipment to clean and polish treads when provided by property.

4. Place all cleaning supplies back on cart.
5. Place elevator/escalator back in service.
6. Close door and clean outside of door; spot clean wall near elevator request button.
7. Report any burned out bulbs, etc., to maintenance.

Performance Assessment Criteria

— *Product:* Elevators and escalators are cleaned according to property policy and procedures.

— *Process*: All performance elements are critical for the cleaning elevators and escalators. The steps are numbered to show an appropriate sequence for completing the skill.

Clean Food and Beverage Outlets

Conditions of Performance

Given the following:

— Property policy and procedures

— Stocked housekeeping cart

— Mop, wringer and bucket

— Chemical solutions
— Floor machine
— Floor finish
— Carpet-cleaning equipment
— Proper signage

Work to be Performed

— Clean and sanitize food and beverage outlets.

Performance Criteria

— Food and beverage outlets are cleaned daily.
— Stripping and refinishing of floors and extraction of carpets are performed on scheduled basis or as needed.
— Carpet is spotted daily.
— Time to complete skill is 20-45 minutes depending on size of area.

Performance Elements

1. Prepare room for cleaning by turning on lights, opening window treatments, and posting proper signage.
2. Pick up trash, empty and sanitize trash cans.
3. Clean seats, table legs and chair rails. Spot seats as needed.
4. Clean table bases.
5. Sweep edges of carpets and hard floors.
6. Dust furniture and fixtures and clean glass surfaces.
7. Remove food residue and spills from carpets.
8. Move chairs away from table. Spot and vacuum carpets. Clean hard floors.
9. Clean window treatments, light fixtures and other pieces of furniture paying close attention to small grooves and other places where dust collects.

10. Follow carpet care schedule.
11. Report/replace burned-out light bulbs and report maintenance problems to appropriate personnel.

Performance Assessment Criteria

— *Product*: Eating area is sanitized and clean.

— *Process*: The performance elements are critical to providing clean food and beverage outlets.The steps are numbered to show an appropriate sequence for completing the skill; however, a different sequence may be used.

Clean Banquet and Meeting Rooms

Conditions of Performance

Given the following:

— Property policy and procedures

— Stocked housekeeping cart

— Vacuum cleaner

— Inspection sheet

Work to be Performed

— Clean banquet and meeting rooms.

Performance Criteria

— Banquet and meeting rooms are cleaned and straightened according to property policy and procedures.

— All banquet and meeting rooms are cleaned immediately after function. Time to complete skill ranges from 20-60 or more minutes per room depending on size of room.

Performance Elements

1. Spot-clean walls.
2. Wipe windowsills where applicable.

3. Clean light fixtures and replace burned-out bulbs according to property policy and procedures.
4. Dust and polish furniture. Spot-clean upholstery as needed.
5. Clean and sanitize telephones.
6. Clean hard floor surfaces.
7. Move chairs away from tables and vacuum carpeted area; spot-clean as needed.
8. Gather cleaning supplies.
9. Perform final inspection according to property policy and procedures before exiting room.

Performance Assessment Criteria

— *Product*: Banquet and meeting rooms are clean and ready for next meal or function.

— *Process*: The performance elements are critical for cleaning the banquet and meeting rooms. The order given is recommended but not required except for numbers eight and nine which are completed last.

Clean Exercise and Swimming Pool Areas

Conditions of Performance

Given the following:

— Property policy and procedures

— Stocked housekeeping cart

— Pool vacuum

— Vacuum cleaner

Work to be Performed

Clean whirlpool, sauna and swimming areas.

Performance Criteria

— Swimming pool and exercise areas are neat, clean and free of wet towels and soiled linen.

— Clean towels and linens are available.

— Swimming pool and exercise areas are cleaned once or more daily depending on use.

— Time to complete skill is 15-30 minutes depending on size.

Performance Elements

1. Collect wet towels and soiled linen.
2. Empty and clean ashtrays.
3. Empty and clean trash receptacles and replace liners.
4. Clean glass areas.
5. Clean wall areas.
6. Sweep and mop hard floor surfaces.
7. Clean and straighten lounge furniture.
8. Restock towels and linen.
9. Vacuum carpeted areas.
10. Report to supervisor any unsafe or damaged conditions.

Performance Assessment Criteria

— *Product*: Swimming pool and exercise areas are clean, neat and ready for use.

— *Process*: The performance elements are all critical for cleaning the swimming pool and exercise areas. The steps are numbered to show an appropriate sequence for completing the skill; however, a different sequence may be used.

Cleaning Administrative Offices

Conditions of Performance

Given the following:

— Property policy and procedures

— Stocked housekeeping cart

— Vacuum cleaner
— Keys

Work to be Performed

— Clean administrative offices to maintain overall cleanliness and neat appearance.

Performance Criteria

— Administrative offices are cleaned according to property policy and procedures.
— Skill is performed on daily basis.
— Some cleaning tasks (e.g., window cleaning) are performed on weekly or monthly basis and/or as needed.
— Nightly cleaning varies depending on size and number of offices. One office is cleaned in 15 minutes or less.

Performance Elements

1. Knock before entering the office and pick up debris and empty trash cans and ashtrays.
2. Spot-clean wall areas.
3. Clean windows and window treatments according to property policy and procedures.
4. Dust furniture.
5. Clean and sanitize telephones.
6. Arrange furniture but avoid moving or rearranging any items on desks or work surfaces.
7. Sweep or vacuum floor.
8. Gather all cleaning supplies and exit office, closing door and checking to make certain it is locked.
9. Clean door hardware and surrounding area.
10. Check and report any burned-out light bulbs to appropriate personnel.

Performance Assessment Criteria

— *Product*: Administrative offices are clean and ready for next business day.

— *Process*: The performance elements are all critical for cleaning the administrative offices. The steps are numbered to show an appropriate sequence for completing the skill; however, a different sequence may be used.

Clean Employee Areas

Conditions of Performance

Given the following:

— Property policy and procedures

— Stocked housekeeping cart

— Vacuum cleaner

— Service elevator key

— Power washer

— Proper signage

Work to be Performed

— Clean areas closed to guests but occupied by employees working at facility.

Performance Criteria

— Employee areas are free of dirt, grime and dust.

— Employee areas are cleaned daily with deep/rotational cleaning tasks (e.g., steam extraction of carpet soil, stripping and refinishing of floors) performed on a scheduled basis.

— Cleaning time, excluding time for deep/rotational cleaning tasks, is 60 minutes.

— Time to complete skill varies according to size of area to be cleaned.

Performance Elements

1. Clean elevator.
   a. Take elevator out of service post appropriate signage.
   b. Sweep and damp mop elevator.
   c. Place elevator back in service.
2. Clean service corridor.
   a. Pick up debris and empty trash.
   b. Clean corridor floor.
3. Clean employee dining room by picking up debris and straightening contents.
   a. Remove food residue and spills.
   b. Move chairs away from table.
   c. Clean floors.
4. Clean and sanitize employee restroom.
   a. Check to see if restroom is vacant. Knock on door first and announce "Housekeeping," and wait for response. After three announcements, assume it is safe to enter.
   b. Prop restroom door open when entering and place an approved floor sign at entrance.
   c. Apply appropriate cleaner to toilets and urinals before attending to other tasks.
   d. Pick up any debris and empty trash cans.
   e. Wipe down mirror with cleaning solution and dry, leaving it free of streaks.
   f. Clean and sanitize basin and countertops using a sanitizing solution.
   g. Restock and clean dispensers.
   h. Clean and sanitize toilets and urinals using bowl brush, and polish bright work.
   i. Clean and sanitize handles on toilets and urinals.

j. Clean and sanitize all exposed floor areas and baseboards.

k. Reassemble all cleaning supplies and return to cart.

l. Remove wet floor warning sign when floor is dry.

5. Clean general storage area.

   a. Prop open door to storage area to be cleaned.

   b. Pick up debris and trash.

   c. Clean exposed floor in storage area.

   d. Close and lock storage area door.

6. Clean back of house floors as needed.

Performance Assessment Criteria

— *Product:* Back of house areas are free of trash and debris and are clean and sanitary.

— *Process*: The performance elements are all critical for cleaning the back of the house. The steps are numbered to show an appropriate sequence for completing the skill; however, a different sequence may be used.

Clean Housekeeping Storage Areas

Conditions of Performance

Given the following:

— Property policy and procedures

— Stocked turndown cart

— Vacuum cleaner

Work to be Performed

— Clean housekeeping areas that may include housekeeping office, laundry and linen rooms.

Performance Criteria

— Housekeeping areas are cleaned according to property policy and procedures.

— Cleaning housekeeping areas is performed on daily basis.

— Time to complete skill is 45-60 minutes but may vary according to size of areas.

Performance Elements

1. Clean linen and uniform area.
   a. Organize linens/uniforms.
   b. Clean linen room floor.
   c. Dust any furniture and shelving in linen room.
2. Position housekeeping carts for ease in restocking.
3. Clean housekeeping storage area floors as needed.

Performance Assessment Criteria

— *Product*: Housekeeping storage areas are clean and neat.

— *Process*: The performance elements are all critical for cleaning the housekeeping storage areas. The steps are numbered to show an appropriate sequence for completing the skill; however, a different sequence may be used.

Preparing Budget

Conditions of Performance

Given the following:

— Financial, quality and employee satisfaction goals of facility

— Corporate guidelines

— Revenue and occupancy forecast

— Cost per occupied room

— Budget constraints

— Computer workstation with appropriate software

— History/analysis reports on amenity and supply usage

Work to be Performed

— Prepare an operating budget and a capital expenditures budget.

Performance Criteria

— Typically prepared for each fiscal year, annual operating budget summarizes anticipated year-end results.

— Housekeeping budget process takes 3 weeks to complete and is completed with 95% accuracy. Time to complete budget may vary depending on property's requirements.

— Reforecasting is performed on monthly or as needed basis.

Performance Elements

1. Establish par levels for each amenity and supply by reviewing occupancy/trend reports in order to identify the amount needed. Upon determination, increase the total necessary by 10% in order to allow for adjustments in occupancy.
2. Determine levels of expense in various categories including wages and salaries, benefits, cleaning and guest supplies, linens and uniforms, contract cleaning services and laundry services to derive a Cost Per Occupied Room (CPOR). Use CPOR to determine expenses such as labour, guest supplies and cleaning supplies. Supplies such as uniforms as well as contract cleaning services need to be zero based. Par levels need to be maintained or changed based on need.
3. Review level of service to be maintained by property.
4. Maximize profits and control expenses in relation to corporate goals and objectives.
5. Prepare budget figures annually for operating and capital budgets.
6. Present budgets to upper-level management.
7. Review and revise budgets as needed until finalized for next fiscal year.

8. Control expenses by comparing actual costs with amounts budgeted and assessing variances.
9. Reforecast and adjust controllable expenses throughout year in proportion to variation in occupancy levels.
10. Capital budgets are prepared annually and replacements of equipment or machines may be part of an overall renovation/modernization or may be purchased as needed throughout the fiscal year. When preparing capital budgets, consider age and anticipated wear life of Furniture, Fixture and Equipment (FFE) items. Any items that will depreciate in 12 months must be budgeted for replacement.

Performance Assessment Criteria

— *Product*: Operating budget and capital budget are prepared and utilized throughout the fiscal year for controlling expenses.

— *Process*: All performance elements are critical for budget preparation. The steps are numbered to show an appropriate sequence for completing the skill.

Purchase Linens, Uniforms, Supplies and Equipment

Conditions of Performance

Given the following:

— Property policy and procedures

— Inventory records

— Requisition forms

— Operational budget/direct budget

Work to be Performed

Purchase linens, uniforms, supplies, and equipment based on need and operating budget.

Performance Criteria

— Requisition forms are completed with 100% accuracy using precise specifications for items requisitioned.

— Linen needs are forecasted on yearly basis and purchased throughout year. (Purchases are made as frequently as quarterly.)

— Uniforms are replaced as needed to maintain par level or when styles are changed.

— Operating supplies are purchased as needed to maintain par level, usually on monthly basis.

— Major machines and equipment are replaced annually according to capital budget.

— Time to complete skill varies from 30 minutes to 1 hour monthly, depending on number of requisitions prepared.

Performance Elements

1. Establish par levels.
2. Examine inventory records to determine linen needs and requisition linens to maintain par levels.
3. Check operating budget to determine which operating supplies to requisition.

   Operating expenses are budgeted on the basis of cost per occupied room and requisitions for purchase are based on inventory records and projected occupancy. Purchases should not exceed operating budget unless there is a large increase in occupancy.
4. Select linens, uniforms, supplies, and equipment to be purchased.
5. Complete requisitions for purchasing replacements.
   a. Requisitions for uniform purchases are based on par levels, and new uniforms are requisitioned to maintain par level.

b. Requisitions for purchasing replacement of major machines and equipment are prepared based on capital budget. Items to be purchased are planned when capital budgets are developed.

c. Price, quality and durability of product are considered when completing requisition requests.

d. Requisition forms are signed ensuring signatures are in appropriate location.

6. Give form to appropriate staff (e.g., purchasing, etc.).
7. File copy of requisition in appropriate file.

Performance Assessment Criteria

— *Product*: Requisition form is completed to meet housekeeping requirements for each day of the week.

— *Process*: All performance elements are critical for completion of requisitions. The steps are numbered to show an appropriate sequence for completing the skill.

Prepare Property Staffing Guide

Conditions of Performance

Given the following:

— Property policy and procedures

— Basic formula to identify specific number of positions needed

— Appropriate form

— Schedule of events

— Occupancy forecast

— Annual/monthly payroll forecast

Work to be Performed

— According to occupancy levels, determine total labour hours, number of staff needed, and estimated labour expense required to operate housekeeping department for each work shift for each day of the week.

Performance Criteria

— Staffing form is completed annually, listing number of room attendants and other housekeeping staff needed on each work shift according to varying occupancy levels.

— Staffing schedule is completed legibly with 100% accuracy.

— Time to complete skill varies from 15 minutes to 1 hour, depending on season of year, events scheduled, and size of property.

Performance Elements

1. Determine total labour hours, number of employees needed according to occupancy levels and estimated labour expense.
2. Locate appropriate form.
3. Determine number of room attendants and other staff (e.g., inspectors, day-shift lobby attendant for public areas, housekeepers, etc.) required for each work shift.
4. Record number of staff needed on staffing form.
5. Sign or initial form in appropriate location.
6. Distribute form to appropriate staff.
7. File copy of form according to property policy and procedures.

Performance Assessment Criteria

— *Product*: Housekeeping employee staffing guide is completed to meet requirements for varying occupancy levels.

— *Process*: All performance elements are critical for developing a housekeeping employee staffing guide. The steps are numbered to show an appropriate sequence for completing the skill.

Develop Employee Work Schedules

Conditions of Performance

Given the following:

— Property policy and procedures
— List of housekeeping staff
— Appropriate forms
— Order request form
— Vacation/absence request forms
— Union contract
— Occupancy forecast
— Local, state and federal labour laws.

Work to be Performed

— Prepare housekeeping employee staffing schedule for each day of the week.

Performance Criteria

— Appropriate form is completed assigning housekeeping staff to service public areas and room attendants for each work shift throughout the week.
— Appropriate form is completed assigning work schedule for other housekeeping staff including executive housekeeper, assistant executive housekeeper, inspectors, etc.
— Staffing schedule is completed legibly with 95% accuracy.
— Time to complete skill varies depending on season of year, events scheduled, and the size of facility.

Performance Elements

1. Obtain appropriate form, schedule of events and occupancy forecast.
2. Determine number of housekeeping staff required for each work shift.

3. Record staff vacations and requested days off.
4. Record number of staff needed on appropriate form.
5. Balance staff schedules by scheduling additional days off (low occupancy) or scheduling overtime (high occupancy).
6. Post staffing schedule.

Performance Assessment Criteria

— All local, state and federal labour laws are followed.

— *Product*: Housekeeping employee staffing schedule is completed to meet staffing requirements for each day of the week.

— *Process*: All performance elements are critical for developing a housekeeping employee staffing schedule. The steps are numbered to show an appropriate sequence for completing the skill.

Develop Departmental Policy and Procedures

Conditions of Performance

Given the following:

— Property policy and procedures

— Employee handbook

— Communication medium

— Federal, state and local regulations

— Union contract

Work to be Performed

— Develop departmental policy and procedures.

Performance Criteria

— Departmental policy and procedures are developed and updated according to current trends and department needs.

— Time required to complete the skill depends on type of policy and procedures to be developed and/or modified.

Performance Elements

1. Identify need to modify or clarify existing policy and/or procedures.
2. Identify need to create new policy and/or procedures.
3. Modify existing policy and/or procedures.
4. Create new policy and/or procedures.
5. Ensure that new/modified policy and/or procedures comply with federal, state and local regulations.
6. Present suggested policy and/or procedures changes to appropriate department/persons for approval.
7. Post new and modified policy and procedures.

Performance Assessment Criteria

— *Product*: Departmental policy and procedures are developed or modified to meet identified needs of property.

— *Process*: All performance elements are critical for developing policy and procedures. The performance elements are numbered to show an appropriate sequence for completing the skill; however, a different sequence may be used.

Contract House Cleaning Services

Conditions of Performance

Given the following:

— Property policy and procedures

— Operating budget

— Resource materials

— Liability document

Work to be Performed

— Contract with outside cleaning services.

Performance Criteria

— Contract is acquired with reliable outside service that will provide services to meet property's quality standards.

— Time to complete skill varies according to service contracted.

Performance Elements

1. Contact well-established companies that provide services required.
2. Obtain at least three bids for new jobs.
3. Ask companies to list equipment and supplies that will be used.
4. Check references thoroughly.
5. Review time expectation, quality assurance, and terms of contract.
6. Verify insurance coverage for workers, guests, property employees, and assets.
7. Greet service people upon arrival and review job parameters.
8. Visit job site after work has begun to ensure property expectations are being met.
9. Walk through project upon completion to review contractor's work.
10. Authorize payment for work when job is satisfactorily completed.

Performance Assessment Criteria

— *Product*: Contract for outside services is obtained.

— *Process*: All performance elements are critical for contracting with outside services and are numbered to show an appropriate sequence.

Maintain Staffing Requirements

Conditions of Performance

Given the following:

— Job descriptions

— Property policy and procedures

— Employment application forms

— New hire packet (e.g., benefit forms, state and federal forms, etc.)

— Scheduling forms

— Training manual

— Local, state and federal regulations

— Current employee union contracts

— Safety manual/property tour/staff introduction

— Annual occupancy forecast

Work to be Performed

— Maintain housekeeping staff requirements of property.

Performance Criteria

— Housekeeping staff requirements of property are determined and met to maximize guest satisfaction.

— Policy and procedures for staffing property are followed without error.

— Time needed to maintain staffing requirements varies with each job classification and recruitment and interview time required.

Performance Elements

1. Determine fixed positions (e.g., housekeeper, supervisor, assistant director of housekeeping, director of housekeeping, rooms division manager/director of facility operations).
2. Determine number of variable staff positions (e.g., housekeepers, inspectors, lobby attendants, etc.).
3. Identify staff vacancies due to vacancies from regular turnover, vacations, sickness, average absenteeism, promotions and increased areas of responsibility.
4. Review and revise job descriptions.
5. Advise human resource department to recruit prospective employees.
6. Review applications.
7. Interview prospective employees.
8. Have prospective employees take appropriate pre-employment tests.
9. Hire new employees.
10. Provide orientation training.
11. Explain benefits to employees.
12. Complete paperwork for personnel files.
13. Communicate personnel policies and procedures.
14. Monitor compliance with state and federal hiring and workplace laws.
15. Monitor performance of new employee closely and determine if they are correct fit for property.
16. Take action, preferably in first 30 working days, if employee is not proper fit.

Performance Assessment Criteria

— *Product*: Property housekeeping staff requirements are identified. Individuals are recruited, interviewed and hired to meet property needs.

— *Process*: Performance elements 1-13 are performed prior to elements 14-16.

Orient, Train and Inform Housekeeping Staff

Conditions of Performance

Given the following:

— Property policy and procedures

— Job descriptions

— Training manual

— Local, state and federal regulations

— Applicable employee union contracts

Work to be Performed

— Orient, train and inform housekeeping staff.

Performance Criteria

— Employees are oriented and trained. Current employees are retrained and informed of all changes.

— New or revised policy and procedures are communicated to employees without error.

— Time to complete skill varies according to activities being performed.

Performance Elements

1. Conduct property and government mandated training and orientation sessions on the following subjects:
   a. Cleaning tasks
   b. Policy and procedures
   c. Handling hazardous products and equipment
   d. First aid

e. Safety and security

f. OSHA standards/reporting processes

g. Blood Borne Pathogens (BBP)

2. Conduct informational staff meetings.
3. Coach and support employees.
4. Communicate property policy and procedures changes.
5. Monitor compliance with local, state, federal and union hiring and workplace laws.

Performance Assessment Criteria

— *Product*: Each employee is oriented, trained and informed of changes to property policy and procedures.

— *Process*: All performance elements are critical for orienting, training and informing employees. The steps are numbered to show an appropriate sequence for completing the skill.

Supervise Employee

Conditions of Performance

Given the following:

— Property policy and procedures

— Scheduling forms

— Training schedules

— Local, state and federal regulations

— Union contract

— Employee evaluation forms including

— current employee union contracts

— personnel action forms (e.g., change of status, benefit request, etc.)

— disciplinary forms

Work to be Performed

Supervise employees.

Performance Criteria

— All supervisory functions are completed in timely manner.
— Job performance expectations are communicated to employees. Employee evaluation forms are completed and discussed with each employee before filing.
— Forms are completed without error.
— Time required to complete skill varies with each job classification and employee.

Performance Elements

1. Determine job performance standards.
2. Communicate job performance standards.
3. Communicate personnel policy and procedures.
4. Review and recommend revisions in salary schedules.
5. Settle conflicts among employees.
6. Complete employee evaluation forms.
7. Discuss evaluations with employees.
8. Enforce property policy and procedures.
9. Coach, counsel and take disciplinary action when necessary.
10. Terminate employees when necessary.
11. Monitor compliance with union, state and federal hiring and workplace laws.

Performance Assessment Criteria

— *Product*: All supervisory functions are completed. Job performance expectations are communicated to employees.

— *Process*: All performance elements are critical for supervising employees. The steps are numbered to show an appropriate sequence for completing the skill.

Developing and Implementing a Preventative Maintenance Plan

Conditions of Performance

Given the following:

— Property policy and procedures

— Written Preventative Maintenance (PM) program

— Preventative Maintenance Order (PMO)

— Established manufacturer's recommendations

— Compliance with standards (OSHA/EPA inspections)

Work to be Performed

— Develop a plan for Preventative Maintenance (PM) and implement following the established manufacturer's recommendations, empirical measurements of degrading performance, or impending failure of unmaintained piece of equipment.

Performance Criteria

— Appropriate maintenance activities are executed to ensure continuous operation of facility, system or piece of equipment.

— Equipment performance operates at proper efficiency without interruption.

— Development of PM program plan is completed in 1-2 days.

Performance Elements

1. Identify and list facility, system or equipment to be maintained.

2. Obtain established manufacturer's recommended maintenance plan. Where entire systems or major system components are mass-produced, manufacturer usually recommends service frequencies and procedures.
3. Develop and implement written PM program.
4. Initiate PMO which is a statement of actual procedures to be used in performance of preventative maintenance task for system or piece of equipment.

Performance Assessment Criteria

— *Product*: Preventative maintenance program is developed and implemented.

— *Process*: All performance elements are critical for completing the skill. The steps are numbered to show an appropriate sequence of completion.

Developing and Implementing a Rotational Cleaning Plan

Conditions of Performance

Given the following:

— Property policy and procedures

— Established manufacturer's recommendations

Work to be Performed

— Develop, implement and monitor plan for rotational cleaning and implement according to facility policy and procedures.

Performance Criteria

— Rotational cleaning is performed on scheduled basis. Rooms are scheduled for rotational cleaning as directed by department management.

— Development of rotational cleaning plan is completed in eight hours.

Performance Elements

1. Develop inspection schedule for determining areas to be scheduled for deep cleaning.
2. Assign staff to perform deep cleaning.
3. Identify deep cleaning to be done on rotational cleaning basis (e.g., bedspread and blanket rotation and cleaning, flipping and rotating mattresses, shampooing carpets, dusting high and hard-to-reach areas, cleaning vents and fans, vacuuming under furniture that requires heavy moving, cleaning and vacuuming window coverings, etc.).
4. Calculate cost associated with rotational cleaning plan for budgeting purposes.
5 Initiate rotational cleaning plan.
6. Track costs and progress for rotational cleaning.

Performance Assessment Criteria

— *Product*: Rotational cleaning plan is developed, implemented and monitored.
— *Process*: All performance elements are critical for completing the skill. The steps are numbered to show an appropriate sequence of completion.

Report Broken or Malfunctioning Equipment

Conditions of Performance

Given the following:

— Property policy and procedures
— Room assignment sheets
— Reporting form

Work to be Performed

— Complete reporting forms listing broken/malfunctioning equipment to be sent to maintenance department.

Performance Criteria

— Reporting forms are completed accurately and with details about nature of malfunction or breakage of equipment.

— Reporting form is completed in less than five minutes but varies depending on number of reporting forms prepared.

Performance Elements

1. Review manufacturers' warranties.
2. Examine reporting section of room assignment sheets completed by housekeepers.
3. Complete reporting form identifying malfunction or breakage of equipment.
4. Describe in detail nature of equipment problem.
5. Sign reporting forms in appropriate location on form.
6. Give form to maintenance.
7. File copy of reporting form according to property policy and procedures.
8. Follow up to assure job is performed and/or performed correctly.
   a. Periodically review outstanding reporting forms. Question why certain items take so long to repair.
   b. When repairs are complete, check to assure quality standards are met.

Performance Assessment Criteria

— *Product*: Reporting forms are completed to include all equipment reported to have malfunctioned or appearing to be broken.

— *Process*: All performance elements are critical for completion of reporting forms. The steps are numbered to show an appropriate sequence for completing the skill.

Report Missing Items

Conditions of Performance

Given the following:

— Property policy and procedures

— Room assignment sheets (reporting section)

— Reporting form

Work to be Performed

— Complete reporting forms for items housekeepers have found or guests have reported missing.

Performance Criteria

— Reporting form is completed with 100% accuracy.

— Skill is completed in 2-3 minutes.

Performance Elements

1. Report any guest items found in guest's room or on property.
   a. Record found item on the room assignment sheet.
   b. Complete report form identifying found items.
   c. Describe in detail item and location where item was found.
   d. Give form to front desk and security.
   e. Place found item(s) in appropriate designated location with tag identifying location where found.

f. File copy of report identifying found item in appropriate file.

g. After 90 day waiting period (or time period established by property), staff member will receive item they turned in.

2. Report property items that are missing.

a. Examine reporting section of room assignment sheets completed by housekeepers.

b. Describe in detail item and location from which item was reported missing.

c. Reporting forms are signed in the appropriate location on the form.

d. Give form to front desk and security personnel.

e. Remove item from inventory.

f. File copy of reporting form in appropriate file.

g. Post charges to guest's room account, if necessary, for items missing.

3. Guests reporting missing items from room should be referred to security/loss department.

Performance Assessment Criteria

— *Product*: Reporting forms are completed to include all items and location from which items were reported missing.

— *Process*: All performance elements are critical for completion of reporting forms. The steps are numbered to show an appropriate sequence for completing the skill.

4

Human Resource Management

Leadership

Though the exercise of leadership is situational, the following traits are considered essential to successful hospitality leadership.

Lead with a vision: Moving large and complex organizations in a particular direction requires the ability to formulate and articulate a vision of what the organization should be.

Inspire others with a sense of purpose and excitement: "Selling" the vision requires constant hammering home of easy-to-grasp themes. Without the "big picture" sense of direction, employees become lost in the day-to-day detail and monotony of their jobs. Leaders must engage with employees on all levels and view such interaction as an opportunity to "spread the gospel".

Transform vision into day-to-day action: Long range vision must be broken down into a concrete plan of action for managers and supervisors at all levels. Performance reviews and goal setting sessions play an important part in establishing and communicating near and long term objectives.

Communicate and provide feedback: Most organizational failures result from faulty or inadequate communication. Informed employees are better employees. Leaders should strive to create an environment that facilitates communication flow; where superiors and subordinates keep each other informed, quality and performance standards are communicated, feedback is constantly given and every employee knows where the organization is going and how it will get there.

Instill dedication to needs and desires of members and guests: The bottom line for any business is customer satisfaction. Shortsighted policies that have a negative impact on this satisfaction will eventually show up on the bottom line. The surest way to keep customers satisfied is to know what they want. Employees at all levels should be required to constantly seek the feedback and input of members and guests. Further, they should be instilled with a complete dedication to customer satisfaction.

Be proactive in finding problems: Every organization has problems and some managers try to hide their problems. A sure sign that there are problems in an organization is that no one ever talks about them. Everything goes too smoothly and no one rocks the boat. It is a simple task to ask questions, to dig a little wherever one goes. Inevitably problems turn up. Often those most familiar with and vocal about problems are the line employees who deal with them every day. A significant step in solving problems is to place a major and positive emphasis on problem discovery. It's the first step in problem solution.

Know and preach that every problem has a solution: Every problem can be solved. It's merely a matter of priorities. Even the most complex problem can be broken down into its smaller solvable components. Sometimes a solution is the result of compromise or many little steps that contribute to an improvement in the overall situation. As much as possible, one should look for system solutions to problems.

Have a bias toward action: Accomplish something every day. There is an insistent time factor in management. New problems crop up every day. When problems are not solved, the sheer volume of accumulating problems can paralyze an organization.

Be a strong organizational team builder: Motivation and morale is built on making every employee part of the team.

Organizational loyalty seemed to be the strong suit of the Japanese, but it is little more than a corporate version of the military's esprit de corps. Much of it goes back to pride and recognition, but it also depends upon building a strong organizational identity and constant communication.

Have strong support for employees: On any level, leaders serve two important constituencies - customers and superiors. There is, however, a third constituency of major importance - employees. Without the willing and committed involvement of this group, the organization will never achieve high levels of success or standards of excellence.

Be self motivated and a self starter: A leader's ideas, words, action and example are major determinants in the success of the operation. No one should need to tell a leader what has to be improved in his or her organization. He or she should recognize what needs to be done, formulate a vision and prepare an action plan to accomplish it.

Recognize the importance of personal selling: Perhaps the greatest marketing tool available is the committed involvement of leadership in the marketing effort. By becoming actively involved with members and selling the club at every opportunity, the leader promotes not only the operation, but him or herself. Since many decisions are influenced by personal loyalties and first-hand recognition of competency, this type of salesmanship is often the most far-reaching and effective.

Pay attention to details: A good leader must have an eye for details. Much can be learned by observing an operation and a leader must spend a good deal of his or her time "out and about" to know what is going on in an organization.

Possess high standards of quality: Leaders must establish and communicate their standards of quality. When employees are left to decide quality standards for themselves, the best that can be expected is inconsistent, and at worst a complete absence of, quality and service.

Have a positive attitude that remains upbeat in the face of adversity: Attitude is all-important in any endeavor.

Employees look to leaders for guidance, reassurance and example. A leader must learn to roll with the small ups and downs while keeping an eye on the larger vision. The proper attitude should also be mixed with an upbeat good cheer that is invariably infectious.

Effective and efficient operations are the direct result of good leadership. While sound management and technical skills are also important in club operations, without leadership the organization will never achieve its fullest potential.

Spring clean your goals and plans

In US, during the spring season, is traditionally a time for spring cleaning, getting rid of the old and making way for the new. It's a time of new beginnings, with a sense of hope and optimism. "What's that got to do with my business and work?" you may be wondering? Well, actually rather a lot. Now is a great time for you to spring clean your life, and your work and business. A time for cleaning out and reviewing parts of your life and business you're ready to commit to improving. It's like pulling out the weeds ready to plant new seeds; seeds of possibilities.

It's an opportunity to examine your goals and clear out the ones you don't want any longer. This may involve spring cleaning your desk and getting rid of piles of clutter. When we're surrounded by clutter, our mind gets bogged down which prevents us from thinking clearly and being focused. Perhaps it's time to dust away the cobwebs on your sales and marketing plans, and throw away the rubbish, i.e. the stuff that no longer forms a useful part of your plans. It may involve spring cleaning your personal life by polishing up relationships, clearing out old habits and attitudes which no longer benefit you. Or stripping back your finances to get them in good shape for the future. Why not take a vacuum to your health and exercise plans and clean out the bits you don't want?

This clear-out can involve taking huge steps or even very small ones. Even these small things which need dealing with drain our energy and it's surprising how much this happens. If left undone, the little tasks, like the filing cabinet drawer which jams, the unmade bed, the pile of papers on your desk, all niggle away at you and sap your energy. When these are sorted out, there is more time for other things in your life and business. Cleaning out leaves space and this space is then available for new opportunities.

Opportunity for more energy, more business, more sales and more of the things you want for yourself. A radical spring clean puts the zest back into your life and gives you the freedom to think bigger and reach for the sky.

Use healthy pressure to achieve the impossible

Do you feel you're capable of doing and being more? Do you have lots of ideas or things you want to do but, with your current workload, you think it's impossible? Well, what if it is possible? What if it's time for you to shake up the status quo; the way it's always been done? What if it's time to put all your ideas and things you want to do on the table and find a way to actually do them? This suggestion isn't for the faint-hearted or those who are likely to feel overwhelmed by everything. It is for you if you feel ready to put some pressure on yourself.

Healthy, positive pressure which requires you to be your absolute best. This is the key point; it's about who you need to be and not what you need to do. Sometimes it's necessary to increase the pressure on yourself to feel truly alive, productive and for life to be interesting. Pressure applied to yourself, if done in the right way, can inspire and get you into action, even massive action. Most people stop short of taking action; they spend more time thinking about what they need to do and analysing it all. This wastes so much time and energy. Time and energy that could be put to better use by taking action. Putting pressure on yourself stretches you personally and breaks through the limits you've set for yourself. If you're ready for this pressure, the first step is to capture all your ideas or things you want to do on paper.

You need to see them in black and white to give you clarity. Once you have everything on paper, keep adding to it as other ideas are uncovered and pop up in your mind. Also, as an entrepreneurial or creative person, some of the things you may need to do include planning, defining processes and putting systems in place. All those things that you see as boring, uninspiring and not necessary. Yet they are essential for success.

This is an area that may be a stretch for you and in which you may need to grow. You need to plan, define processes and implement systems to give you the freedom to focus on doing what you do best and the things you love. With these in place, most of it can be done by other people and will ensure that they do it in the way you want, giving you even more freedom. As an employee, when you have clarity about the things you truly want to do outside of work, whether it's setting up a business or indulging in leisure pursuits, the stretch you may need to make is to complete your work during your working day and not feel compelled to do more or work longer hours, which are usually unnecessary. Put the pressure on yourself by asking, "What will it take to complete my work during the working day?" Perhaps your growth lies in needing to be more focused, productive, to delegate more or to find ways to be more effective.

The way to unleash your ideas and do what you truly want to do is to focus only on those that utilise your strengths, talents and unique abilities. It's now necessary to make the shift and be your absolute best. Anything that doesn't utilise all these fully, needs to be done by someone else. Ask yourself, "In what way can these things happen without me?" This isn't about doing more and more; it's about who you need to be in order for these things to get done.

Change is usually inconvenient, especially when good staff hand in their resignation. And sometimes it's a relief, but either way, with preparation and practice you and your business can be much less at the effect of inevitable staff changes. But the cost of recruiting and training replacement staff is enormous. There will always be staff leaving, but check the following list to see how you can improve procedures to minimise the disruption and expense. No-one is indispensable. Some staff will be missed, but as you write down and record your systems - phone numbers, ordering sheets, stock lists, recipes and procedures, you will feel more and more confident that the business will continue even if some of the faces driving it have changed. How many systems and recipes do you have written down?

Be ready to handle discipline confidently and fairly – most owners and managers are nervous about disciplining or warning staff who are no longer performing. If there is a clearly written Job Description, you will have a list of 'failure points' to check against performance. Stay in touch with your friendly Industrial Relations adviser so you can check procedures. Your performance in this vital role is being watched by all your staff! Pre-written discipline and warning letters will help with your confidence – sometimes even a practice session with a close friend on running the interview!

Manage the timing – it's rare for someone who has resigned to give the same degree of enthusiasm and loyalty in their remaining days. In some situations it may be better to pay them out on the spot to avoid disruption. The extra cost is usually minimal compared to the alternative of having disgruntled staff sticking around. There will be minimum times for notice under the relevant Award, but make sure staff know what you expect and keep communication lines open so that when they planning changes, they will let you know well in advance eg students returning to study.

Protect your assets – ensure return of uniforms and tools. A Uniform & Tool Agreement signed when staff commence covers you for items that don't come back. A Key Register keeps track of what has been issued to whom. Protect computer information – make sure there are clear rules about accessing computers after a resignation or dismissal. Generally it should not be allowed, unless under supervision. Passwords and access codes may need to be changed. Sometimes it may be necessary for staff to be escorted from the premises.

Industrial relations experts advise against elaborate references when staff leave – have a clear policy on what will and will not be provided. A pre-written Statement of Service should be ready at the time they finish with covering dates and work title. A more generous letter may be appropriate for some. Help with a CV and job opportunities is always appreciated by staff who may have to leave because of a downturn in business, and once again, other staff are watching the generosity of how you handle good staff who are moving on.

Final pay is calculated accurately and ready for the final shift. Are you ready for questions about holiday pay, status as a casual or permanent and any discrepancies that may not have been handled properly? Exit Interviews are an excellent opportunity for a candid view of your business from someone who no longer has an obligation to just repeat the 'official line'.

Generally, any staff visiting outside their shift times is to be avoided. You can't prevent outside fraternisation, but staff who leave because of poor performance or dissatisfaction will be disruptive if their call back to visit. Have your rules written in the staff manual. If you strengthen your procedures and practice your responses, you'll be less buffeted by unexpected resignations, your staff less affected and your business more resilient. Some people you will miss, but no-one is irreplaceable, and it's surprising how the gap is often filled by someone even etter!

Handle your frustrations

As a human being, chances are you've said this many times, either out loud or in your mind. The great thing about accepting you're frustrated is that you've identified and acknowledged what's going on. It's too easy to carry on struggling with something and being unaware that it's causing you frustration. Once you've realised that you're frustrated, you're free to make choices about how you handle it. The way you handle your frustrations is a key to successfully moving on. One of the first choices you need to make is to shift away from being a victim and from saying "Why me?" or "Why did this have to happen?" Being a victim wastes your time and energy and often leaves you feeling even more frustrated.

Instead, make the shift to tapping into your own resourcefulness and discover solutions. Part of the reason we often stay stuck and frustrated is that we don't believe we can do something about it. You are more resourceful than you think. The first step is to identify specifically what you're feeling frustrated about. It may seem obvious but often when we feel frustration, we start to pile other unrelated things on top of it and this clouds the issue. Specifically naming your frustration is half the battle. Once you've identified this specifically, then be an observer of yourself.

This isn't an opportunity to beat yourself up. It's an opportunity to observe what's going on without judgement, leaving you able to make effective choices. As an observer, you'll often see a different perspective. As you're observing yourself, see what you most need, what's truly important to you and what it will take to move forward quickly. Observe the chatter that's going on in your mind. Is your mind chatter keeping you stuck? What is worth listening to?

One of the best ways to be an observer and to see the situation more clearly is to take a break. Once you've stepped back from the frustration, you'll find it easier to tap into your creativeness and come up with ideas and solutions. Tap into the creative and resourceful part of yourself by asking empowering questions. Empowering questions such as "What is important to me about this?", "What is the intended result?", "What choices are available to me?", or "What is the next action I need to take?" When you're asking these questions, listen carefully for your own response. This is where your own personal resourcefulness will show up and give you the answers and solutions to enable you to move forward. You'll quickly move beyond the frustration and get back to achieving what you want.

When frustrations have occurred, it's well worth getting to the source so that you can handle it once and for all. What often leaves us frustrated is when the same problems come up time and time again. Get to the source of your frustration and from that, learn what needs to change or needs to be done differently in the future. Frustrations can also present an opportunity, although it may not feel like it at the time. They're an opportunity for growth and improvement.

Mistakes job candidates make searching for a new job

Understanding the job search game can result in more qualified interviews. Job seekers looking for a new position in 2004 should be aware of the most common mistakes made in conducting a job search. Knowing the "rules of the job search game" can help candidates be more successful in their efforts.

"When clients come to me searching for a new job, I spend a great deal of time not only preparing their resume, but also educating them on the job search process," said Kathy Sweeney, a Certified Professional Resume Writer and president of The Write Resume in Phoenix, Arizona. "I always want to make sure they understand how a successful job search is conducted."

According to Sweeney, the top six mistakes made are:

1) Sending unsolicited resumes. Most employers have a policy against accepting unsolicited resumes. They simply do not have the room to keep these resumes on file. If the candidate has a contact within a company, then walking in a resume that meets the qualifications of an upcoming position may be acceptable.
2) Ineffective networking. Networking is not about asking friends or neighbors if they have any "openings" at their company. Networking is about building lasting relationships with individuals in a certain industry. Networking is a two way street – you have to give to receive. Sweeney says that candidates should make a name for themselves, but they should be "famous, not infamous."
3) Using an ineffective objective on the resume. Most candidates put a broad objective statement on their resume

hoping to land "any job." A better approach is to use a "profile" or "summary of qualifications" on the resume. The benefits are two-fold; a summary tells the employer what hard skills are possessed and also offers an opportunity to place "keywords" in the resume, which are searched by computer job management programs.

4) Applying to every type of job - no matter what it is. More recruiters and hiring managers are receiving resumes from candidates who are not qualified for positions. This is a waste of time and effort on the part of the jobseeker. If the candidate is not qualified for the job, he/she will not get a call. Instead, candidates should focus on the type of work they would like to do and then go after that position, getting the training or education necessary to meet the qualifications.

5) Being unprepared for the interview. Many candidates do not perform thorough research on the company prior to the interview. Research can be done on the internet or at the public library. Knowing information about the company and key products or services will give the candidate a competitive advantage in the interview process.

6) Not following up after the interview. Countless job seekers never follow up with the employer after the interview. Sending a personalized letter, thanking the interviewer for their time, in addition to reiterating interest in the position, should be mandatory. Get the business card of the hiring manager to ensure the letter is addressed to the correct person. If a candidate really wants the position, impress the interviewer by sending the letter FedEx.

Sweeney, who has conducted several hundred job search and interview preparation seminars, in addition to serving as the career expert for numerous internet based job search boards, said the most common mistakes that job seekers make can be corrected if they take the time to educate themselves on the job search process.

In Singapore, there was support for a zero increase in pay levels for 2003, with any rewards being reflected in bonus pay. Company contributions to the Central Provident Fund have also been reduced to stimulate employment levels in the city.In Thailand, competition for skilled staff remains a key factor in determining any payroll increment, and other industries have targeted hotel staff as they are perceived as having essential basic business skills. Although this year's budgeted salary increases were generally not implemented,there will probably be a modest increase in 2004 to match cost-of-living increases.

In South Korea, negotiations with unions determine salary levels, and it is predicted that increases will range from 5-9%. Hong Kong has one of the highest salary costs in the region, thanks to almost two decades of rampant payroll inflation. Although the Employers Federation has taken a lead role in recommending that employers hold off pay rises, amazingly - after over five years of patchy economic performance - employers still largely maintain a fixed 13th -month bonus. Part of the problem in Hong Kong is that overall civil-service pay has risen steadily, despite poor economic performance and private-sector practice. The challenge is to introduce independent governance in civil-service pay, which will ensure that government compensation decisions are not administered by those who are the beneficiaries of the system. And here lies the secret of appropriate pay practice: independent oversight. It is unreasonable and unrealistic to subject an individual manager to the suspicion that a pay proposal that he/she is championing has been determined against a consideration of "what's in it for me?"

It takes extraordinary courage and objectivity to recommend and implement appropriate pay policies that may not be in the interests of certain individuals or groups of colleagues. Independent oversight is required, and smart companies form an independent compensation committee to oversee their compensation programmes. This committee ensures that the company's compensation programme is designed to attract, retain and motivate employees at all levels, and takes into account the compensation practices of companies competing for hotel-industry talent.

Rules for Bringing out the Best in People

Dr. McGinnis outlines twelve rules for bringing out the best in people. These principles can be applied to any team you lead: the front desk, the sales department, housekeeping, servers, the kitchen, or even the management team of your hotel or restaurant. These skills are valuable in creating a motivational environment where your employees want to work and feel the can contribute to the success of your organization. Following are the twelve rules:

Rule 1 – Expect the best from the people you lead

In the hospitality classes there are two theories—motivational theories and strategies. One theory, the Pygmalion Effect, states that the expectations your employees have of themselves determines how they will perform. If we expect great things as managers, great things will happen. If we accept and expect average performance, average performance is what we will get. By emphasizing the positives and what employees can do, employees will believe in themselves and perform at higher levels. To do this, we must communicate our belief in their skills and abilities.

Setting high performance and quality standards and communicating to your team so that they can achieve them will yield positive results. Housekeepers will clean rooms to the cleanliness levels you set. Servers will up-sell menu items because you set the standards and expectations high. Positive expectations can yield positive results.

Unfortunately, when people become managers or leaders within an organization, they immediately feel like a police officer and must watch every employee move to make sure standards are being met. This watchdog role is looking for failure and creates an adversarial relationship between management and line employees. Good managers, on the other hand, look for the strengths in employees and discover ways to encourage the skills and abilities of each person.

Rule 2 – Make a through study of the other person's Needs

One of the more enjoyable parts of teaching at the college level is working with students and helping them discover what excites them about the hospitality industry. When a student makes a true connection with their passion for what they want to do, it is easy to push them to succeed. Their interest level is higher when studying as they develop a passion for what they are studying. The fear of pleasing other people, like parents, disappears and the passion for discovering success becomes so clearly apparent. Whether it be working for a baseball park in the minor leagues, becoming a leader in the housekeeping department, or working toward a vision of owning a restaurant or club, discovering what a student wants makes the educational experience far more motivating for both the student and the instructor.

McGinnis says, "Too many leaders ignore this essential early step. They see motivation as mere hype – slapping people on the back and giving rah-rah pep talks. But it is more than hype. A good motivational plan must be as carefully fitted as a designer dress. We must ask a lot of questions about where people have been and where they are going, what they believe, what are their sore spots, what they love and what they hate. In other words, we must make an inquiry into people's present need systems." Motivation is therefore situational. It is unique to each person.

Rule 3 – Eestablish high Standards of Excellence

"So far," says McGinnis, "I have been saying that the best way to bring out the best in people is to treat them in a positive, encouraging manner, capitalize on their gifts, and begin with their present needs and desires. But that does not mean that the good motivator is soft. To the contrary, most highly motivating leaders are hard as nails on standards of excellence. They hold to certain values tenaciously, and they set out to build a group of like-minded persons who share those values."

The best-run restaurants, the best-run hotels, the best-run food service facilities allow for individuality in their teams while enforcing certain standards. It is important that restaurants and hotels set standards and enforce them. Employees like to have clear-cut objectives that are attainable. We can't as managers set out standards so high that our employees can't achieve them or are always falling short. People want to have their skills and abilities challenged and tested – stretched, so to speak – but they must have regular successes to feel that their efforts are valued.

McGinnis concludes this rule by communicating an important lesson: "In pressing for excellence, we must be careful to have goals that are both challenging and realistic, and we must devise a graded progression of objectives so that our people can enjoy the regular feedback of success."

Rule 4 – Create an Environment where failure is not Fatal

People handle failure in different ways. Failure, in some cases, is motivational and ignites a fire within to learn and not repeat mistakes. Others, however, start with such great energy only to have the motivational fire extinguished after one failure or miscue. If we as managers in the hospitality industry can help our employees handle failure effectively, we will create an environment that is motivating and encourages high performance. A student who worked at a theme park one summer told me how one of the worst managers he worked for followed him around and regularly pointed out all the faults in the performance of his job duties.

Managers are faced with a unique challenge: creating high expectations and expecting high performance while still tolerating failure at times. Harshly criticizing a new employee for not performing a task correctly will only create a feeling of defeat and discouragement. Effective managers use whatever tactics are necessary to help employees identify the failure, what the cause is, learning from the mistake, and moving on to a higher level of performance. At times, we may need to cheer them on to try harder. Other times we may have to simply push them back into a position forcing them to start over and create a series of successes that will instill confidence.

Rule 5 – Management by Encouragement

Scudder N. Parker once said, "People have a way of becoming what you encourage them to be – not what you nag them to be."

Rule 6 – Employ models to encourage success

Coaches sometimes use the tactic of talking about the success of former students and players to motivate their players. "Win one for the Gipper" is one of many examples of such motivation. Success breeds success and using the examples from the past can help motivate today's employees to move forward and upward.

Rule 7. Recognize and applaud achievement

Praise and positive reinforcement is an essential art for a manager or supervisor. As Dr. McGinnis states, it is the difference between saying "I'm expecting great things from you" and saying "you've done a terrific job running the housekeeping department" or "you did a great job handling that lunch hour rush in the kitchen this afternoon." A restaurant is successful if its servers and cooks are successful. If employees are doing well in their jobs, they will be highly motivated. The systems we have in place should not only be designed to produce winners and recognize them on a periodic basis, the systems should be in place to recognize achievement at the moment it occurs. "There are right ways and wrong ways of expressing appreciation and reinforcing positive behavior," says Dr. McGinnis. Here are some suggestions:

— *Hand out commendations in public* – praise in front of others and acknowledge success

— *Use every success as an excuse for celebration* – success breeds success, so why not celebrate as often as possible

(sales goals, up-selling goals, occupancy goals, daily, and weekly goals)

— Employ some gesture to give weight to your commendation – A trophy, an award, a prize, and not always the same gesture

— *Put your compliment in writing* – make it a part of their file so you can review it during performance reviews and copy the letter to those who need to know

— *Be very specific in your praise* – tell a server "I like the way you sold that additional bottle of wine" or to the room attendant, "Thanks for cleaning two extra rooms today."

Rule 8 – Employ a mixture of positive and negative reinforcement

Every day of our lives, we do things because we are motivated by fear. We fear losing our jobs and that can spur us on to high performance levels. Thus, we avoid certain kinds of behavior in our work environments because we fear the repercussions of doing otherwise. It is foolish to work in an environment where we do not use discipline or reprimand employees. Yes we ought to use the carrot more than the stick, but the stick has its uses. We must follow undesired behavior with immediate corrective action. If your busperson is late one day, we need to ask why. If the tardiness becomes regular, progressive disciplinary procedures should be used to correct the behavior. As soon as the correction is made, the negative reinforcement should stop. Offer a plan for improvement which shows your busperson you care about them, and how their actions impact the operation.

"The proper way to use negative tools for motivation," states Dr. McGinnis, "is not an easy question for any of us dealing with people. What is the proper balance between negative and positive reinforcement? For now, let us agree that praising should far outweigh scolding, and that in the long run what we are aiming for in our use of fear and guilt is an allegiance to high values rather than fear of our displeasure."

UNDERSTANDING JOB ORIENTATION

You've hired a new employee – or maybe several. They are scheduled to walk into your restaurant or hotel later today. What is your plan for making this new employee, or these new employees if it is the case, to get them to be a productive member of your team in short period of time? You want them to be productive and to start contributing to the success of your organization – right? Orienting employees to their workplaces and their jobs is one of the most neglected functions in many organizations.

The most frequent complaint about new employee orientation are that it is overwhelming, boring, or that the new employee is left on their own fending for themselves. The result is often a confused and unproductive employee who is more likely to leave you within a year. With an ongoing labor crunch, developing an effective employee orientation experience is crucial. It is important that new hire programs be carefully planned to educate the employee about the corporate values and history and who is who in the organization. A well thought out orientation program, whether it lasts one day or six months, will help not only retain employees, but will also make them more productive in a more shorter time period.

Benefits of Orientation

Orientation isn't just a nice gesture put on by the organization. Orientation serves as an important element of the recruitment and retention process. What benefits does it provide?

Reduces Startup Costs: Proper orientation gets the employee get "up to speed" faster and reduces the costs associated with learning the job. A thorough orientation provides new employees with knowledge and information that will make them make few mistakes.

Reduces Anxiety and Stress: New employees, when put into a new, strange situation, will experience anxiety that can hinder job performance. An orientation program reduces anxiety resulting from entering into an unknown situation, and provides guidelines for behavior and conduct, so the employee doesn't have to experience the stress of guessing.

Reduces Employee Turnover: Employee turnover increases when employees feel they are not valued, or are put in positions where they can't their jobs effectively. Statistics show that most people who leave a new job do so in the first 90 days of employment. Orientation shows that the organization values the employee and helps provide the tools necessary for succeeding in the job.

Saves Time for the Supervisor: The more effective the orientation program, the less likely supervisors and other staff members will have to spend time training the employee, answering questions that arise, and correcting problems made. Taking the time to orientate employees effectively will eliminate questions and save time because fewer errors will be made in the process.

Develops Realistic Job Expectations, Positive Attitudes, and Job Satisfaction: In addition to learning about the values and attitudes of the organization, it is important that employees quickly learn what is expected of them, and what to expect from others they will be working with. While people can learn from experience, they will make many mistakes that are unnecessary and potentially damaging to productivity and profits. A big reason why employees who struggle initially with their jobs is that they are unaware of the job requirements and do not feel welcome or a part of the team.

There is no perfect orientation program that fits every organization. The purpose of the program, how it is conducted, and even what it is called may vary from one employer to another. The main objectives are clear though:

— help employees become productive as soon as possible, and

— develop a sense of pride and commitment to the company and its purpose.

These two objectives are best achieved through two separate orientation components: job specific orientation and general company orientation.

Job specific orientation communicates the information that will make the employee successful in doing their job and establishes the foundation for initial training.

General company orientation is designed to introduce the organization mission and values to the new employee. By meeting people, discussing the operation, understanding why things are done, the employee will gain an clear picture of how they fit into the big picture and feel more comfortable in their role.

In designing a program that best fits your needs, consider the following questions:

— What do employees need to know about this work environment that would make them more comfortable?

— What impression do you want to make on an employee's first day?

— What key policies and procedures must employees know on the first day to avoid making mistakes on the second day? What vital pieces of information do they need to understand?

— What specific things can you do to ensure that employees will begin to meet their co-workers and begin developing relationships with some of them?

— What special things (work area, equipment, special instructions) can you provide to make new employees feel comfortable and welcome on their first day?

— What positive experience can you provide that the employee can discuss with his or her family at the end of the first day? The experience should be something to make the new employee feel valued by the organization.

— How can you help the new employee's supervisor be available to the new employee on the first day to provide personal attention and to convey a clear message that the new employee is an important addition to the work team?

Once you have determined what to include in your program, create a checklist so that each new employee receives the same information, same treatment, and develops the positive attitudes you desire in your employees. Use the checklist for each new employee and have them sign the document so they see what the program included.

Your orientation program has slick, pre-printed handouts. The program is colorful and a friendly presenter uses good visuals such as overhead transparencies and a whiteboard. The employee or employees receive a guided tour of the facility. They have their employee handbook in hand. You've covered everything, so you think, yet the employee feels confused, overwhelmed, and like a stranger in a foreign land. Not your intention at all! What's missing?

How can you take your program from conveying a lot of information to making new team members feel a part of the organization in the short period of time? Many employees question their decision to change companies by the end of their first day. Anxiety is created by mistakes that companies often make during that first-day orientation program. Common mistakes include:

— overwhelming the new hire with facts, figures, names, and faces

— showing boring orientation videos/dvds back to back – and just using them "the orientation program"

— providing lengthy lectures, presentations, and speeches (yawn!)

— failing to prepare for the new hire - providing no phone, no e-mail, no computer, and no work.

Before you completely redo your current program or process, ask yourself those questions stated earlier: "What do we want to achieve during orientation? What first impression do we want to make?" There is no doubt that a positive first impressions can "seal the deal" for a newly recruited employee. Since first impressions are crucial, here are some tips for putting your best foot forward.

— Begin the process before the new person starts work. Send an agenda or outline to the new employee so they know what to expect. Stay in touch after he or she has accepted the position to answer questions or help in other ways.

— Make sure the work area for the new employee is ready for the first day of work.

— Make sure key co-workers know the employee is starting and encourage them to introduce themselves when the time is appropriate.

— Assign a current employee to show the new person around, make introductions, and start training. Let this have sufficient notice so he or she can make preparations and perform these activities properly.

— Start with the basics. People become productive sooner if they are firmly grounded in the basic knowledge they need to understand their job. Focus on the why, when, where, and how of the job. Don't overwhelm them with too much information on the first day or two.

— Provide samples about how to complete forms as well as the individual's job.

— Have some fun. Do not spend all the time allowed on the employee handbook. Just cover the very important topics.

— Provide a list of frequently asked questions with a contact person/department, and phone number.

— Plan to take the new employee to lunch, or ask a supervisor or co-workers to join the new employee in the lunchroom. The first day on the job is not the day to leave the new employee alone. This is a good time for the manager/ supervisor to take the employee to lunch, include other co-workers, and make sure the employee feels a part of the team.

— Keep the new person's family in mind. A new job means adjustment for the entire family, especially if they have relocated. Do what you can to ease the transition and help them feel comfortable in the community. If you work for a restaurant, offer a free dinner to the whole family so they can experience the service provided. If you work in a hotel, provide the family a free night stay say they all understand what the company does and how it operates.

First impressions of your organization, both good and bad, are made the first day. Decide the objectives of your program and meet them honestly and positively. Getting integrated into the organization will happen only if the new employee decides he or she has made a wise decision to join your team. Your effective orientation can help make or break that decision!

MENTORING

With the tremendous growth of the lodging industry over the last two decades, the industry's ability to develop competent management staff has been severely strained. The most significant source of the future leaders remains line employees or people moving into this industry from others. This means that company training programs and OJT (on the job training) are key to developing managers with technical and leadership skills that will contribute to the success of the organization. Regardless of the source of the emerging managers, they need support and nurturing to develop into the leaders of tomorrow. Mentoring is one way to do this.

Mentoring, from the Greek word meaning enduring, is defined as a sustained relationship between a youth and an adult. In the working world, we define it as a relationship between two people – typically one with many years of experience, the mentor, and one with very few years of experience, the protégé. Through personal involvement and contact, the mentor offers support, guidance, and assistance as the protégé learns, faces new challenges, and develops in their professional career.

The roles that the mentor may play are those of the teacher, supporter, and/or sponsor. As a teacher, the mentor teaches the protégé the skills and knowledge needed to perform the job and provides inside information about the organization, such as politics and personalities. The role of supporter is one in which the mentor helps the protégé deal with career and personal conflicts and pressures, and helps build self-confidence. And, as a sponsor, the mentor intervenes on the protégé's behalf in conflicts that might endanger the protégé's career as well as markets the protégé to upper management.

Types of Mentoring

The two types of mentoring are formal mentoring and informal mentoring. Informal mentoring occurs through friendship, collegiality, teaching, coaching, and counseling. In contrast, formal mentoring is planned and occurs through structured programs in which mentors and protégés are selected and matched through a selection process. Mentoring, whether it be formal or informal, aims to accomplish the same thing - the pairing of a skilled and experienced senior person, the mentor, with a less experienced and junior person, the protégé, to help the protégé grow and develop under the guidance of the mentor.

Mentoring relationships generally occur on an informal basis in the hospitality industry. This is typified by the general manager who takes a junior manager or supervisor under his protective wing and grooms him for greater responsibility. The relationship is based on an unspoken agreement and is subject to the availability and good will of the senior manager and the relationship that is established. Unlike the informal mentoring relationship, a formal mentoring program clearly defines the mentoring relationship by ensuring that the mentor, protégé, and organization clearly understand what to expect and what is expected of each party. The goals are the same but its process is different.

Although mentoring provides an attractive training and development alternative, it may not be right for your hotel or restaurant. Mentoring programs work best when specific human resource needs and conditions exist. In the absence of these conditions, a mentoring program could actually hurt rather than help your hotel. Some basic questions need to be answered before launching a mentoring program.

— Does your organization need to prepare people within the organization to fill future management positions? Protégés join a mentoring program with the implicit promise that excellent performance will be rewarded by career advancement. If there is no room at the top for successful protégés, the organization will be burdened with a surplus of ambitious, overqualified, and frustrated individuals who will eventually take their skills and talents elsewhere.

— If future human resource needs are forecasted, are they continuing or one-time needs?

— Does your organization represent an expanding chain where continued growth insures an on-going need for upper level managers, or does your organization represent a single property dealing with attrition-related human resource needs? If this is an infrequent, one-shot occurrence, then a structured mentoring program would not be cost-effective.

— Does your corporate culture value the veteran employee or does it prefer to buy "new blood" from outside the organization? Developing talent from within the organization takes time, resources, and long-term commitment from upper management, making their support vital to the success of the program. A high level of upper management interest and commitment is needed from the outset since mentors come from the upper management ranks.

— Does your organization have enough suitable managers available to pair with protégés? Mentors should be at least two position levels above the protégé (to prevent mentors from feeling threatened by their protégés), competent, widely respected, secure in their jobs, skilled coaches, and possess excellent interpersonal skills. They should have the time and the willingness to volunteer for the job.

— How will a mentoring program fit in with your other human resource programs? If successful succession planning and management development programs are already in place, will a mentoring program replicate, replace or enhance it? How will a mentoring program link to other training programs? Is there someone who can initiate and oversee the formal program? A successful mentoring program requires someone to coordinate the selection and pairing of mentors and protégés, establish orientation programs, perform periodic reviews of the pairs, and to help conclude the relationship when the time is appropriate.

Mentoring is not a panacea for all organizations; however, given the right conditions, its organizational benefits can be enormous. Good mentoring programs: attract the best candidates for a job, reduce turnover of talented people, help people achieve their optimum potential and productivity, assure a smooth transfer of leadership from one generation to the next, and encourage communication up and down the organizational hierarchy.

Steps to Implement a Formal Mentoring Program: Implementing a mentoring program requires the same careful planning, monitoring, and evaluating that any major project requires.

Select mentoring program coordinator: The coordinator will be responsible for helping the mentor and protégé negotiate an agreement, conduct orientations, monitor the relationship, and assist with concluding the relationship.

Select protégés: They should be intelligent, ambitious, committed to the organization, have good interpersonal skills, be positively perceived by the organization, and be willing and able to accept greater responsibility.

Determine the developmental needs of the protégé: This can be accomplished by reviewing the protégé's work record, interviewing the protégé, their current and former supervisors, and testing.

Select mentors: They should be technically competent, supported by peers and upper management, have power within the organization, be highly regarded in the organization, feel secure in their positions, have the time and the desire to assume responsibility for a protégé' career development, and be able to teach, coach, and motivate others.

Pair protégés and mentors: Considerations in the paring would be the developmental needs of the protégé and the skills and knowledge of the mentor as well as the personalities of the individuals involved.

Familiarize mentors and protégés with their roles: Subjects that should be addressed are time commitments, expectations of mentors and protégés, available resources, relationships between mentor, protégés, protégé's manager, and the mentoring coordinator, and the benefits of mentoring to the mentor, protégé, and organization.

Mentors and protégés negotiate an agreement: Mentors and protégés negotiate an agreement which includes their expectations and responsibilities, confidentiality, duration of the relationship, scheduling of meetings, and the amount of time that will be spent on mentoring activities.

Develop a plan: The mentor and protégé develop a plan for meeting the needs of the protégé.

Implement the plan: The mentor and protégé meet periodically for coaching sessions, evaluating progress, and reviewing the development plan. Progress is periodically reported to the coordinator.

Conclude the relationship: Relationships might be concluded when all goals are achieved, the agreement date is reached, or the protégé and mentor feel that the relationship is no longer productive.

TRAINING AND DOCUMENTATION

Documentation is not just a restaurant industry issue, it is an issue in every business that has many employees. The law is definite on the issue when it regards the termination of an employee. Documentation does not have to be a bad thing, as some of us have come to view it. If you are performing job reviews when you are supposed to, and you are informing your staff of the wonderful things they do and some of the areas they could use improvement, you are documenting. Having a form that each staff member signs at the end of his/her review will show that you have done your job and they have agreed that you have done so.

Their complaint is that they feel insignificant and not valued by their management and company. Good attitudes go a long way to a more productive employee. A pat on the back goes a long way in this business. Documenting bad behavior, such as tardiness, no-call/no-show, bad attitude, etc., is the kind of documentation that will keep you out of trouble with the law. Ultimately, it is your responsibility to ensure your entire staff understands the rules and regulations. Having signed documents by them that they understand the rules is one way to ensure that.

Training Outside the Box

Restaurant owners wouldn't be owners if they didn't know everything about every position in the business. While that is certainly true, owners/managers are not always able to make sure that training is being handled in the way that is the most productive and profitable. Managers hold weekly or monthly staff meetings in which they remind staff to really push those sides and appetizers. Try to get check averages above the usual $9 per person, do your side work, pick up trash if you see it laying on the floor, be a team player, don't run with scissors, etc. They have heard it before; they're not going to listen this time either, because they know all of that.

Most restaurants put a manager or trainer/server in charge of training. They feel confident that it is being handled properly. No one would dispute that fact. Maybe you have books, manuals or videotapes that you encourage your staff to read or watch. That's all fine and good, but is anyone interacting with them? Is anyone spending quality time with them and letting them practice the routines until they feel comfortable? Sure, they are learning exactly what they are being taught, and that is the menu items, where the coffee is made, where to get bread, etc. They aren't being taught up-selling and increasing the check average.

People come into your restaurant to eat, not to browse and look through your menu and see if you have the entrée they want to purchase. It's easy to fall into the trap of thinking that waiting tables is the easiest job in the world because of that reason. It's not like buying a car. People come in because they are hungry and they need to eat. There is no choice in our survival; we must eat. They may or may not need a car. The fun part is guiding their experience and making it enjoyable so they feel like they get more than their money's worth! They feel compelled to tip their server because he/she has displayed knowledge, charm and true customer service skills, which is really a caring attitude.

Hiring an outside trainer doesn't mean you are incapable or don't know enough about your own business to run it; it simply proves a fact that you do not have enough hours in the day or week to accomplish everything you would like to. Practice makes permanent, not perfect. Let's face it, no one is perfect and, try as you might, you are not going to have a perfect team. But you can come close! You will not lose control of what your staff does; you have the right to tell an outside trainer the goals you are trying to reach with your staff. Two or three hours in a fun, interactive class on a day off really isn't too much to contribute to the improvement of a career. Make an outside trainer work for you; one certainly wouldn't want to work against you.

Keep in mind that most people won't tell you that they like your food but would rather not have to deal with your staff. It's usually little things that wait staff don't perceive as significant, or they think that your guests don't care one way or another how they are served, just as long as they are served! Your guests tell people like me. They tell people who are in the business, but never directly. They may even tell a competitor about their experience.

We live in a society where people don't want to hurt others' feelings, but they do so at their own detriment. They would rather tell someone else. Statistically, people tell 10-12 other people about a bad experience. They have begun to expect the usual, mundane, just take the order and leave as quickly as possible attitude. Therefore, they don't tip any more than they feel the service is worth. In between meetings, interviews, inventory issues, disciplinary action, and the list goes on. People who are offering you a service are going to be as accommodating as possible. Your staff will come back with more tools to make more money.

Bad habits are hard to break. It is proven that people, when breaking one habit, will replace it with another habit. Why not make it a good habit? Last but not least, if you are skeptical or you don't want to send your people into a class without first checking it out for yourself, ask if you can attend a class and observe. Imparting that information to your staff is much more difficult in the restaurant because there are so many distractions. Sometimes servers are intimidated by your presence. Sometimes they are intimidated by guests and don't feel comfortable trying out new things in front of them, so they never move out of the "order-taker" mode.

Payments

In the wake of the economic conditions and corporate scandals of the past few years, shareholders are monitoring the actions of their respective companies with renewed and concerned interest. It has reached the point where bonuses in general seem to be increasingly viewed in a negative light, whether as the subject of shareholder revolt or of employees gossiping around the water cooler. Bonuses however are not a bad thing if awarded appropriately.

A bonus should be a key component of a well structured performance related compensation programme. Indeed, over the past couple of decades the implementation of bonus schemes has become more and more prevalent and the majority of employers now recognise that a well-designed programme can have a positive impact. In a recent survey of compensation practices among hotel companies in Europe, HVS found that the vast majority of companies have a bonus scheme in place for executives at hotel department head level upwards.

The grant of a bonus however should not be based merely on job on title or an employee's seniority. The most appropriate manner in which to reward an employee is through a performance linked incentive bonus. Incentives strengthen the link between an individual's performance and that of the company, and overall business performance improves as a result. When designing a bonus plan it is worth bearing the following points in mind.

A successful bonus plan does not stand alone but is part of a larger, integrated reward scheme and Human Resources strategy. Before implementing a bonus scheme an organisation or department must carefully define the goals of the scheme, how it fits into the overall HR strategy, and how much weight the bonus carries in the overall reward package. There is no one-size-fits-all bonus scheme. Rather, each company must tailor its bonus strategy to its corporate culture and operating philosophy.

For example, an assertive, rapidly growing company many decide to pay a low base salary with a high bonus potential component. A conservative company however may prefer to pay a high base with a minimal bonus element. By their nature, bonus plans are typically aimed at rewarding short-term performance, i.e. less than twelve months. An effective scheme needs appropriate, significant and measurable performance targets. In addition, the plan needs to be simple to comprehend and easy to communicate.

A bonus programme contains two to four criteria upon which performance targets are based, although a company can have as many as it feels appropriate. Financial criteria can include measures such as EBITDA, Department or Company Profit, Earnings per Share (EPS), and Revenue Growth. Additionally, recognition should be given for the achievement of personal objectives, such as winning a new contract for the company, or the implementation of a new training programme. These measures can be weighted accordingly for each position. For example, in a public company where EPS is a key measure for all executives, it may represent a larger part of the CEO's bonus potential than of the Chief Technology Officer's. This would then reflect appropriately the contribution of each individual to the company's EPS.

One of the benefits of having two or three criteria is that it still rewards employees in a year when one of the measures may have suffered through external influences. For example, if EPS are down due to factors outside of a company's control, such as the performance of the stock market, then the employee still has an incentive to excel against the other two measures. Qualification for bonus award should be clear and straightforward. Once goals are met then a bonus is paid. The threshold for qualification of bonus is typically around 95% achievement of goal. In cases where goals are exceeded, a company can introduce an override bonus to reward the superior performance.

For example, if an employee exceeds his department profit target by 10% then his related bonus component increases by 2%. A company can then introduce a cap which corresponds to the maximum percentage as determined in the overall bonus plan. Bonus plans based on immeasurable criteria, such as 'being a jolly good chap who has put in 20 years service', are to be avoided and will no longer be tolerated by investors. Well implemented, performance linked bonus schemes however are to be encouraged and should be regarded in a positive light. They motivate staff, lead to improved business results and are based on measurable targets rather than on someone's whim.

Offense and Defense

Offense and defense are words of opposite meaning, yet often linked together. Their obvious meaning is demonstrated on the football field. One team attacks an area defended by another, trying to reach the goal. The purpose of the defense is to stop the attack, to defend their territory, to protect the goal. Though these terms have most often been applied to armies at war, they can also be used to describe less physical competitions such as a game of chess. What characterizes each of these examples is a conflict or competition. Two words derived from these terms are the adjectives offensive and defensive. The dictionary defines offensive as:

— Unpleasant or disagreeable to the senses; obnoxious, disgusting.

— Causing anger, resentment, giving offense; insulting.

Defensive means:

— Intended or suitable for protection.

— Carried on for the purpose of defending against attack or danger.

— Having an attitude of defense.

Everyone has heard the phrase "a good offense is the best defense." This idea is especially useful on battlefields, football fields and even chessboards. By keeping your opponent so off balance by relentless attacks, he has no time or resources to plan attacks against your positions. In this way your offense becomes your defense. People have natural tendencies. Whether inborn or created by longstanding habit, they are part of our makeup and we express them without thinking. One such habit is the tendency to personally associate ourselves with that which we do. Just as the farmer has a proprietary interest in the fields he labors so hard to till and harvest, we all identify with our company, organization, or place of work.

A corollary to this sense of association is the natural inclination to protect that which we consider our own or with which are associated. So it is natural for us to feel pride in our work and place of employment. When someone attacks it with criticism, disparaging remarks, or complaints, the natural tendency is to defend it, to assume a defensive attitude. This is all well and good unless you depend upon that someone's goodwill for your livelihood.

When you work in the service industry, you literally cannot afford to become defensive. When you become defensive, many things happen physiologically and psychologically. Adrenaline starts flowing; you tense up, ready to repel any further attack; your heartbeat and respiration quicken. Likewise, your mind races ahead to your next move or response so you don't hear what is being said and you don't focus on the moment.

Knowing that a good offense is the best defense you become antagonistic; you raise your voice; you develop an attitude; you become abrupt and huffy with the other person. At this point, without even knowing it, you have become offensive; that is by definition, "causing anger, resentment, giving offense; insulting." So how can you avoid this natural tendency to become defensive? The first step is to become aware that you become defensive when criticized or listening to a guest complaint. Notice the dead giveaways. Do you get tense and nervous? Do your hands shake or your voice quaver? Do you have trouble breathing or feel tightness in your chest? Do you raise your voice? Any of these symptoms reveal your defensiveness. Realizing this, what can you do about it? First of all, understand two important things:

— Complaints are not usually directed at you, so don't take it personally. Allow some distance between yourself and the complaint. Not too much, though; you must show a sincere concern to resolve the problem.

— When a guest complains, there is, in his mind, a problem. Whether we think there is a problem or not is immaterial. Furthermore, because of the nature of the service profession, the problem is ours. When considered in this light, the guest is doing us a favor by making us aware of the problem. We should be appreciative and thankful instead of defensive. In addition, there are some particular things you can do when confronted with a complaint.

— Where there is no conflict, there is no need for offense and defense. Don't allow a conflict to arise. Disarm the situation by cheerfully accepting our problem. Listen carefully to what the guest is saying. Apologize sincerely for our shortcomings. If you can solve the problem, cheerfully and quickly do so. If you can't, get a manager who can.

— If you find yourself becoming nervous or defensive, take a deep breath. The inflow of oxygen will help quiet your system and the moment you take to breathe has a calming effect on your nerves.

— If you find yourself losing control, try to leave the room on some pretext. If you are a server, tactfully excuse yourself "to check with the kitchen." Once there, take a deep breath and get control of yourself. Try to put the guest's anger into perspective. It's not the end of the world. Resolve to overcome that anger. Take another deep breath and go back to the guest.

— Go on the offensive in a positive away. Take control of the situation. Ask pertinent questions about our problem. Take notes as necessary. This taking ownership of the problem demonstrates a proprietary concern and a desire to correct the problem.

— While apologies must always be given, remember that easy apologies and facile excuses do not impress.

— Be sincere. You should have a sincere desire to help any guest with a need or concern. If you don't, you're in the wrong business.

Two things you must never do:

— Pass the buck or evade responsibility. You may not have created the problem, but now that it's been brought to your attention, you need to resolve it.

— Don't become defensive. It is not us against the guests. We're on their team!

Responding to guest complaints is one of the most difficult things we face in the service profession, but when we avoid becoming defensive, we often can create a turnaround situation where the problem is solved and the guest satisfied. There is no more satisfying situation in service.

Improving Guest Services

Smart service providers care about their customers. That's a given. But those who really care don't need to go out of their way to convince customers. Caring is part of their service philosophy and it shows in the way they treat customers. Conversely, those who make an issue of their service philosophy often seem to fall short.

Customer satisfaction is based on service delivery, not claims about service delivery. And it's service delivery, not claims, that customers describe when they sound off to friends and colleagues. So it might be worthwhile to examine your own service philosophy and analyze how well that philosophy translates into action. Conversely, examine your service delivery, and question — really question — whether it reflect or contradicts your service philosophy.

Improving guest services really doesn't require the latest and greatest tools. In this day and age of throwing every conceivable amenity and trendy technological perk at hotel guests, it is a fact that all the amenities in the world won't improve the basics of a well-run hotel. To begin improving guest services, take a look at your people, product and performance. If your hotel is under performing, it is not the brand's fault, the economy's fault or the war's fault. The fault comes from directly within and is directly linked to the services you provide for your guests. The front desk is your guest's first impression of your hotel. Before the clerk begins to speak, the guest forms an opinion. Today, in this industry, the state of the front desk is horrible.

The basics are barely addressed. Uniforms are a rarity. Front desk staff in polo shirts and an array of unacceptable pants, skirts or worse, too-tight jeans, is not a substitute for a well-put-together uniform. Consider name-tags. This is basic "curb appeal," and it should be a priority. A consistent pulled-together appearance enables your guests to place confidence in your hotel and its staff representatives. The multi-cultural aspect of the hotel industry is wonderful. However, a hotel general manager should ensure that the desk staff can clearly communicate with the guests. Travelers expect language barriers in foreign travel, not domestic properties.

There are plenty of frustrated travelers with stories to tell about desk clerks they could not understand, either face-to-face or on the telephone. Not only does this harm your guest appeal, it may put you at risk. If a guest needs to communicate an emergency, and the staff member cannot communicate information back, you will most certainly face an unpleasant liability. "The winning hotel has ensured that its product meets and exceeds guest expectations."

Today's guests are faced with more choices and levels of quality than they ever thought possible. However, the hotel that maintains an excellent product (a good night's rest) has succeeded in not only sustaining decent occupancy levels; it has also succeeded in stealing business from competitors. Why? The winning hotel has ensured that its product meets and exceeds guest expectations.

Guest expectations are basic: cleanliness, comfort and convenience. Cleanliness is priority one. Guests will no longer accept stained carpets, worn blankets and sheets or threadbare towels. They simply don't return. Guests have come to expect bedding like they have at home. Foam mattresses, flat pillows and worn bedspreads won't make it. The very purpose of any hotel is a good night's rest. Your absolute best investment would be good bedding. Sleep in your own beds and honestly assess if they're worth the rate you charge. Pillows are a cheap investment that make a huge guest impression. Guaranteeing a great night's rest is absolute guest service.

In-room comfort is important to the traveler. Make sure your rooms are well lit. Is the lighting where the guest needs it? Are your lampshades dirty or dusty? Are the chairs you provide comfortable? Are they soiled or stained? Rent a steam cleaner and make them look new. Guest comfort starts with impressions; if the chair they will sit on is stained, they will start wondering what's on that bedspread that they cannot see.

Convenience is important too. Does a guest have to reach behind furniture to plug in his cellphone charger? Buy a power strip so he has easy access. Is the bathroom vanity cluttered? Is the desk cluttered? How many times have you seen a stayover room where the guest moves all the "stuff" so he has room to work? Think like a guest, and look at your rooms like a guest. You can add all the amenities in the world, but if a guest can't spread out his own things, he won't be happy. Give him room to relax and rest easy. Finally, there is the issue of performance.

Front desk teams must be trained properly and should be re-trained regularly. Would you hand the keys to your new car to a 16-year-old without a thought? When you leave poorly trained desk agents at the desk, you are handing over the keys (and potential liabilities) of your hotel and the lives of all its guests to that same 16-year-old, figuratively speaking. Teach your staff the basics of guest services. Make eye contact. Smile! Greet every guest. Try to remember names. Don't express frustration in front of the guest. Do everything possible to make the guest feel important and valued. Your staff does that, right?

Air Traffic Controller

This is a major, major job. One mistake may go unnoticed, two show up at some level, and three in the same day, let alone the same shift, regardless how small, have a rippling effect. Mis-connections, late departure, misplaced luggage, lost luggage, gate not available after a twenty-minute early arrival, curt if not rude gate attendants, plans altered, meetings cancelled, long waits, disappointing service, poor damage control, and of course, the insincere, "I'm really sorry, but there's nothing I can do about it." If you fly you've been there. If you don't fly and you own a restaurant, you've been there. If you've been a customer in a restaurant you've gotten that same insincere excuse from the host staff when they failed to do their job properly. "I'm really sorry but there's nothing I can do about it." When this happens, you get the same result from your guests that airlines get from passengers. In effect, your Host staff is your watchtower of success.

This correlation between Air Traffic Controllers and your Host staff is an incredible observation that has been overlooked for far too long. Simply put, pay the money, hire the right person who knows how to do the job, and your near air collisions and fatal accidents decrease dramatically. Following are the facts and areas of responsibility:

(1) Air Traffic Controllers schedule incoming flights and monitor them. Hosts make reservations and monitor them.

(2) Air Traffic Controllers compare flight plans and book terminals for maximum efficiency. Hosts estimate table turnaround time, reset time, and prepare tables for the next seating.

(3) Air Traffic Controllers observe and record early arrivals and approaching aircraft. Hosts acknowledge and accommodate early arrivals and plan for approaching guests.

(4) Air Traffic Controllers ensure a gate is ready, with proper staffing and equipment in order to deplane. Hosts ensure tables are ready and there is proper staffing.

(5) Air Traffic Controllers estimate on-ground time. Hosts estimate table turn time.

(6) Air Traffic Controllers plan next turnarounds. Hosts plan next turnarounds.

(7) Air Traffic Controllers ensure all requirements are met before takeoff. Hosts ensure that the staff is monitoring their guest for proper turnaround time.

(8) Air Traffic Controllers clear runways and wish happy flying to the pilots. Hosts open doors, thank guests, and invite them back.

(9) Air Traffic Controllers start the same process for the next incoming flight. Hosts start the same process for the next incoming party.

The job of an Air Traffic Controller is to avoid collisions not only in the air, but also on the ground. They keep the runways clear and they keep the traffic moving to make sure everyone is working to the maximum potential, resulting in timely service.

When compared to the Host position, the worst thing that can happen is a near or mid-air collision in your restaurant because the Host has not calculated the arrival times and departure times correctly.

The Host serves as the Air Traffic Controller to prevent those incidents that happen when there is a delay in one flight. And if you've flown, you know that just one flight delayed, has a trickle down effect throughout the country, causing delays for all other flights. When it's more than one flight, the problems grow exponentially just like they do in your restaurant when your Host makes one or two mistakes in the same shift. There are many comparisons to be made with regard to Air Traffic Controllers and Hosts, and that fact alone dictates that you need a skilled, educated person to coordinate the incoming and outgoing traffic. That person requires maturity, sophistication, knowledge of working a restaurant floor, and quite likely more money than you're currently paying. How much more? Probably not a lot, but certainly more than what you're paying.

There is no need to measure the importance of each job; they really are the same job, just different industries. As such, the same level of people should be hired. While this is a strong message, it is one that needs to be heard. If you don't, your restaurant is truly on a collision course. To avoid the collision course, we need to shift the industry perception in reference to the position of Host. We must acknowledge the importance of the position, rather than simply staffing it with, for no better term, "a pretty face." The person hired for the position needs to be analytical, methodical, and have an understanding of the elements of air traffic control. If you want to ensure safe flying for your customers, spend the money on the front side and you'll reap it on the backside.

Assessment

The various assessment tools available in the marketplace are universally devised to aid in gaining an understanding of how someone will fit into your business culture, work in a team environment, offer creative input, handle cultural diversity, and solve everyday problems that occur in their job. All these things are impossible to deduce from a reading of their resume, or even the most exhaustive unstructured interview. Furthermore, many assessment tools can be customized to fit the particular needs of our industry, or your organization. Hiring more effectively leads to lower turnover.

Reducing your turnover is not simply alleviating a headache for human resources; it has a significant impact on profitability. There are many types of tools currently in use for the purpose of making the hiring, and human capital development process more effective, but they fall into two main categories: structured interviews, or written examinations. The following are ways in which these tools can be used to advantage:

Benchmarking

By administering the test to groups of existing employees who already have a known level of success with your organization, you can map a group of trends and repeated traits that form a competency model for those positions. Depending upon the cost of the assessment tool you choose, this can be done at all practical levels of the organizational chart.

Final Screening

Your assessment tool of choice should be one of the last elements used in the screening process to provide backup, or possibly counterpoint to the opinions of the interviewer(s). Assessment is particularly potent in this regard when you have already used the tool to set benchmarks for the position.

Development and Succession Planning

Whether assessing a future CEO, Vice President, or department head, personality profiling should be part of identifying an internal candidates aptitude for the position. In this case again, when combined with benchmarking, assessment can be a very valuable tool to help identify the "best" candidates for training and development to be the future managers and leaders for the company.

Choosing a Tool

The U.S Department of Labor, Employment and Training Commission has published a guide to "Testing and Assessment – An Employers Guide to Good Practices" which is available on-line. Beyond the exhaustive criteria supplied there for making certain that the assessment tool you choose is bona fide, there are many other factors that may influence your choice. Companies like Talent Plus provide "structured interviews", that determine many of the previously mentioned personal characteristics based on verbal response to customizable question sets posed by an interviewer.

Lab Profiles (Language &Behavior Profile), developed by Rodger Bailey in the early '80's is another type of interviewing technique created to predict individuals' personal, and professional characteristics. The time spent researching and choosing the tool most appropriate for your company will be time well spent. Though there is training and cost involved in using any type of assessment in your hiring and development process, we believe the long-range value to your firm far more than outweighs them.

Values in Practice

A company's values are put into practice in several ways: the choice of measurements that will be used to gauge performance and success, the treatment of employees, the allocation of wages and benefits, and the kinds of performance that will be recognized, rewarded, and talked about. Regardless of what a company says its philosophy is, what it measures is one of the biggest determinants of what its values really are. If food costs, labor costs, and inventory turnover are all it measures, talks about, and uses to evaluate performance, people will adapt to that and the company culture will be control-oriented. The frequency of measurement also has a profound impact on the organizational culture in communicating the true values of the company.

An organization must decide whether its systems are there for the convenience of the guest or the accounting office. If your employees believe their first priority is keeping proper inventory and accounting records, in reality "service" isn't your philosophy. If you want service, you have to place equal or greater emphasis on measuring service. This may mean evaluating guest satisfaction by measuring repeat business, responding to guest reactions, comments, and suggestions, and even conducting guest surveys and gaining other guest feedback.

How you treat your employees will also communicate how you think guests should be treated. If you want guest satisfaction, you also have to measure employee satisfaction, since their behavior is part of the product. Employees must be happy and content themselves before they can make guests happy. When people feel good about themselves and are comfortable with their skills, they're more willing and able to perform in public. The happier they are, the likelier they are to go out of their way to help a guest or co-worker.

If your human resources strategy is working, you won't need a customer service training program to teach workers to smile. You won't need a customer service training program to teach workers to smile. On the other hand, employees in uncomfortable situations will generally tend to be ruder to guests and one another. Employee turnover, absenteeism, attitude surveys, and accident rates are all indicators for measuring employee satisfaction.

When managers know that employers consider achieving guest and employee satisfaction to be as important as achieving financial results, they're likelier to give proper emphasis to service and the importance of their employees in achieving successful service. When that happens, employees know that management means it when it says, "Our employees are our greatest asset."

Compensation policies will also communicate the values of a company. If a company wants to emphasis service, employees who are on the service line should be adequately compensated. If front desk agents, cashiers, and telephone operators earn minimum wage, while clerks in accounting, the storeroom, or the mail room are paid substantially more, this communicates that service isn't the company's top priority.

Values can be reinforced through recognition programs and the rewards provided to employees. When employees perform consistently according to your values, they should be recognized and rewarded. These employees should be turned into heroes who become role models and examples for others to follow. Others who see them being rewarded will know what's important to the company and what it takes to get ahead, and they'll want to follow suit. It's only when everyone understands what the goals and values are and can see that the company really does operate by them that they can begin to identify with and commit to them.

Your human resources policies and procedures are a practical application of your mission and values. In essence they are the translation of a philosophy statement into a working operation. No area of management communicates and controls your values more forcefully than the development and day-to-day administration of your personnel policies and procedures. These are the rules and how-tos that determine what you require and permit, who you hire, how you train, what you praise and pay for, and why you discipline or terminate someone.

Art of Storytelling

One of the most effective ways of reinforcing values is to talk about the people who best represent them. Every organizational culture is characterized by traditions and legends of which all employees quickly become aware. The process, sometimes known as storytelling, has a powerful influence on the behavior and attitudes of workers, because it summarizes the beliefs and values of the company. A favorite example of many in the hospitality industry is a story Disney employees tell all about Walt Disney taking his children to an amusement park. After observing the level of maintaining there, he's said to have vowed that if he ever had an amusement park, he'd never want to have chipped paint on the horses on his carousel. Clearly, that determination is understood and upheld by employees in the Disney organization today.

5

Maintenance of Culinary Services

Refrigeration Facilities

Refrigeration facilities shall be adequate to provide for the proper storage, transportation, display, and service of potentially hazardous foods. Specific refrigeration needs are based upon the menu, number of meals, frequency of delivery, preparation in advance of service.

1. All potentially hazardous foods requiring refrigeration shall be kept at or below 45F except when being prepared or served.
2. Walk-in freezers shall be designed, constructed and maintained to keep frozen foods frozen. Temperature indicating devices will be required.

Point-of-use refrigerators should be provided at workstations for operations requiring preparation and handling of potentially hazardous foods. Refrigeration units, unless designed for such use, shall not be located directly adjacent to cooking equipment or other high heat producing equipment, which may tax the units cooling system.

To plan reserve storage, the following will need to be considered: menu, type of service, number of meals per day, number of deliveries per week. The following is a suggested formula to establish required reserve storage for walk-in refrigeration units.

Total Interior Storage Volume Needed:

$$\frac{\text{Vol. per meal (Cu. ft.) x number of meals}}{\text{40\% usable Space}}$$

Below are typical meal volumes for each of three types of refrigerated storage:

Meat and Poultry = . 010 - .030 Cu. ft. per meal

Dairy = . 007 - .015 Cu. ft. per meal

Vegetables and fruit = . 020 - .040 Cu. ft. per meal

Thus for a restaurant serving 1000 meals between deliveries (assume a minimum of 4 day storage) the following storage capacities are needed:

Meat refrigerated storage =

$$\frac{\text{.030 cu. ft./meal x 1000 meals = 75 Cu. Ft.}}{.40}$$

Vegetable refrigerated storage =

$$\frac{\text{. 040 cu. ft./meal x 1000 meals = 100 Cu. Ft.}}{.40}$$

Dairy refrigerated storage =

$$\frac{\text{.015 cu. ft./meal x 1000 meals = 37.5 Cu. Ft.}}{.40}$$

To calculate the interior storage space required for the above example in square feet, simply divide the cu. ft. (volume), in each case, by the height o of the unit.

Example for meat storage =

$$\frac{\text{75 cu. ft}}{\text{6 ft. (height)}} = \text{12.5 sq. ft.}$$

of interior floor area would have to be provided to accommodate storage of meat for 1000 meals. To estimate total interior volume or space, add the requirements for each type of food. To convert interior measurements to exterior floor area simply multiply by 1.25. Thus, for meat storage, in the above example exteriors floor area = 1.25 x 12.5 sq. ft., or 15.6 sq. ft. would be needed.

The following is a suggested formula to establish required reserve storage for reach-in refrigeration units.

Total interior storage volume needed

Vol. per meal (Cu. ft.) X number of meals X 75% usable Space

Thus for a restaurant serving 1000 meals between deliveries (assume a minimum of 4-day storage) the following storage capacities are needed:

Meat refrigerated storage =

$$\frac{.030 \text{ cu. ft./meal} \times 1000 \text{ meals}}{.75} = 40 \text{ Cu. Ft. unit}$$

Vegetable refrigerated storage =

$$\frac{040 \text{ cu.ft./mealx1000 meals}}{.75} = 53 \text{ Cu. Ft.}$$

Dairy refrigerated storage =

$$\frac{.015 \text{ cu. 'ft./meal} \times 1000 \text{ meals}}{.75} = 20 \text{ Cu. Ft. unit}$$

All refrigeration units must have numerically scaled indicating thermometers accurate to $\pm 3°$ F with the temperature-sensing unit located in the unit to measure air temperature in the warmest part. All such thermometers should have an externally mounted indicator to facilitate easy reading of the temperature of the unit.

— Refrigerators and freezers shall be capable of maintaining appropriate temperatures when evaluated under test conditions. Maximum operating temperature (cabinet air) shall be:

Max. Compressor Type	*Max. Temp*
Rapid Cool down	Food temp cooling from 140° F to 45° F within 4 hours
Refrigerated	Cabinet air temp 33-41°F
Buffet units	Food temp 45° F
Storage & display Refrigerators	Cabinet air temp 41°F
Storage & display Freezer	Cabinet air temp 0° F

— Approved cove juncture base shall be around the interior.

— Approved cove junction base shall be around the exterior.

— Approved enclosure between the top of the unit and the ceiling will be required as per manufacturer specification.

— Outside remote refrigeration units shall be for unopened standard packaged goods only. These units shall meet National Sanitation Foundation or equivalent.

— If the walk-in floors are water-flushed for cleaning or receive the discharge of liquid waste or excessive melt water, the floors shall be non-absorbent (i.e. quarry tile or equal) with silicone or epoxy impregnated grout, sloped to drain outside of the box to a floor drain or trench drains located within 2 feet of the cooler door.

— Walk-in units should contain moisture-proof lamps providing a minimum 10 foot candles of light at 30" above the floor.

Hot Holding and Reheating Facilities

The hot holding facilities must be capable of maintaining potentially hazardous foods at an internal temperature of 140° F or above during display or holding. Reheating equipment must be capable of raising the internal temperature of potentially hazardous foods rapidly to at least 165° F. Appropriate product thermometers will be required to monitor temperature.

FACILITIES TO PROTECT FOOD

Food Preparation Sink

Adequate facilities must be provided to promote good hygienic practices, sanitary food handling and to minimize the potential of cross contamination between finished and raw products. Separate areas should be designed to separate food handling operations involving raw and finished products.

Separate vegetable washing facilities shall be provided in establishments that wash raw vegetables. Where it can be documented by low volume, infrequent preparation or where items are purchased prewashed and pre-packaged, a separate preparation sink may not be required. Establishments that scale or eviscerate fish, wash raw poultry, or other raw meats shall provide separate sinks with preparation space for these processes. Where it can be documented by low volume, infrequent preparation or where items are purchased prewashed and packaged a separate preparation sink may not be required. For facilities that have a low volume of vegetables, fish, poultry or other raw meats that are being prepped or washed then the operator may want to install a chief table to accommodate this operation.

The minimum recommended drainboard length for food preparation sinks when installed is 18". All food on display, during service or while being held must be adequately protected from contamination by the use of: packaging; serving line, storage or salad bar protector devices; display cases or by other effective means including dispensers.

Where frozen desserts are being portioned and dispensed, running water dipper wells should be provided for the in-use storage of dispensing utensils.

DRY STORAGE CONSIDERATIONS

The dry storage space required depends upon the menu, number of meals, quantities purchased and frequency of delivery. The location of the storeroom should be adjacent to the food preparation area and convenient to receiving. Where possible the storeroom should be free of uninsulated steam and water pipes, \water heaters, transformers, refrigeration condensation units, steam generators or other heat producing equipment. Temperatures of 50° F to 80° F are recommended. Foods shall not be stored under exposed sewer lines due to the possibility of contamination from leaks in the overhead lines. Two suggested formulas used in estimating required storage space is as follows:

Formula 1

Linear feet of shelving for storage (ft.) =

$$\frac{\text{volume per meal x number of meals between deliveries}}{\text{D x H x C}}$$

Volume per meal = .025 to .050 cu. ft. per meal served

D = Depth of the shelves in feet

H = Clearance between shelves in feet

C = 80% effective capacity of shelf height

For example assume 400 meals per day and a 10 day storage between deliveries = 4000 meals for which to provide storage, Volume of .035 per meal, shelf depth of 18 inches, clearance of 18 inches between shelves and 80% effective capacity of shelf height:

Linear feet of shelving for storage (ft.) =

$$\frac{\text{.035 cu. ft x 4000 meals}}{\text{1.5 ft. x 1.5 ft. x 80\%}} = \text{77.77 Linear feet}$$

Formula 2

$$\text{Required Storage Area (sq. ft)} = \frac{\text{Volume per meal x number of meals between deliveries}}{\text{Average height x fraction of usable storeroom floor area}}$$

(1) Volume per meal = .025 to .050 cu. ft. per meal served

(2) (2) Useful storage height = 4 to 7 feet

(3) Storage time between deliveries = 3 to 14 days

(4) Fraction of useable storeroom floor area = .3 to .6

For example assume 100 meals per day and a 10 day storage between deliveries = 4000 meals for which to provide storage:

Required Storage Area= .05 cu. ft.x1000 meals 5ft.x.3

Required Storage Area = 33 square feet

Clearance between the shelves should be at least 12" to 18". Sufficient moveable dunnage racks and dollies (with smooth surfaces, cleanable in case of food spillage or package breakage) should be provided to store bulk food or bulk containers at least 12" above the floor for fixed storage shelves and 6" for portable storage units. Dunnage racks, etc. should be spaced from walls sufficiently to prevent vermin harborage, monitoring and inspection. Food containers shall not be stored under exposed sewer lines or leaking water lines. Approved food containers with tight-fitting covers are required for storing broken lots of items such as flour, cornmeal, sugar, dried beans, rice and similar foods. Scoops are recommended for each food storage container in use. Facilities that have a large amount of take-out or use single items will need to increase the amount of storage in order to handle these items.

HAND WASHING

Lavatory facilities shall include hot and cold running water supplied through a combination faucet or tempered water, sanitary towels or approved hand drying devices, and soap. Antibacterial soap should be provided at each employee lavatory facility. Any self-closing or metering faucet should be designed to provide a flow of water for at least 15 seconds without the need to reactivate the faucet.

For employees, at least one lavatory facility shall be provided in the kitchen area in addition to any lavatories which may be provided in the toilet rooms. Additional lavatories may be required in food preparation or utensil washing area which are more than 25' from a lavatory or when the food preparation areas or utensil washing facilities are located in a separate room. Splashguard protection is required if spacing to adjoining food, food contact surfaces, or utensil washing and storage area surfaces are less than 18 inches.

Splash guards shall not hinder access to the lavatory, should extend from the front of the sink to 12 inches above the rim of the sink, and be of easily cleanable construction. Lavatory facilities shall remain free of storage, shall be used exclusively for hand washing and shall be kept clean and in good repair.

WATER SUPPLY AND SEWAGE DISPOSAL

Where a non-municipal water supply or sewage disposal system is utilized, the location of these facilities shall be noted on the plans and certification provided that state and local regulations are to be complied with.

Cross-connections with sewage lines; unapproved water supplies or other potential sources of contamination are prohibited. Hot and cold running water under pressure shall be provided to food preparation, utensil and handwashing areas, and any other areas in which water is required for cleaning. Running water under pressure shall be provided in sufficient quantity to carry out all food preparation, utensil washing, hand washing, cleaning, and other water-using operations.

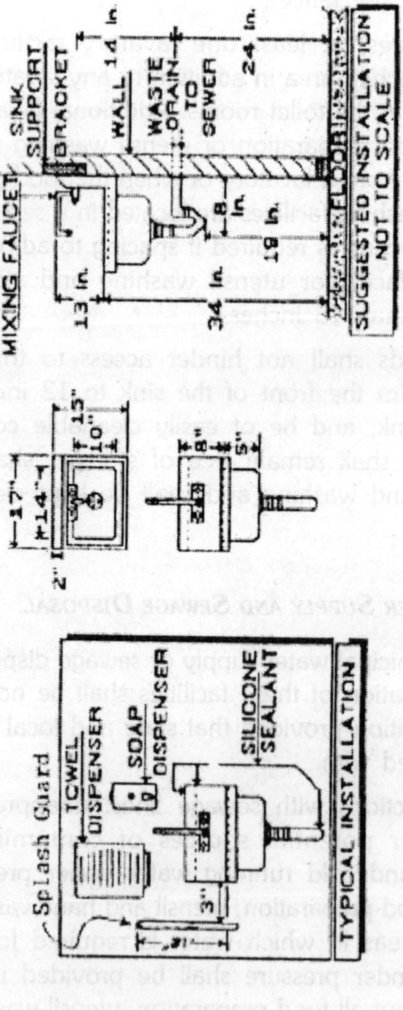

Figure 1

Illustrates a typical hand wash installation with a splash guard

Wastewater from food service equipment such as utensil wash sinks, prep sinks, dishmachines and other equipment that discharge liquid wastewater should be discharged to a sanitary Floor- Type sink wastewater receptor as illustrated below in

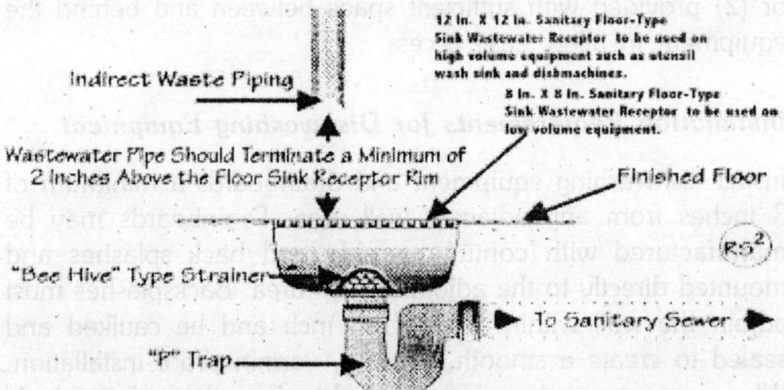

Typical Floor Sink Installation Detail

Figure 2

Food Equipment and Installation

The following outlines some of the equipment installation requirements to insure proper spacing and sealing to allow for adequate and easy cleaning: Food equipment shall be installed as follows:

1. Counter-mounted equipment shall be on 4-inch sanitary legs, sealed to the counter or be portable.
2. Floor-mounted equipment shall be on 6-inch sanitary legs, on casters, or sealed to the floor.
3. Equipment not on casters or not portable shall be sealed to the wall and/or adjoining equipment, or spaced to facilitate cleaning.
4. Portable equipment and equipment installed on casters shall be installed with flexible utility lines and/or quick-disconnect couplings.

The above criteria shall be applied to permit all exposed areas of equipment and adjacent surfaces to be accessible for cleaning. If an item of equipment is not portable, is not installed on casters, or is not otherwise easily moved, it shall be (1) sealed to adjoining surfaces with an approved sealant or metal flashing, or (2) provided with sufficient space between and behind the equipment to allow easy access.

Installation Requirements for Dishwashing Equipment

Install dishwashing equipment and drainboards a minimum of 3 inches from any adjacent wall area. Drainboards may be manufactured with continuous side and back splashes and mounted directly to the adjoining wall area. Backsplashes must adjoin the wall within 1/32 of an inch and be caulked and sealed to create a smooth, sanitary, vermin proof installation. Where equipment does not effectively adjoin the wall within 1/32 of an inch it should be installed a minimum of 3 inches off the wall. Soiled Drainboards are recommended to be located a minimum of 18" from food contact surfaces or equipped with splash protection. Splashguard protection is required if spacing to adjoining food, food contact surfaces, or utensil washing and storage area surfaces are less than 18 inches. Splashguards shall not hinder access to the lavatory, should extend from the front of the sink to 12 inches above the rim of the sink, and be of easily cleanable construction.

Portable Equipment

Food equipment that is small and light enough to be easily moved by one person shall be considered portable and is exempt from equipment installation requirements. (Figure 3 illustrates some examples of portable equipment)

Counter Installation of Equipment

Food equipment, which is not readily movable because of size, weight, or rigid utility connections, shall be installed on counters or tables as follows:

1. On 4-inch sanitary legs; or
2. Sealed to the counter; and
3. Properly spaced to facilitate cleaning; or
4. Equipped with an integral lift lever, pivoting foot, polyethylene wear strips, or a similar device, which allows easy access under and around the equipment for cleaning.

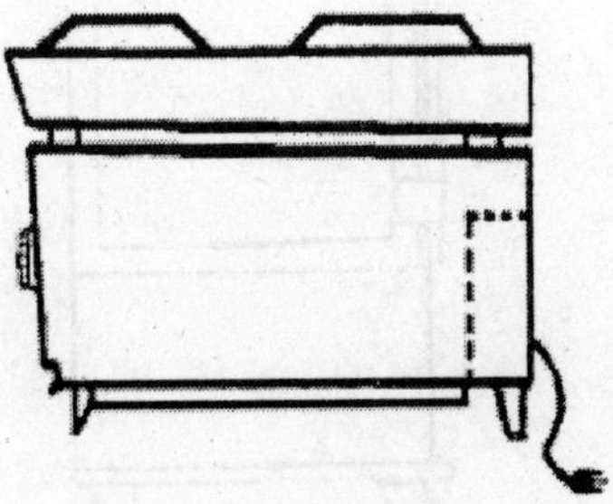

Electric Hot Plate

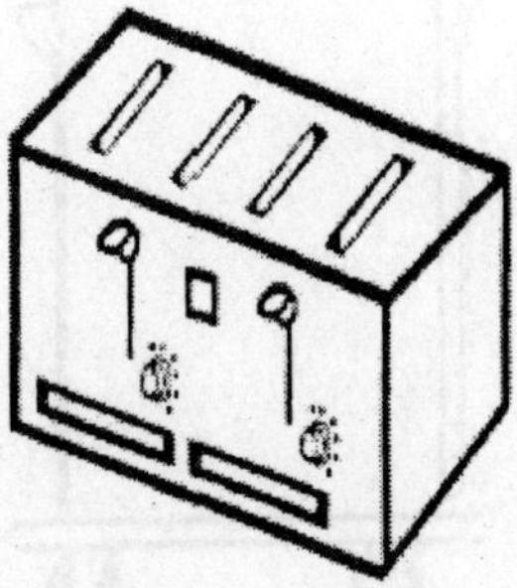

Toaster

Figure 3

Undercounter Installation of Equipment

Undercounter equipment installed on the floor shall be equipped with casters or sanitary skids, or on 6-inch sanitary legs and sealed to adjacent surfaces or properly spaced to facilitate cleaning.Casters shall be properly sized for the equipment served, and should be compatible with the cleaning materials used. It is strongly recommended that equipment be installed on casters when possible. Equipment installed on casters allows easy movement and facilitates the cleaning of surrounding surfaces and equipment. Casters also allow for maximum utilization of space by reducing or eliminating spacing requirements for cleaning.

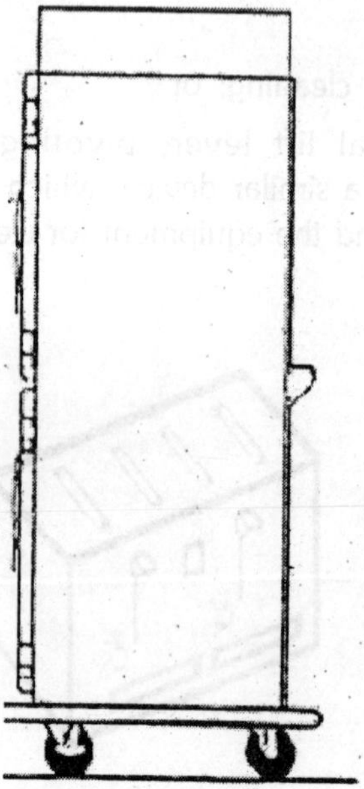

Holding Cabinet

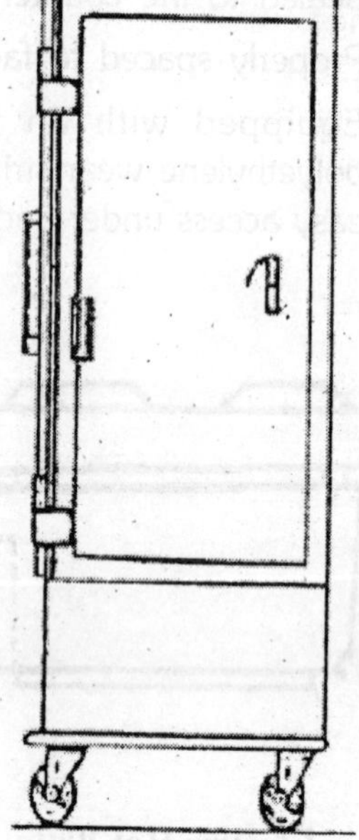

Reach-in-Refrigerator

Electric Fryer

Figure 4

Casters can be installed on most food equipment, including ice machines and deck ovens. Flexible or quick-disconnect couplings are needed on caster-mounted equipment with utility connections. Due to safety concerns, some tilting braising pans, equipment receiving direct steam lines, and some top-heavy equipment should not be installed on casters. Casters may not be the appropriate when floors are severely degraded.

Sanitary legs

When equipment is supported on legs and installed on the floor, the legs shall:

1. Provide at least six inches of unobstructed space between the equipment and the floor;
2. Be of a design that is easily cleanable and constructed of approved materials; (Angle iron, bricks, and concrete blocks are not approved)
3. Be arranged and built to prevent internal harborage of vermin or accumulation of liquids and debris;
4. Provide a minimum of interference with cleaning at the leg-floor contact,
5. Contain no exposed threads, or embellishments, or overhanging edges that serve as places for accumulation of dust, dirt, and debris. (Figure 5 illustrates equipment with Sanitary Legs.)

Masonry Islands

Island installation of equipment reduces the total floor area that must be cleaned. Masonry islands should be a minimum height of six inches with a cove of at least ¼" inch radius at the juncture of the island and the floor. The edges of the equipment should overhang the island (but not more than the height of the island) to prevent grease or other liquids which may spill over or run down the sides from running underneath. The juncture between the base of the equipment and the island shall be sealed to prevent vermin harborage.

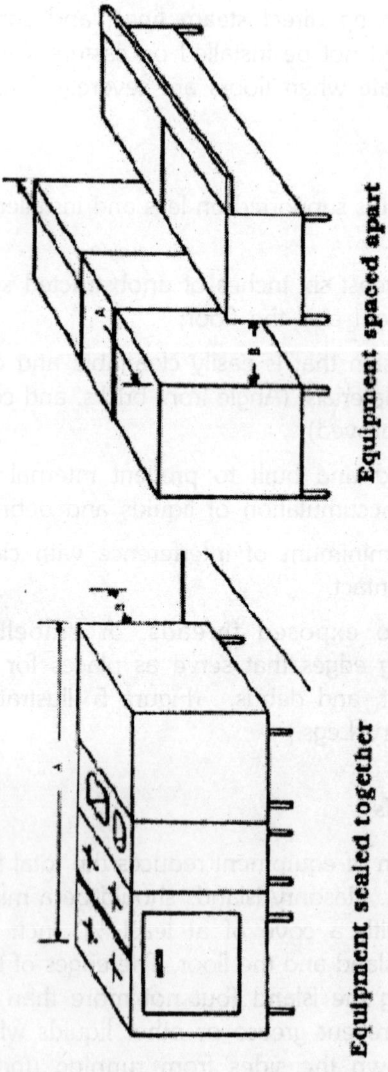

Figure 5

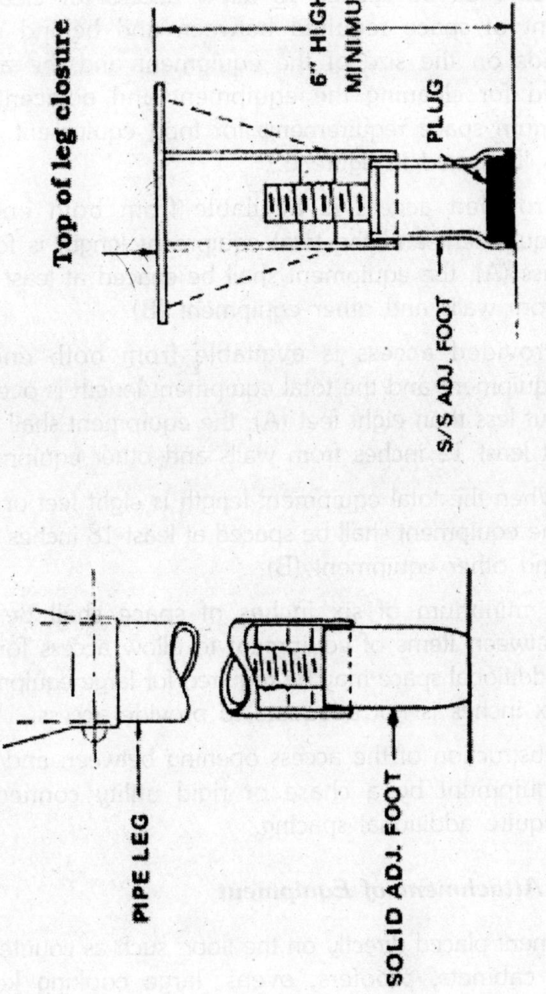

Figure 6. illustrates equipment with Sanitary Legs

Remember to plan for a of 30 inches minimum and 36 inches preferred for a single aisle, 48 inches minimum and 60 inches preferred for a double aisle.

Equipment not readily movable or sealed to adjacent surfaces shall be spaced to allow access for cleaning. The amount of space required between and behind equipment depends on the size of the equipment and the accessibility needed for cleaning the equipment and adjacent surfaces. (Minimum space requirements for food equipment installation are as illustrated in figure 6.)

1. Provided access is available from both ends of the equipment and the total equipment length is four feet or less (A), the equipment shall be spaced at least six inches from walls and other equipment (B).
2. Provided access is available from both ends of the equipment and the total equipment length is over four feet but less than eight feet (A), the equipment shall be spaced at least 12 inches from walls and other equipment (B).
3. When the total equipment length is eight feet or more (A), the equipment shall be spaced at least 18 inches from walls and other equipment (B).
4. A minimum of six inches of space shall be provided between items of equipment to allow access for cleaning. Additional space may be required for large equipment when six inches is not adequate to provide access.
5. Obstruction of the access opening between and/or behind equipment by a chase or rigid utility connection may require additional spacing.

Floor Attachment of Equipment

Equipment placed directly on the floor, such as counters, display cases, cabinets, proofers, ovens, large cooking kettles and retarders shall be effectively sealed to the floor using silicone, metal flashing, vinyl coved base, or other approved material. Metal kick plates which are readily removable will not be required to be sealed to the floor, provided the base of the equipment is sealed to the floor or the areas behind the kick plates are easily cleanable. (Figure 7 illustrates floor-mounted equipment.)

Wall Attachment of Equipment

Equipment attached to walls, such as lavatories, preparation sinks, utensil washing sinks, dish tables, counters, and cabinets shall be effectively sealed to the wall to prevent splash, debris accumulation, and vermin harborage. If the equipment is open underneath, such as a drainboard, dish table, or open base table, it may be installed at least three inches away from the wall. This provision is made due to the fact that dish tables, drainboards, and immobile open base tables are accessible underneath the counter top and a space of three inches from the wall to the equipment is enough to facilitate cleaning.

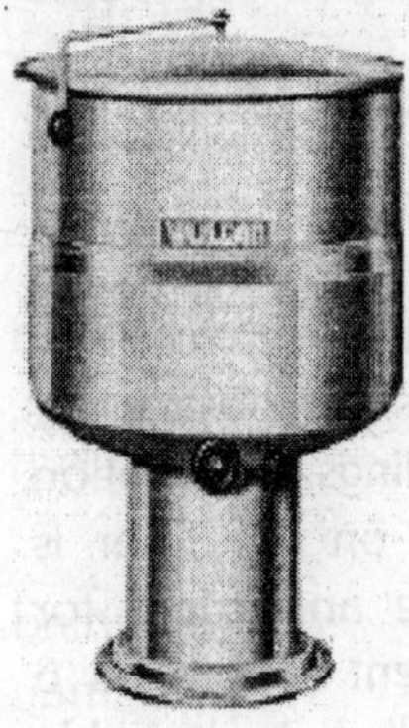

Cooking Kettle

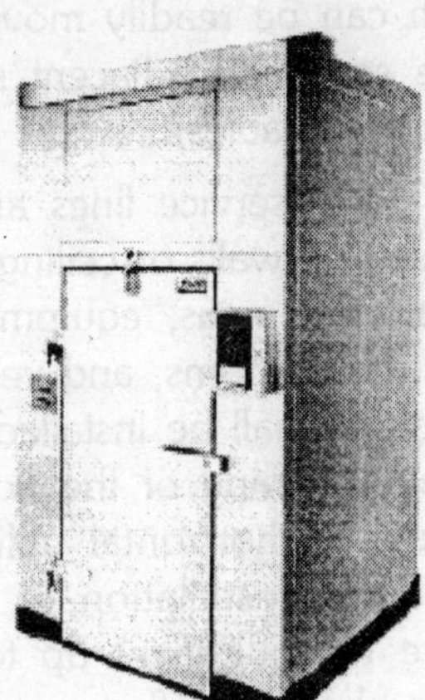

Bakers Oven

Figure 7

Free Standing Attachment

Utensil wash sinks, prep sinks or any sink that requires water to the unit can be either mounted to the wall or off the wall.

The equipment can also installed free standing (not attached or bracketed off) if the equipment is installed with flexible water lines that allow for the unit to be pulled 6 to 12 inches away from the wall for cleaning. This method will allow for easier installation and will prevent the problem of having to replace the sealant on a wall attached unit approximately every year.Sink with flexible water lines and wasted indirectly to a floor sink

In cases where the space between the equipment and the wall is too large for use of a silicone sealant, metal or other approved flashing is necessary for an effective seal. Examples of equipment that frequently require metal flashing are walk-in coolers and freezers, retarders, proofers, and large ovens. Some installations may require a combination of flashing and silicone sealant.

Equipment mounted on legs and placed against walls and which can be readily moved for cleaning will not be required to be sealed to adjacent surfaces (i.e. work tables and some equipment tables).

Utility service lines and pipes shall not be unnecessarily exposed on walls or ceilings, in walk-in refrigeration units, food preparation areas, equipment washing areas, utensil washing areas, toilet rooms, and vestibules. Exposed utility service lines and pipes shall be installed in a way that does not obstruct or prevent cleaning of the floors, walls, and ceilings. Installation of exposed horizontal utility lines and pipes on the floor is prohibited. Installation of exposed utility line and pipes for service to equipment up to point of attachment should be 6 inches above the floor and 1 inch off the wall. It is desirable that switch boxes electrical control panels, wall mounted electrical cabinets, and etc. is installed out of the cooking or dishwashing areas.

All utility and service lines and openings through the floor must be sealed adequately. Exposed vertical and horizontal pipes and lines must be kept to a minimum. The installation of exposed horizontal utility lines and pipes on the floor is prohibited. Any insulation material used on utility pipes or lines in the food preparation or dishwashing area must be smooth non-absorbent and easy to clean.

Sneeze Guard Installation

1. *Sneeze Guards (food Shields):* Display of unpackaged foods shall be effectively shielded to intercept the direct line between the customer's mouth and the display of food, and shall be designed to minimize contamination by the customer.
2. Shields shall be mounted to intercept a direct line between the customer's mouth and the food display area at the customer -use- position. The vertical distance from the average customer's mouth to the floor shall be considered (1.4 m) 4 ft 6 in to (1.5 m) 5 ft. Special consideration must be given to the average customer's mouth height in educational facilities and other special installations.
3. Shields shall be fabricated of easy-to-clean and sanitary material.
4. Edges of glass or other hazardous material shall be trimmed with a smooth protective member or have a safety edge of parent material.
5. Where the ends of equipment are designed to allow for customer self service, or customer view food shields complying with these standards shall be installed.

Dishwashing Facilities

Hand dishwashing facilities should include an approved three-compartment sink. The sink shall be of sufficient size and depth to submerge, wash, rinse and sanitize all utensils. The sinks shall have splashback protection and drainboards that are an integral part and continuous with the sink. Minimum recommended dimensions are as follows:

Food Stand: 18" width x 21" length x 14" depth with 24" drainboards; facilities with only selfserve hot-dog may use 18" drainboards.

Restaurant: 18" width x 21" length x 14" depth with 36" drainboards, if single-service restaurant or restaurants utilizes multi-use utensils or has 50 or less seats, 24" drainboards are acceptable. Establishments with more than 50 seats should have pre-flush or pre-scrapping equipment should be provided.

If additional holding space for soiled utensils is required, this may be accomplished by storage carts. Adequate facilities shall be provided to air-dry utensils. This may be accomplished by approved drainboards, dishtables, portable or stationary air drying racks, or wall and/or overhead shelving units located in close proximity to the dishwashing area. Floor drains should be provided in areas where wet pots, utensils and equipment are air-drying on approved racks or dish tables away from the sink.

Mechanical Dishwashing

Full service facilities that utilize multi-use eating and drinking utensils and seat in excess of 100 people and facilities with 50 seats that utilize self service buffet units should provide mechanical dishwashing facilities. The capacity of the dishwashing machines shall be based on the peak number and type of dishes, utensils, flatware, etc. that must be washed each hour. The following formula offers the minimum acceptable method for determining the required rack capacity per hour; seating turnover is assumed to 1.5 times per meal and a minimum of 5 pieces of tableware are assumed for each place setting.

Formula for a 100 seat food service facility:

100(seats) x 1.5(seat turnovers per hour) = 150 x 5(utensils per place setting) = 750

750(utensils used per hour) / 20(utensils per rack) = (required # racks per hour)

OR

100 x 1.5 = 150 x 5=750 / 20 = 37

For this example a dishwashing machine rated by the manufacturer to wash a minimum of 37 racks per hour must be provided. Consult the manufacturers specification sheets for optimum capacity.

An adequate facility for preflushing or prescrapping shall be provided on the soiled dish side of the Dishwashing machine. The requirements for air-drying shall be the same as for hand dishwashing. Where lowtemperature dishmachines are used, additional drying space may be required.

Dishwashing facilities are recommended to be located such that dirty dishes from the dining area are not carried through food preparation, storage or display area. Dishwashing equipment should be located immediately inside the kitchen door when entering from the dining area. This location will reduce the possibility of contamination that can occur when dirty dishes are transported through the kitchen and food preparation areas.

Adequate facilities shall be provided to air-dry utensils prior to final storage. This may be accomplished by approved drainboards, dishtables, portable or stationary air drying racks, or wall and/or overhead shelving units located in close proximity to the dishwashing area. Floor drains should be provided in areas where wet pots, utensils and equipment are air-drying on approved racks or dish tables away from the sink. For air drying of utensils it not necessary to have large drainboards.

FINISH SCHEDULE: FLOORS, WALLS, CEILING

1. All floor coverings in food preparation, food storage, utensil-washing areas, walk-in refrigeration units, dressing rooms, locker rooms, toilet rooms shall be smooth, nonabsorbent, easily cleanable and durable. Anti-slip floor material should be used in traffic areas.
2. Any alternate materials not listed in the below chart must be submitted for evaluation.
3. Joints between floors and walls shall be coved or radiused with appropriate materials.

4. Properly installed floor drains should be provided in floors that are subject to water splash from sinks, basins or equipment. Floors shall be sloped to the drain.
5. Grouting shall be non-absorbent and impregnated with epoxy, silicone or polyurethane.
6. All walk-in refrigeration units should be installed according to the NSF guide "Special Consideration Regarding Installation of Walk-In Refrigerators and Storage Freezers" or equivalent.
7. Carpet is not recommended in the immediate area adjacent to the buffet units.
8. Sealed concrete and commercial grade vinyl composition tile may be used on floors. However, their applications are limited.

Walls

1. The walls, including non-supporting partitions, wall coverings and ceilings of walk-in refrigerating units, food preparation areas, equipment washing and utensil washing areas and toilet rooms shall be smooth, non-absorbent and easily cleanable. Light colors are recommended for walls and ceilings. Exposed studs, joists and rafters are not considered acceptable wall finishes.
2. All alternate materials not listed in the above chart must be submitted for evaluation.
3. Glazed surfaces include glazed block or brick or ceramic tile. Grouting must be nonabsorbent and impregnated with epoxy, silicone, polyurethane or an equivalent compound. Concrete block if used must be rendered non-porous and smooth by the application of an approved block filler followed by the application of an approved paint or other approved martial.

   All mortar joints should be tooled and finished to render them easily cleanable.

4. Plastic laminate panels may be used. Joint finishes shall be smooth and compatible with the wall finish.
5. FRP and plastic laminated panel is not recommended behind heat radiating equipment such as fryers, griddles, ranges etc.
6. Finished drywall is not recommended behind utensil wash equipment, can wash, mop sink areas or behind prep sinks.

Ceilings

Finishes should be light-colored, and must be smooth, non-absorbent and easily cleanable. Vinyl faced drop-in ceiling tile or drywall finished with epoxy paint are considered approved materials for installation in kitchen and food service areas.

Plumbings and Cross Connection Control

Once a potable water system (also referred to as "safe drinking water" or just "drinking water") has been contaminated by the inadvertent actions of the user or installer, the foreign or toxic material can be distributed throughout the facility's potable plumbing system and adjacent premises on the same supply. The contaminated water, if undetected and utilized, may subsequently cause illness or death. Therefore each business, institution, residence, or other user has the ultimate responsibility to protect its potable water from any actual or potential introduction of contaminants or pollutants. The entire piping network for a water system, from the point of origin to the point of use, is divided into two categories: Primary (containment) and Secondary (isolation) systems.

The primary system is composed of the water mains used by the water purveyor to deliver water to the various buildings (or service connections) on the system. The water purveyor is responsible for delivering safe drinking water to the point of delivery for the customer's or users water system (secondary system). To protect the system from foreign or toxic materials being introduced via the customer, a backflow prevention assembly or device is installed at the water service entrance for "containment" on the premises.

The secondary system is the plumbing network that distributes potable water from the down stream side of the water meter or service connection to the points of use throughout the facility and/or premises. Remember that few people are aware of what is occurring inside the building and/or premises (secondary system). The determination of cross-connections is, in part, the function of the inspector; however, it is the ultimate responsibility of the owner to comply with state and local plumbing codes specific for that jurisdiction. Safeguarding the system is met by "isolation," providing backflow protection at each actual or potential cross-connection on the premises.

Cross Connections

A cross-connection is an actual or potential link between the potable water supply and a source of contamination (sewage, chemicals, gas, etc.). This link can be envisioned as a conduit or hose permitting the transfer of foreign material into a safe drinking water system. A crossconnection can be any temporary or permanent direct connection (hard plumbed), bypass arrangement, jumper connection, removable section, swivel or change over device, etc. that could connect a potable system to a non-potable source. Ideally, it is best not to have any crossconnections, but in certain situations they may be unavoidable. When an installation requires a cross-connection (as a last resort or unavoidable situation i.e., boiler, injector units, chemical aspirators), it must be properly protected with an acceptable backflow prevention assembly or device to eliminate any potential for a reverse flow back into the potable supply. Unprotected cross-connection threatens the health and safety of individuals and food or beverage products utilizing water from that system. There are two types of cross-connections are there:

1. *Direct Connection*: Direct connections are a physical connection between a potable and non-potable system. An

example of this would be a water supply line connected directly to a boiler, sewage line, or other nonpotable auxiliary water source. A direct pathway exists between the two separate systems for contamination to be transferred into the potable system as shown in the diagrams below. A direct connection is subject to both back-siphonage and backpressure.

2. *Indirect Connection* : An indirect connection between a potable and nonpotable supply does not exist under "normal" conditions; however, under "unique" circumstances a pathway for contamination can occur. Usually the source of contamination may back-up, be blown across, siphoned, pushed or diverted into a potable water supply. An indirect connection is only subject to backsiphonage.

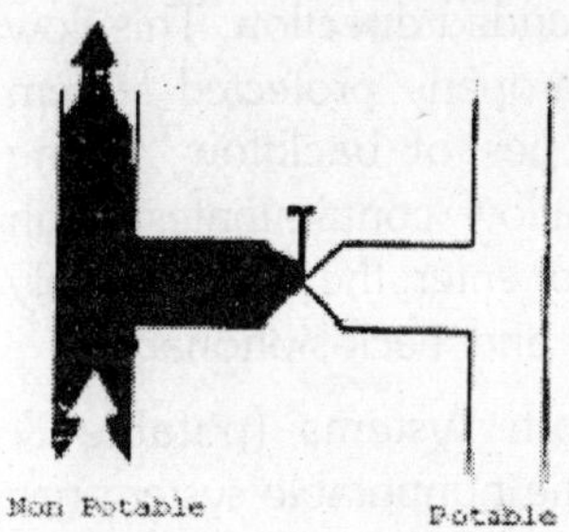

Valved connection between potable water and nonpotable fluid.

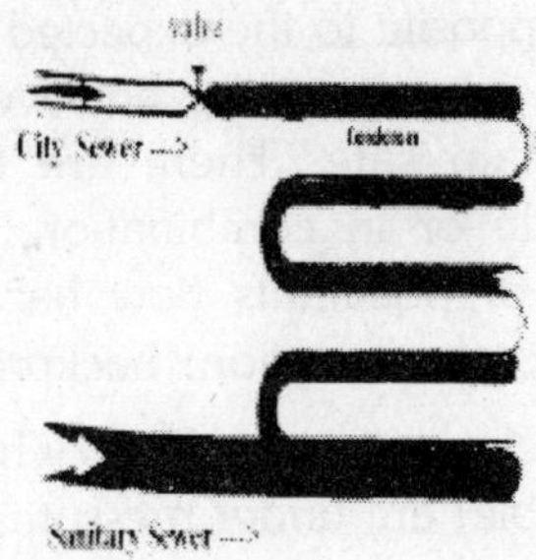

Valved connection between Potable water and sanitary sewer.

Example scenario, the end of a faucet terminates below the flood level of a sink, and the waste backs up or the sink becomes clogged to the point that the water inlet becomes submerged. If a vacuum or negative pressure should develop in the potable supply, the contaminant could be siphoned into the water supply.

Forces acting on Cross-connections

Some cross-connections are immediately obvious, but others can be subtle and difficult to find. Contamination or pollution occurs when the pressure differentials between the water supply and another system, via some connection, are sufficient to transfer the contaminant or pollutant into the potable supply. The temporary reversal of pressures or momentary vacuums in the water supplies can be freakish and unpredictable. These hydraulic forces can either PUSH (forced by higher pressure than the potable supply) or Pull (vacuum/siphon, the potable supply drops below normal levels) the contaminant into the drinking water system.

Backflow

Backflow is a reverse flow in the primary or secondary system that is opposite to the expected or intended direction. This flow reversal is undesirable; however, a properly protected system can remain safe. There are two types of backflow, acting separately or in combination, that allow contaminates (high hazard) or pollutants (low hazard) to enter the water supply via a cross connection: backpressure and back-siphonage.

Backpressure occurs when both systems (potable & nonpotable) are under pressure, but the nonpotable system has a greater pressure than the potable system. This pressure differential pushes the contaminant or pollutant into the potable supply. Pumps or thermal expansion from boilers connected to a supply are examples of how these pressure differentials can be created. Causes of backpressure are:

For backpressure to occur, a "direct connection" to another system must exist. This other system would actually or potentially be operated at a higher pressure than the potable supply, i.e., a fertilizer injector system, booster pump, boiler, fire sprinkler system or other auxiliary water source.

Back-siphonage occurs when the pressure in the water supply drops below zero (less than atmospheric pressure or negative head pressure), and the adjacent nonpotable source is drawn or siphoned into the potable supply. Causes of back-siphonage are:

1. Undersized sections of pipe can create an aspirator effect in the restricted area.
2. A break or repair in a supply line can create a vacuum or siphoning effect (as gravity drains the water out) on the elevated portions of the system above the effected area.
3. A high water withdrawal, such as fire fighting or water main flushing, can create a vacuum. This withdrawal is more likely to create stronger negative pressures at the higher elevations on the system.
4. A vacuum can be induced on the suction side of a booster pump, such as high-rise buildings and processing plants.

Evaluating Cross-connections

There are several different types of assemblies (units that can be tested after installation) and devices (can not be tested after installation) available for controlling cross-connections and preventing backflow. The type of assembly or device needed depends upon the type of cross connection, the intended purpose of the plumbing configuration, and what could backflow into the water supply under various scenarios.

1. Evaluate the plumbing supply, equipment attached to it, and any waste lines attached or near by. Think about what could do wrong with this design and what can be done to make it safe.
2. Determine the degree of hazard involved, either a high or low hazard will exist with a cross-connection. The degree of hazard depends on whether the nonpotable source is deleterious or not.

High Hazard situations exist when there is an actual or potential connection for any toxic or infectious substance, to be introduced into the water supply, and may create a danger to the health and well-being of anyone using the water. Examples of contaminants are pesticides, chemicals, and infectious microorganisms.

Low Hazard situations exist when there is an actual or potential connection for a nontoxic substance (also referred to as a pollutant) to be introduced to the water supply and create a nuisance, or be aesthetically objectionable to the water user. Examples of pollutants are turbidity, beverages, and food coloring.

3. Evaluate the use of the backflow prevention device relative to the TIME that supply pressure is present on both the "up stream" and a down stream side of the device.

Continuous pressure conditions exist when the water pressure remains on both sides of the device for more than 12 hours. Continuous water pressure can exist under dynamic conditions (the water is "on" and flowing in the intended direction through the device) or static conditions (the water is "on" but a shut off device down stream in the "off' or closed position results in no flow through the device).

Non-continuous Pressure conditions exist when the device is only subject to intermittent water pressure on both sides of the device that does not exceed 12 hours.

Physical Backflow Prevention Methods Air Gap

It is simple, economical, non-mechanical (no moving parts), fail safe, and can be used for potential backsiphonage or backpressure situations. An air gap is an unobstructed, vertical air space that separates a potable system from a nonpotable system. This air gap is necessary to prevent any contaminant or pollutant from being siphoned or pushed back into the potable water supply. Although this is an extremely effective backflow preventer, the interruption in the piping creates a subsequent pressure drop on the "down stream" portion. Consequently, most air gaps are used at the end of the supply line or faucet such as at a sink, vat or storage tank. The air gap installation and use:

1. The air gap must be the greater of the two—a minimum of one inch or twice the inside diameter of the supply pipe. This distance is measured from the supply pipe to the flood level rim (the point of over flow) of the receptacle or fixture.
2. Air gaps require inspection for any compromised "2xD or 1 inch" requirements and any splashing problems, but no testing is necessary.
3. An air gap can be installed in a continuous piping system to protect the source from any potential contaminant on the down stream side of the system. Providing an air gap within the supply system (versus at the end of the supply line) would require a reservoir and possibly a booster pump. An open reservoir can subject the water to air borne pollutants and the loss of free chlorine in a treated supply. If a reservoir is utilized, then there needs to be a means to periodically drain and clean the tank.

The barometric loop is an extension of the supply line that can be construed as a giant upside down "U". This configuration is designed based on the fluid dynamics of water and is utilized to protect all down stream inlets against "back-siphonage" only. An absolute vacuum on a pipe can only "pull" the water up 33.9 feet; to go any higher, a pump would be necessary to push the water up the column. The barometric loop must be at least 35 feet tall and the base must be at a higher elevation than any of the inlets or fixtures that are on the down stream side of the loop. The size of the 35-foot high loop limits its practicality for application (processing plant) for protecting against negative pressure.

Barometric Installation and use

1. The loop must be at least 35 feet upright and all plumping inlets or fixtures must be no higher than the loop's base.
2. Approved for continuous pressure and no potential backpressure.

Mechanical Backflow Assemblies and Devices

The type of mechanical assembly or device selected must be appropriate for the degree of hazard and specific application relevant to the potential backflow possibilities. Mechanical backflow preventers consist of single or multiple check valves that open from the flow pressure of the potable water. These valves are fabricated to seat tightly on a machined surface and when closed, prevent any flow in the wrong direction. Also, some devices have air inlets or ports that are vented to the atmosphere to relieve any vacuum or negative pressure developed in the system. All backflow devices must be installed so they are accessible for inspection, service and repair.

Grease Interceptors

Oil and grease entering a facility's drainage waste system will eventually solidify somewhere'- down stream and eventually clog the sewer line and/or cause potential problems for the onsite or public sewage system. The oil and grease from foods and cooking liquefy at high water temperatures primarily originating from the three compartment sink, warewashing machine or some pieces of equipment such as an oriental wok cooker. Oil and grease can occur in a combination of four forms:

1. Dissolved oil is oil that has dissolved in the water via a degreasing compound and will not separate from the water.
2. Chemically emulsified oil is oil that has been broken down into very small particles via a detergent and will not float to the surface.
3. Free oil, which is the majority of the oil produced in a food service facility, is not dissolved or chemically emulsified but is in a liquid form that is available to float to the water surface-when it is -allowed to-coalesce.
4. Mechanically emulsified oil is free oil that has been agitated in water to form small droplets. These droplets will congeal, as free oil does, provided enough time is allowed for the process. A grease interceptor (or grease trap) is a chamber

designed for wastewater to pass through and allow any free or mechanically emulsified oil to float to the top for retention as the remainder of the effluent passes through.

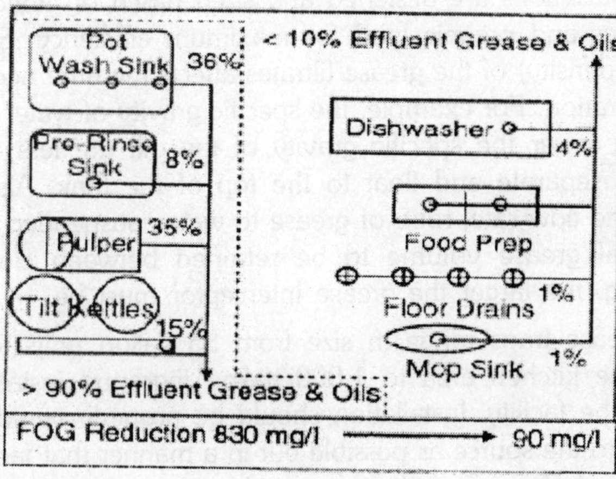

Figure 8. Typical Institutional Kictchen

For the oil to float to the top, it is necessary to calm the water as turbulence only perplexes the separation. To assist in the ponding or calming process, the waste water enters through an inlet baffle and may pass through additional baffles before exiting through the outlet baffle. Flow rate (volume of water per unit of time, i.e. 7 gallons per minute [GPM]) affects time and turbulence in the interceptor. Too fast a flow rate does not allow the "time" necessary for separation and creates turbulence.

Thus, many of these installations are equipped with a flow control valve prior to the inlet baffle. Only the facility's grease laden waste should be plumbed to the grease trap, otherwise suspended solids would fill the unit and a larger tank would be needed for the higher volume of waste water. Also, some installations are designed with a solids strainer prior to the interceptor, to prevent solids from interfering with grease separation.

Sizing the Interceptor

Trap installations are designed and sized based on anticipated flow rates and organic load for maximum efficiency. Specific gravity (density) of the grease filtrates affects the time necessary for separation. For example, the specific gravity of water is 1.0, thus the lower the specific gravity of the oil, the less time it takes to separate and float to the top of the tank. Also, the higher the flow rate, ratio of grease to water, suspended solids, and total grease volume to be retained between cleaning/emptying, the larger the grease interceptor must be.

Grease traps range in size from 35 gallon units located inside the kitchen area to 1,000 gallon inground installations outside the facility. Installation should be properly vented and as close to the source as possible but in a manner that facilitates the ease of cleaning and service without creating a nuisance.

Automatic Grease/Oil Removal Units Used In Conjunction Or In Place Of Standard Vault Type Grease Interceptor.

Trend Analysis: Good News - Bad News

The good news is that there are record numbers of restaurants in the U.S.A. The bad news is that these restaurants are discharging record amounts of grease and foodstuffs into sewage collection systems. The salient factors affecting a restaurant, hospital kitchen, school cafeteria, casino or other food processing facility are:

a. Ware-washing equipment.

b. Production equipment

c. Menu

d. Management/operating practices

Although there are a wide span of restaurants and food handling facilities, they tend to fall into four distinct categories: 1) Past-

Food, 2) Full-Service Restaurants, 3) Institutional Kitchens and 4) Special Sites. The choice of automatic grease removal system relates to these four categories. In all cases, ware-washing and production equipment is taken into consideration as you design to reduce FOG (fats, oils and grease) and BOD (Bio-chemical oxygen demand - the amount of digestible foodstuffs) present in the effluent.

Fast-Food Restaurants

Fast-food restaurants have the simplest production equipment. In a fast-food kitchen nearly 93% of all fats, oils, greases and other foodstuffs pass into the three compartment pot washing sink.

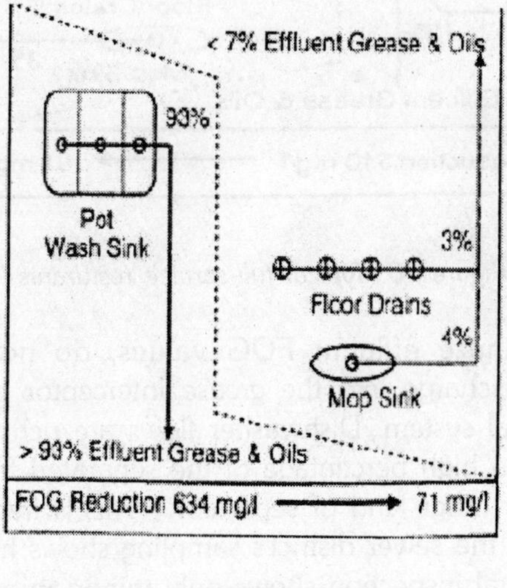

Figure. 9. Typical Fast food Grease Source of Fixture

Tips: The more fryer-type cooking appliances, the high levels of effluent grease and oils. An one automatic grease/oil removal unit point source system in a fast food restaurant servicing a three compartment sink typically removes 6 to 9 lbs. (2.7 - 4.1 kg) of grease per day.

Full Service Restaurants

Full service restaurants offering table service with washed, nearly 90% of all fats, oils, greases and other foodstuffs pass into the three compartment sink (75%) and the pre-rinse sink at dishwashing (15%).

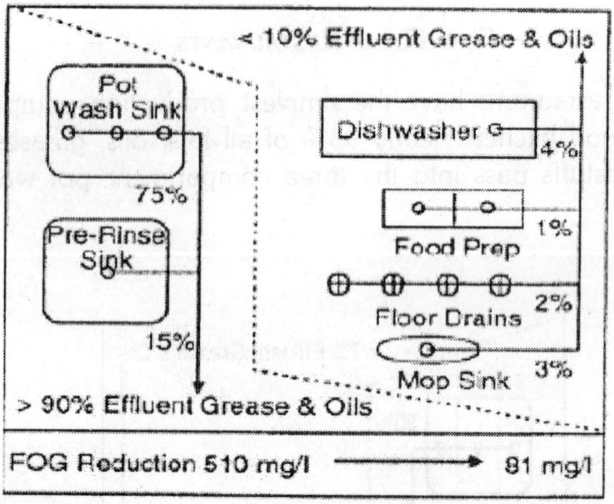

Figure 10. Typical full-service resturants

Tip: To minimize effluent FOG values, do not route the dishwasher discharge into the grease interceptor or automatic grease removal system. Dishwasher flows are rich in detergent and emulsify a high percentage of the separated fats held in a grease trap or other kind of separator. This is frequently seen at sites where the sewer district's sampling shows high levels of FOG, but visual inspection shows only minor amounts of free-floating fats and oils in the grease trap.

Institutional and Large Commercial Kitchens

These large, multi-purpose kitchens utilize a wide range of warewashing and food preparation equipment. The increased number of grease bearing point sources generally mandates use of central-type automatic grease removal systems. One large automatic grease/oil removal unit system servicing a 300 bed hospital kitchen typically removes a barrel of grease every 10 to 14 days.

Tips. Rarely seen in full service kitchens, tilt kettles which are used to cook large volumes of cooked meats, soups, sauces and other foods are installed in more than 70% of institutional kitchens. Tilt kettles can put large volumes of greases and foodstuffs into the drainage system. Large institutional kitchens such as prisons, hospitals, and college cafeterias also frequently incorporate potato peelers, pulpers, bakery sinks, wet hoods and other equipment that can discharge high volumes of greases and other foodstuffs into the drainage system. When specifying central removal systems for institutional kitchens, determine the maximum drainage flow value and provide at least 100 pounds (45 kg) of grease removal capacity per day.

Special Food Preparation Sites

Casinos, military mess halls, large correctional institutions and food processing plants often have a negative effect on a sewer system. For example, casinos serve high volumes of food 24 hours per day. The casino is often in a location such as a waterfront, which requires the sewage to be pumped through one or more lift stations. This leads to high sewer maintenance costs and high effluent FOG numbers. Automatic grease removal systems are steadily gaining favor with casino operators because of their round the clock operation. More than 40% of all U.S. casinos are equipped with automatic grease removal systems ranging from the smallest one automatic grease/oil removal units to the largest systems.

INSECT AND RODENT CONTROL

Openings to the outside shall be effectively protected against the entrance of rodents and insects by the installation of tight fitting self-closing doors, closed windows, self-closing windows at drive-through, screening, controlled air currents at delivery doors, vestibules or other approved means. Screening for windows, doors, skylights, transoms, intake air ducts and other openings to the outside shall be tight fitting and free of breaks in the screening material. Screening material should not be less than sixteen mesh to the inch. Doors, door jams and openings between the floor and bottom of outer doors shall be adequately flashed with a rodent proof material to eliminate any openings. Openings within the establishment around pipes, or conduit shall be tightly sealed.

Openings on the outside of buildings shall be sealed with sheet metal, concrete or brick and mortar. Eliminate potential vermin harborage by sealing all cracks and crevices. Cracks and crevices in excess of 1/32" shall be sealed with an approved caulking compound to provide a smooth and sanitary installation. Caulk used in a food zone area shall be FDA or NSF approved for use. Horizontal spaces, which will be rendered inaccessible after construction or equipment installation (such as wall cavities and areas underneath walk-in coolers or cabinets), should be treated with an approved material to prevent the possibility of roach infestation. Loading docks and delivery doors should be provided with effective air curtains, vestibules, or with self-closing doors to preclude the entrance of insects. It is recommended that outside lighting around loading areas and entrances to be sodium vapor rather than mercury vapor to decrease insect attraction.

LIGHTING

Permanently fixed artificial light sources shall be installed to provided in all areas in which food is prepared, or in which utensils are washed, shall be provided with at least 50 foot-candles of light on food preparation work levels and at utensil washing work levels. At least 10 foot-candles of light at 30 inches above the floor shall be provided in all other areas, including storage rooms and walk-in units. This shall not include dining and lounge areas except during cleaning operations. Fixtures shall be kept clean and in good repair. Light bulbs in food preparation, storage, and display areas shall be shatter-proof or shielded so as to preclude the possibility of broken bulbs or lamps falling into food. Shatter-proof or shielded bulbs need not be used in food storage areas where the integrity of the unopened packages will not be affected by broken glass falling onto them and the packages, prior to being opened, are capable of being cleaned. Heat lamps shall be protected against breakage by a shield surrounding and extending beyond the bulb, leaving only the face of the bulb exposed.

VENTILATION

All rooms of a permitted retail food establishment should be adequately ventilated and kept reasonably free of grease, excessive heat, steam, condensation, vapors, smoke, and fumes. Mechanically introduced make-up air shall be provided as necessary. Ventilation systems shall be designed and installed according to state building codes. The following information is provided to offer guidance in meeting the requirement for ventilating cooking equipment. There are several methods used in calculating the volume of air movement, measured in Cubic Feet per Minute (CFM), necessary to effectively and efficiently ventilate cooking equipment. While these methods are used in general applications, it must be noted that engineered exhaust systems which are customized for specific equipment under specific use conditions may also be approved by the building code official or fire marshall.

General Principles of Exhaust

The purpose of an exhaust hood is to provide a method of collecting, as nearly as possible, all of the grease produced from the cooking process, while furnishing a means of removing heat, smoke, and odors from the cooking area. For the hood to fulfill its purpose there must be a sufficient volume of air movement (capture velocity) to draw grease particles and cooking vapors directly from the cooking surface to the grease extractors. This air flow removes cooking odors and keeps grease particles from settling onto nearby surfaces.

An effective capture velocity shall be sufficient to overcome opposing air currents, capture the grease and cooking vapors, and transport them directly to the grease extractors. Grease extractors are ineffective in removing grease vapors. Only when grease vapors cool and condense can an extractor remove grease particles by directed air flow, contraction, and expansion (drop out). It is essential to have a sufficient volume of air flowing to cool and condense the grease vapors into grease particles prior to reaching the grease extractors. Non-toxic smoke bombs may be used to evaluate and regulate kitchen exhaust hoods and supply systems. No fabricator of exhaust hoods can create all the conditions in the plant that the hood must cope with on the job site to function correctly.

In the case of heat and steam producing equipment, the purpose of the hood or ventilation system (such as a pants-leg duct system) is to control humidity, heat, and unwanted condensation. A major cause of unacceptable hood performance is a lack of coordination between the Heating, Ventilation, and Air Conditioning (HVAC) system and the exhaust hood system. These systems should be coordinated prior to installation, and balanced when installation is completed, to ensure the proper performance of both.

Fire Protection

Exhaust ventilation systems for all grease producing cooking equipment is under the jurisdiction of the State Fire Marshal's Office and local fire and building officials. System designers and/or owners should contact these officials regarding fire safety plan review and inspection.

Hood Size

1. Canopy hoods and island hoods shall have a minimum depth of two feet and shall extend at least six inches beyond any equipment being ventilated, except that no overhang will be required on sides where aprons are installed. The dimensions of the hood are, in all cases,

larger than the cooking surface to be covered by the hood. The amount of overhang of the hood depends upon the clearance or distance between the base of the hood and the top of the cooking equipment. A rule of thumb for the overhang on canopy hoods is 0.4 of the distance from the cooking surface to the bottom of the hood, but in any case, no less than six inches.

Example

1. Hood overhang = distance from bottom of hood to top of range = 0.4 x 3.25 ft. = 1.30 ft., or approximately 1 foot, 4 inches Canopy hoods shall be installed so that the bottom of the hood is between 6.5 feet and 7 feet above the finished floor.
2. Ventilator, or "backshelf", hoods are designed to mount to the wall directly behind the cooking equipment. This type of hood is often used where ceiling height is a factor. It is normally placed closer to the cooking surfaces than a canopy hood, and works well in light to medium duty cooking applications. The ventilator hood is not recommended for charbroilers or similar high heat and grease producing cooking equipment. It does not have the capture area of a canopy hood and is not able to effectively handle large surges of cooking emissions (steam, heat, vapors, etc.)

Several dimensions are essential in the proper installation of a ventilator hood. Ventilator hoods shall extend from the wall a minimum of 16 inches, and shall be installed so that the distance from the top of the cooking equipment to the bottom of the ventilator hood is no more than 24 inches. Equipment placed under a ventilator hood shall not extend beyond the sides of the hood or more than 36 inches from the back of the hood. These restrictions are necessary to ensure maximum capture and removal of cooking emissions.

3. Pants-leg exhaust systems are designed to remove the heat or steam close to the point of discharge from warewashers

or conveyor cooking equipment. These systems must be sized to effectively ventilate the equipment served.

4. Eyebrow hoods are designed to immediately remove heat from an oven at the point of emission or as the door is opened. These hoods must effectively ventilate the door openings of the equipment served.

Exhausted Air

The amount of air exhausted through a hood exhaust system is dependent upon the size of the hood, its particular installation, and its use. There are several methods available for determining the amount of air to be exhausted. With the exception of systems engineered for specific equipment and specific applications that are approved by the health authority, the following criteria shall be used to calculate the amount of air exhausted:

1. Canopy hoods.

Standard square foot method

This method of calculating exhaust air volume is based on the size of the opening in the hood (length x width) and the capture velocity relative to the installation of the hood (see Table I). Hood length x hood width = square feet (ft.^{2}) of hood opening.

Ft.^{2} of hood opening x factor from Table I = CFM of air exhausted.

Table I.

Exposed sides	*Factor(CFM/ft.^{2})*
4 (central island hood)	125
3 (wall hung hood)	100
2 (corner hung hood, or with aprons)	85
Steam or heat exhaust only	70

Exposed linear foot method

This method of calculating the exhaust air volume is based on the total exposed linear footage of the hood and the capture velocity relative to its application (see Table II). Exposed linear footage of hood x factor from Table II = CFM of air exhausted.

Table II

Application	*Factor (CFM/in. ft.)*
Light duty (no grease, light grease)	150 - 250
Medium duty (fryers and griddles)	250 - 350
Heavy duty (heavy grease, charbroiler)	@350+

Square feet of cooking surface method

This calculation of the volume of exhausted air depends on the size, temperature, and design of the cooking equipment and the minimal capture velocity required to keep smoke, vapors, and fumes under the hood. The amount of air to be removed is calculated by multiplying the surface area of the equipment (f t.^{2}) by the appropriate updraft velocity factor (see Table III); total air exhausted is the sum of exhaust air volumes of all the equipment added to the minimal capture velocity.

Ft.^{2} of cooking surface of each piece of equipment (length x width) x the updraft velocity factor from Table III = CFM of exhaust required for each piece of equipment.

Table III.

Application	*Updraft velocity factor*
Steam kettles, ranges, ovens, non-grease producing equipment	50 fpm
Fryers/griddles, grease Producing equipment	85 fpm
Charbroilers, high heat and grease producing equipment	150 fpm

DUCT LOCATION AND SIZE

Exhaust ducts should never be located at the sides of the hood. For hoods that are six feet or less in length, only one outlet should be provided. Long hoods should be provided with multiple outlets no closer than six feet apart and no further than 12 feet apart. For hoods equipped with multiple ducts, it is advisable to install a manual air volume damper on each outlet so that the system can be easily balanced.

A duct velocity of no less than 1500 fpm shall be provided to maintain suitable conditions in the duct work. In some cases, a greater duct velocity (i.e. 1800-2200 fpm) may be necessary for the system to function at its best. The cross-sectional area of the exhaust duct (in ft.^{2}) can be calculated by using the following formula:

$$\text{Duct area required (ft.}^2\text{)} = \text{Volume of air exhausted (CFM) - Duct velocity (fpm)}$$

Once removed, the grease is drained into a collection container in the hood or elsewhere. Extractors have generally replaced wire mesh filters where grease removal is of prime concern and compliance with National Fire Protection Association (NFPA) codes is required. Wire mesh filters may be used to exhaust pizza ovens, bread and pastry ovens, and other similar equipment where grease is not of prime concern. Both wire mesh and extractor type filters have an efficient operating velocity range of 200 to 500 fpm; the operating velocity of the filters shall not be less than 200 fpm.

There are two general types of grease filters: wire mesh and extractor filters. The extractor filter removes grease in the exhaust process by centrifugal motion or by impingement on a series of baffles. The manufacturer's optimum rating of the filter should be used in calculating the filter area required in the exhaust system. Standard size filters should be used to avoid additional cost and to allow ease of replacement. Any space in the filter bank not covered by filters/extractors shall be fitted with sheet metal blanks. If calculations indicate that a fraction of a filter is needed, add an additional filter. The filter area required for an exhaust system can be calculated by using the following formula:

Filter area needed (ft.^{2}) =
Volume of air exhausted (CFM) - operating velocity of the filters (fpm)

Calculating Static Pressure

To select the proper size fan, the volume of air to be moved and the total resistance to its movement must be known. There are a number of restrictions in an exhaust system which affect air flow. The resistance to air movement is measured in inches of water, and this friction loss is called static pressure (S.P.). The static pressure against which the exhaust fan must work is considered to be the sum of the following five items:

1. The resistance of the grease filters measured under heavy use. A value of .2 inches of water is ample for most filters.
2. The "entrance loss" of static pressure occurring where the exhaust duct attaches to the hood will be about .1 inch of water.
3. The resistance created by natural winds blowing on the exhaust duct opening is a matter of judgement; the average wind pressure is approximately .15 inches of water.
4. The energy, or accelerating pressure, required to accelerate the air to the duct velocity, usually about .20 inches of water.
5. The resistance of the exhaust ducting, which is determined by the total length of the straight duct plus the number and type of elbows.

Make-up Air

The term "make-up air" is used to identify the supply of outdoor air to a room or building to replace the air removed by an exhaust system. For a consistent and regulated flow, make-up air should be mechanically introduced by a fan, swamp cooler, etc. Mechanically introduced makeup air shall be supplied as part of the exhaust system when the amount of air to be exhausted exceeds 1500 CFM. Make-up air is critical to the design of a ventilation system. It is generally recognized that all systems exhausting more than 1500 CFM need mechanically introduced make-up air to ensure a balanced system. Mechanical engineers recommend that make-up air be supplied at 85 to 90 percent of the exhausted air.

Make-up air controls should be interlocked with exhaust controls to ensure that the units operate simultaneously. Replacement air shall be filtered and may also be tempered by a separate control. The air velocity through the make-up air system should be low enough to avoid the possibility of drafts. It is desirable to have the kitchen under a very slight negative pressure to prevent any filtration of cooking odors from the kitchen into the dining room.

Can and Mop Cleaning Facility

A curbed can wash/mop basin with a floor drain shall be provided. Cleaning facilities shall include combination faucet, hot and cold water and threaded nozzle with appropriate backflow prevention device.

— If located inside the building, it may have combined use for cleaning mops and disposal of mop water or similar waste. Minimum recommended size is 3' x 3'.

— If located outside of the building, an additional mop basin for cleaning mops and disposal of mop water or similar waste may be required inside the building. Minimum recommended size for can wash is 3'x 3', minimum recommended size for mop basin is 2'x 2'. If chemical storage and hose reels are used in this area the unit will need to be increased in size to accommodate these additions. Minimum recommended size for can wash with chemical storage and hose reel is 3'x 4'.

— If located outside of the building some local municipal authorities may require the facility to be protected from rain water intrusion.

— Separate cleaning facilities may be required for portable food service equipment for catering operations.

— When food service equipment which will not be cleaned in place and is to be removed from the establishment then facilities shall be provided for cleaning and shall be approved prior to use.

Garbage and Refuse Storage Facilities

— All sewage and other liquid waste shall be disposed of in a public sewer system or in the absence of a public sewer system, by an approved properly operating sanitary sewage system.

— Garbage shall be collected and stored in standard, watertight garbage cans or other approved containers or methods and provided with tight-fitting lid. Lids shall be kept in place, except for cans inside the kitchen which are being used frequently during normal operation. The contents of these cans shall be removed frequently and the cans shall be washed.

— Garbage and trash, including recycling items and all other refuse resulting from the establishments operation and other sources, shall be removed from the building and premises as maybe necessary and disposed of in an approved manner.

— Facilities shall be provided for the cleaning and storage of all garbage, recycling containers, grease storage containers and mops.

Dumpster Pads, Recycle Containers and Facilities

Cleaning facilities shall include a combination faucet, hot and cold or tempered water, threaded nozzle, and curbed impervious pad sloped to drain or other approved methods at the facility.

Where containerized systems (compactors) are used for garbage storage, facilities shall be provided for the cleaning of such systems.

Cardboard storage containers shall be stored on concrete pads or other impervious surfaces so as to prevent rodent harborage. Dumpsters shall have drainage holes plugged when not being cleaned. Water should be accessible to cleaning area and not over 50 feet away.

Surface water restricting valves shall be used where Municipal Sewage Departments or on site sewage disposal system requires restriction of surface water. The problem that has come up in many municipalities is that some will not allow for these drains to be installed for fear of rain water coming off the pad will overload the municipal sewage treatment system.

This can be avoided be installing a sump in the pad which has a double outlet. One outlet will allow for rain water to be discharged to the storm drain and the other outlet to drain directly into the sanitary sewer system with the use of a submersible trash pump.

The concept behind this is when the dumpster is being washed an individual can turn on the switch to the pump and pump this liquid directly into the sanitary sewer system. When the cleaning operation is finished the switch is turned off and any rainwater that enters the sump will drain directly out into the storm drain. By installing this type of system two concerns are addressed; one being that the waste is now properly disposed of, and the other is satisfying the concern of excessive rain water impacting the municipal sewage treatment system.

Dressing and Locker Rooms

Rooms or areas separate from food preparation, storage or service areas, and separate from utensil washing or storage areas should be provided if employees will routinely change clothes within the establishment. Lockers or other suitable storage facilities shall be located in dressing areas. If dressing rooms are not provided, separate facilities shall be provided for coats, sweaters and other personal belongings.

Food Safety Management

The era of the me-to restaurant that duplicate current styles is over. The successful restaurant is now more than ever the main event of the evening — the show and the whole patron experience must be memorable. In this environment you need every tool at your disposal to gain a competitive edge. Including distinctive décor — it's the marketing tool that immediately visually position's the restaurant in the market and tells customers who you are and what makes you different from the guy down the street.

In larger more cosmopolitan markets it may be possible to be more daring. For example, the Strip House in New York unabashedly displays pictures of strippers from the 1920s. It is daring in a fun way without being distasteful. Another spot is Felix in Hong Kong. At this international spot the patrons are on display making them as much a part of the décor as static elements. Its high ceilings give it a sense of grandeur while exterior and interior views work together to create its total look.

Such international cities draw from enormous markets and can push the extremes — after all you can eat out at a different restaurant every night in these towns and never have to go back to the same place as long as you live. In smaller markets, dining-out budgets are more modest and a greater percentage of the customer base may be drawn from the region or may be local regulars. The percentage of leisure travelers is likely to be higher and increase in the coming year or so. This observation is reinforced by recent Travel Industry Association of America (TIA) statistics.

According to TIA, in the wake of 9/11, business travel fell 9 percent while leisure travel was actually up 2 percent, but more leisure travelers arrived by car — attributable both to budget constraints and fear of flying. Those wishing to expand during the coming decade can no longer target the upscale, businessperson for whom dining out is less of a novelty, spends more and may be more focused on high quality, consistency and convenience. The leisure traveler, especially those who are less frequent restaurant patrons, crave a unique experience along with a friendly more approachable environment.To achieve individuality visit all the competition in your category and take detailed notes. A word of caution, while it is tempting to go upscale during a renovation, many successful restaurants risk pricing themselves out of the market or losing segments of their customer base, such as the lunch crowd.

Ten Steps for Profitable Food Service

While creativity and innovation are hallmarks of a truly outstanding culinary experience, it is a daily focus on the basics that makes a foodservice operation profitable. The following ten basic guidelines are taught in every restaurant or hospitality program; it is, however, the daily application of these principles that will make a difference on your bottom line.

1. Standardised and costed recipes

Every recipe for every menu item, both à la carte and catered, must be standardized and costed. This basic discipline ensures consistency of product and ongoing profitability. While the initial set up requires some effort on the part of the chef, it allows each item to be priced based upon its raw ingredient cost. Given the volatility of some ingredients, it is important to revisit recipe costing on a periodic basis. One way to simplify this process is to set up each recipe on a separate worksheet in an MS Excel® file. By linking each recipe ingredient to a master ingredient list, the chef can easily update the master list, hence all recipe costing, on a monthly basis.

2. Pricing-based on known cost structure

The standard method of pricing is to take the cost of each menu item and multiply it by an appropriate multiplier to cover the cost of labor, other expenses, and overhead. For instance a 2 ½ times multiplier should yield a 40% food cost; a 3 times multiplier yields a 33% food cost. This simple formula is all well and good, but if your revenues are below projections and/or your payroll cost or overhead are higher than expected, you may still lose money. Given the interplay of revenues, pricing, volume of business, and cost structure, these numbers must be tracked closely and reviewed frequently.

3. Portion control

Standardized recipes are costed based upon specific portion sizes. If untrained or poorly supervised employees routinely serve larger than costed portions, you can kiss your profitability goodbye. Costly meat and fish products should be weighed to ensure correct portion size. Ladles of specific sizes should be used to plate specific menu items. Pies, cakes, and other baked desserts should be cut and served using templates to ensure the correct number of portions are realized. Cooks and pantry workers must be trained to prepare and serve appropriate sized portions.

4. Labour control

Labor, both front-of-house and in the kitchen, is the single largest expense in a foodservice operation; it is also a continuing challenge to control. Electronic timekeeping systems make it easier for supervisors to verify employee hours, but regardless of system used, supervisors must monitor payroll hours daily. Close monitoring of employee hours will reduce overtime and milking the clock, while allowing daily comparison of payroll cost to revenues. Front- and back-of-house supervisors should also keep a daily log that notes revenues, meals served, payroll hours, and a subjective evaluation of the smoothness of service.

5. Benchmarking revenues and expenses

Benchmarking is the act of measuring and analyzing operating performance. In a food service operation there are many things to benchmark, such as meals served and average check per meal period by day of week; payroll hours by position by meal period or day; and beer, wine, liquor sold per meal period and day of week. When tracked over time, these statistics become the baseline to project and monitor future performance. Benchmarks also allow measurement of member reaction to foodservice initiatives such as new menus or pricing. Most importantly, benchmarking makes supervisors more knowledgeable about their operations. Such knowledge translates to improved operations and bottom lines.

6. Routine and consistent inventories

Inventories are critical to monitor stock levels, avoid shortages, control pilferage, and determine cost of goods sold. Inventories can also be time consuming and inconvenient for hard working chefs. Inventories sometimes get delegated to poorly trained subordinates who miss or miscount key items. Sloppy inventories contribute to erratic cost of goods sold. Poorly organized storerooms contribute to sloppy inventories. Keys to accurate inventories include well-organized storage areas, knowledgeable individuals conducting inventories, routine and timely inventories, and organized receiving documents, invoices, and credits slips. Delegating counts is acceptable if employees are trained. However, having the same employee conduct all inventories without spot-checking and oversight will invite problems.

7. Sugggestive selling training for employees

Service employees who are trained in the techniques of suggestive selling can improve your average check and bottom line. Whenever a new menu is put in place, all servers should be provided a "selling sheet" that gives key information about each entree. Such information should include cooking method, ingredients, time of preparation, and enticing descriptors to help sell each item. Just as standardized recipes are important in the kitchen for consistency of product, selling sheets provide the service staff with the knowledge and information they need to sell the product. In addition to entrees, special training should be given for the suggestive selling of appetizers, desserts, wines, and specialty alcoholic beverages. The time spent providing servers with the information and confidence to sell your food and beverages will yield consistently higher average checks.

8. Continual feedback to employees

Every month's budgeted food sales is made up of how many meals are sold and how much each guest spends on average for a meal. By breaking your projections down into meals and average check and posting your daily targets prominently in the pantry, you provide your servers with goals that connect their daily efforts to your profitability. By comparing month-to-date actual meal counts and average check to projected, you give your employees a day by day record of their progress. Most people are competitive by nature and this simple technique will become a powerful incentive to servers. The same technique can be applied to appetizers, desserts, and bottles of wine sold.

9. Forecasting and scheduling

By tracking key benchmark statistics and keeping a daily log of business levels and staffing, foodservice supervisors can develop a routine system of forecasting business levels. While some level of volatility can always be expected in guest patronage, the act of forecasting, when formally done and evaluated after the fact, will assist in maintaining service levels while controlling labor cost.

10. Guest feedback

While some guests are vocal with their opinions, many are not. Foodservice supervisors should make it easy for guests to provide feedback. Comment cards must be readily available, periodic surveys should be conducted, revenue benchmarks should be analyzed to measure guest responses to offerings and initiatives, and employees should be trained to routinely report comments made or overheard to supervisors.Every professional food and beverage manager is aware of these necessary elements to success. Unfortunately, in the ongoing rush of business they are often overlooked. At its root the problem is one of organization. By taking the time to establish systems to address each guideline, by training and delegating tasks, by making each guideline part of the daily routine, each of these steps can be easily integrated into your operation. While the initial exertion may be great, so also is the ongoing payback.

Listen to What Customers Aren't Saying

Some of you put customer comment cards on your tables and ask that guests fill them out and let you know how you're doing. Unless someone was given absolutely outstanding service or the food was just phenomenally prepared, your guests aren't going to take the time to tell you some of the things you really should know. They might tell you that the potatoes were cold or the salad was wilted, but do they ever mention how the server handled the situation? Probably not; the server is usually only mentioned as an extra in the bad scene. That is because servers sometimes act as if everything that goes wrong is the kitchen's fault. If we really think about it, they are the last pair of eyes to see the food before it reaches the table; they should have the final say in its appearance.

Servers are getting the kinds of tips they deserve for their lack of attention to guests and the details that go along with them. Your guests are giving what they think the service is worth. When they walk out your door they might tell you that the food was great, or maybe the food was a little less tasty than usual, but they will never tell you that the service was only ok or even bad. Understand that we live in a society where it isn't ok to be confrontational and tell someone that they aren't performing well.

What guests will do is tell you about the food because they never have to meet your kitchen staff. They know they may have to deal with the same server again. We don't feel like our comments are going to be heard and treated as a comment. We feel like we're going to be labeled a nasty customer and treated worse. Most customers are forgiving and will give you another chance and return. If, however, they receive the same lack of care in service, they will quietly go away.

When a server suggests wine or particular dishes and sides to go along with them, your guests don't perceive them as being pushy. On the contrary, when done in a professional manner and with some charm and class, they perceive it as great customer service! Guests may not be able to articulate these ideas to you. They just know that something is missing. Ask any businessperson who frequently dines with potential clients and he/she will tell you he/she knows the best places to take someone for smooth, seamless service. Your staff deserves to know that they could be earning more money. You could be earning more money because they earn more money.

The High Cost of Loss

Forks, spoons, knives, plates, ramekins, napkins, side plates and bowls, all of these things cost money. It's very painful to see them in the trash and know that you are the only one who feels that pain. How to stop the careless throwing away of those non-disposable items is not an easy task at all.

Tell your dishwasher that you are rewarding him/her for every utensil and dish that he/she recovers from the trash. He/she will receive a quarter for each and every item recovered. You should have a tally sheet for him/her to fill out at the end of every day. At the end of a shift, go through and make sure you have the right figures, etc. and pay him/her cash on the spot. Where does the money come from?

Tell your servers that at the end of every day they will each have to donate the money that is to be paid to the dishwasher! If there are five items found and you have four servers that day, they each donate $.31. One will have to donate $.32. This is not a lot of money. You may alter that amount accordingly. This is merely an example. Servers should not be terribly upset over this amount of money. If you have bussers, include them in this game. You understand that servers don't intentionally throw those items away; they get in a rush and don't take the time to make sure they are only throwing away paper and uneaten food. You must make them understand how much those items cost. If you are so inclined, make up a chart of some sort that outlines your costs, focusing on those items, of course. Doing this is just a way to make everyone aware and to better police themselves and others when bringing dishes and trash to the dish room. Remind them that this is a team atmosphere and this game is something you want to try to reduce the cost of the lost! You might also let them know that you will be better able to give raises and do more fun things for them if you can all reduce the cost of the lost.

6

Risk Management

Hotel Identity Theft

Did you hear the one about the guest who checked in to a luxury hotel room and found a guest folio print out for the previous guest in the waste paper basket in the guest room? Personal information was located on the guest folio and was in the hands of a stranger who had ample opportunity to steal the previous guest's identity. This happens all too often in large and small facilities.

Identity theft can occur in hotels and motels and should be taken very seriously. The Federal Trade Commission has stated that identity fraud is one of the fastest growing white-collar crimes nationwide and affects one in four Americans. In 2002, the FTC received 161,819 complaints about identity theft and it is estimated that it costs each victim more than $1,000 to correct the damage made to their accounts and their reputations. Identity thieves capture information about your guests and use it to commit fraud, steal money, and charge items to credit accounts and even create new accounts.

How can you protect your patrons and guests from being victims of identity theft? Here are some basic security rules for you to pass on to your managers and supervisors to decrease the likelihood that your patrons and guests will be the next victims of identity theft:

— Training is the most important rule. Hotel personnel should never announce out loud the guest's name and room number at the front desk during check-in or in the food and beverage outlets in the hotel or facility. If during the check-in process, you or any of your employees overhears a guestroom number being announced, immediately assign a different room for the guest. In addition, instruct your wait staff not to request a guest's room number out loud in restaurants. Have the guest write it on a piece of paper then destroy the paper. Never, ever say the room number out loud. Believe it or not, this is still happening at hotels and motels across America.

— Instruct your housekeeping staff to leave a kind note for the guest reminding them to never leave important papers containing personal information in plain view in your guestroom, the lobby, any of the food and beverage outlets or in any meeting room space. Remind them to put all personal information, such as airplane tickets, passports, etc. in the in-room safe located in the guestroom when absent from the room.

— Remind guests, and meeting planners so they can advise their attendees, to make sure all computers, including laptops and PDAs (which usually contain valuable and personal information) are secured in all meeting rooms or hand carried by the owner from the guestroom or meeting room space.

— Have your front office and accounting office procedures that address your efforts to safeguard guests' personal information in writing and available for your guests to see. Find out if there are any leaks or holes in your process. Who has access to guests' data and is it secured? Are the employees trained on maintaining the privacy of guests, and how so and how often? How secure are your fax machines? Does personal guest information lie around for anyone walking by to see? Hotels and motels need to focus on these issues and if you haven't, you need to do so immediately.

— Do not place calls directly to guestrooms without the caller knowing the name of the guest assigned to the guestroom for that day. Although your telephone operators want to be helpful to callers, they should never give out names or partial names of any guests to outside callers.

— Do not slip guestroom folios under the guestroom doors the evening prior to checkout. Mistakes by your night shift hotel staff can and do happen and valuable personal information may find it's way into another guestroom or worse yet, stranded in the middle of the hallway for all guests and employees to see.

— Check the credit card receipts printed from all outlets in your hotel, such as retail shops and restaurants. Some receipts still print the entire credit card numbers. Others only print the last four digits of the credit card number. Having the entire number printed on the receipt can be hazardous to your guests' financial health. This is usually a simple software programming issue and it will protect your guests if you promptly remedy this situation.

— Remind all meeting attendees to remove their convention badges outside the meeting venue as it provides immediate personal information to any stranger the attendee passes by. Also, remind meeting planners to be careful as to what information is stored on the back side of the convention badges because if it is lost or misplaced, the information displayed, albeit intended for the ease and convenience of the attendee (such as cell phone numbers of colleagues), can end up in the wrong hands.

— Inspect your wastepaper refuse system or trash dumpsters for your hotel or facility. It is in a secure area? Is it inaccessible to the general public? Does a fence or wall surround it? If thieves will go through your personal household trash receptacles to gain personal information, imagine what they could find if they gained access to the waste paper dumpster located at your hotel or motel. Some thieves have admitted that they go dumpster diving at accounting and law offices to gain proprietary information. What will they find if they dive into your dumpsters?

— Be aware of the potential for identity theft with your hotel if you engage shoptalk or shop call systems. This is when you contract with a third party provider to record live reservation calls for purposes of spot checking the reservation agents for compliance efforts and for training purposes. These audio recordings which include names, addresses and credit card information are now in the hands of someone, other than the hotel staff, that can abuse the process and use this information to steal personal information. Make sure you have written agreements with these companies, together with clear and precise language in the contracts prohibiting any type of use of the information contained on the tapes. The information on the tapes should be limited to hotel use only.

They just seem to be a sign of poor organizational skills and a lack of focus on orderliness and cleanliness by management. These unkept areas influence the employees' attitudes about their work quality and timeliness. Almost, everyone is aware that unkept employee restrooms are not only a sign of management's lack of concern for staff but they also set a poor example of the standard management expects from those same employees in cleaning guest areas.

Accounting offices usually are indicators of what is going on at a hotel. If you can't keep score you probably can't play the game. Its really three issues: gathering data on a timely basis from around the hotel (payroll, revenues, statistics and accounts payable), compiling it quickly and accurately in the form of financial statements followed by interpreting and acting on the information. If the data in a hotel is not gathered efficiently and compiled quickly and accurately it is another symptom of poor organization and lack of attention to detail. Without that information management cannot effect changes for the better in a timely manner.

Management, of course, must know what the data mean and what they can do to cause the relevant numbers to improve. Over half of the problem hotels we have assumed management of have had financial statements that do not conform in any way to the Uniform System of Accounts for Hotels and Motels. What is amazing is that most of the owners and managers involved were aware of the Uniform System but didn't think it was worthwhile to change to it because they had a better system. What they are really saying is that they think they have a better way of looking at their accounting data than over 80% of the other hoteliers in the world! It reminds me of the soldier in the Chinese army who was marching to a slightly different cadence and told his sergeant, "The entire army is out of step but me."

The condition of printed and other materials with which a guest comes in contact are usually in poor condition in problem hotels. If it is a full-service hotel, menus are one of the first things to get threadbare. Telephone books in the rooms and at the pay phone are another example of things no one pays attention to, and they don't cost anything. If you are not proud of every corner and detail of your hotel and you don't have an active plan to improve it, you may beheaded towards trouble. Make lists and delegate them. Maybe a good place to start is with organizing and cleaning the front desk area and working your way through the back-of-the-house areas your guests don't see.

Managers Should Focus on Pulling Weeds

Manager: One who handles, controls, or directs, especially: one who directs a business or other enterprise. Do you want to be a good manager? If so, you need to learn to pull the weeds first. History shows that if you become a good "weed whacker", you won't have to worry much about damage control. Years ago in this industry, when you were interviewing to be a manager or interviewing a manager, you wanted to know if they knew how to pull an employee out of the weeds. Does the prospective manager have the capability of seeing an employee getting into the weeds, and are they able to save that employee?

In management interviews, operators will often ask the candidate if they know how to read a P&L statement, if they understand average per-person guest checks and how to calculate food and beverage costs, if they mind long hours, working holidays and weekends, doing inventory, and so on. All of which is important to know, but if you can't pull the weeds, why go any further with the interview process? Many managers walk around clueless to the fact that their employees are buried, that they are so deep that they are never going to get out of it. Others just ignore it because they don't know how to be a weed whacker. Yes, they can do labor schedules, calculate pour counts and handle other intricacies of a management position, but if they can't pull the weeds when they're on the floor, they shouldn't be a manager.

In the Weeds: A situation considered undesirable, unattractive, or troublesome. Any of us who have ever waited tables, tended bar or simply work in this industry, know the feeling of being buried, or "in the weeds." It's the point where critical mass is reached, when two hands and 60 seconds per minute simply aren't enough. Maybe the hostess flat-seated your section, and you have tables of guests waiting for their drinks, their salads, or their checks.

When an employee finds themselves in the weeds, it's usually one or two insignificant things that put them there. Once there, without a good weed whacker, it's hard to get themselves out. By the time they do get caught up, the guest has paid the price and the operator has taken the loss. The onset of being in the weeds is usually instantaneous. At one moment the employee is fine, and then...BAM! They're buried. It can be something as small as having five customers at the bar and having a glass break in the well. The ice has to be burned, the well cleaned out and refilled with ice. When something like this happens, the five customers turn into 10 or 15.

The manager walks by and sees the bartender trying to burn the ice and simultaneously service the customers, but does nothing about it. "That guy better get it together," he thinks as he strolls by. Instead, the manager should be pulling the weeds.

"Managers should pull the weeds before employees get into them and then there will be less damage control to perform"

Damage control: An effort to minimize or curtail damage or loss. Damage control is essential, and no establishment can operate without it, but there should be more "weed whacking" than there should be damage control. You need to look at your operation and see how much damage control your managers are performing. This could be an indicator that your managers are not very good at working the floor. If this is the case complimenting them on the great damage control they've done is proper, but the correct action would be teaching and instructing them on how they get their hands dirty by pulling the weeds. The equation is simple: pulling more weeds = less damage control; less damage control = happier guest; happier guest = higher profits.

Allowing a situation to get to the point where damage control is needed is not hospitable. It defies the total purpose of the business that we're in. It's easy to understand when you look at it in its simplest form. This is not a difficult business. All you have to do is keep the customer happy. In order to do that, you have to do be hospitable to your guests and attentive to what your employees are (or aren't) doing.

Hospitality is defined as: the act, practice, or quality of receiving and entertaining strangers or guests in a friendly and generous way. Hospitality wins every time. It's that time-tested honored formula. Most employees won't warn you when they are on their way down, when they are about to be buried, or when they are in the weeds. They're too busy trying to catch up. Once they're in the weeds, there's nobody to blame but management. It's easier for a manager to do damage control and then reprimand the employee than it is for them to actually pull the weeds.

We live in ever-changing times, where consumers are increasingly aware, lawyers are ever more litigious and the media increasingly willing to expose any weakness in a hospitality organisation or tourist destination. A company or region in the midst of a crisis cannot completely control these factors, as events in Asia Pacific have demonstrated loud and clear over the past 12 months. However, sufficient preparation and effective management can take the edge off the above factors.

Companies and destinations are now realising that they not only have a moral obligation, but also may need to take a legal stance to be prepared to cope with incidents that involve their clients. Planning, though critical, is not the only component. Training, conducting drills, testing procedures and providing additional external resources are other important functions.

By doing the above, organisations can go a long way to emerging from such incidents with their reputations and/or corporate image intact. In essence, the following "components" are required in order to handle any crisis situation effectively:

- — Leadership (crisis coordination);
- — Adequate emergency response (ambulance/paramedics/ medical support);
- — Victim identification;
- — Media relations;
- — Family assistance;
- — Information dissemination;
- — Internal and external communications.

An effective emergency response and good family assistance will reduce the frustrations that many people experience when caught up in the aftermath of a major incident. Besides going a long way to ensuring effective crisis management, it is also a humane, caring and compassionate way to respond. When your crisis occurs, the hardest part of dealing with it can involve answering the public call for information - as personified by a TV correspondent or newspaper reporter who shows up on your doorstep or on your telephone line to get the story.

How well you respond depends on how well you are prepared. While the existence of some of the above components may be based on the assumption of the pre-existence of a structured and experienced emergency services (police, fire and ambulance), this would be an unrealistic expectation. in many situations. However, there are still some basic steps that governments/regions can look at in order to enhance their level of preparedness. This involves the triad of:

— Planning (developing written plans);

— Training (selecting and training the initial crisis responders); and

— Regular rehearsals (conducting "major incident" exercises).

Local governments—or, even better, regional organisation like ASEANTA and/or PATA—could take the lead in this, and enhance their image, by

— Creating awareness amongst the industry;

— Organising training sessions for all stakeholders; and

— Communicating their efforts to the consumer.

The key to success is intensive training, although indepth consultations towards establishing the exact needs of the participants is needed to tailor the final curricula to local, regional and inter-regional training activities. The focus of the training sessions must be on senior and intermediate levels of management, with the aim that, by the end of the course, all those attending will be knowledgeable about the following :

Stage 1 : Before the Crisis

— What constitutes a real crisis;

— Why crisis management is necessary;

— Assessing potential crisis issues;

— Crisis-management team responsibilities;

— Setting up the emergency communication system; and

— Major elements of crisis management planning.

Stage 2 : During and after the Crisis

— Structuring the media centre;

— Designating spokespersons;
— Preparing "message points";
— Interview techniques and guidelines;
— Controlling the story; and
— Starting the "back-to-normal" plans.

In almost every instance of successful response to a crisis, management and response activities consisting of sound operating execution, coupled with superior communications, predominate. Operational response is essential - it's the one that saves lives, property and other assets. The ability to communicate is no less important - it's the one that saves the business. The simple fact is: perception is reality, and public perception of your company's reaction to a crisis is as important as your operating response.

There are no clear boundaries with any crisis. There is rarely a single moment when one can say an incident or issue has transformed into a crisis. Crisis-management experts recommend adopting a low threshold when defining a crisis, erring on the side of caution and assuming that a small episode can escalate into a crisis at warp speed. The repercussions and impact of crises in tourism is manifested across a series of stakeholders. To avert mismanagement of crises and its consequences, organisations and destinations need to enhance their capacity to understand and respond to crisis crisis situations.

Trial By Media — Do's and Don'ts.

1. Don'Ttmake the media your primary means of communicating on pending or current litigation in progress. Journalists are not a reliable means of ensuring that your key audiences receive your messages, nor is it a reporter's job to make sure everything you think is important gets to the right people.
2. Do communicate directly with your important audiences, internally and externally, to ensure they have the

information you want them to have about matters being tried in the media.

3. Do consider the option of informing certain key audiences of the probability of media coverage on a legal matter before it appears in the press.
4. Do remember that employees are a critical audience—all employees are PR representatives for the organization whether you want them to be or not.
5. Do integrate legal and PR strategy, because you'll be educating the jury pool while also minimizing damage that could occur to your organization in the short-term, even if you win the legal case in the long-term.
6. Do explore the use of publicity about generic or related issues relevant to your particular case or client as a legitimate means of bringing attention to issues that might result in pre-trial settlements, or to develop similar examples to illustrate the issues in your case.
7. Don't say "no comment" if you haven't had a chance to review the case. Say "I'd very much like to comment on this as soon as I've read what's been filed." If appropriate, add: "I still don't have a copy of it myself, could you fax or email one over?"
8. DO tell journalists that you want to respect their deadlines, but would appreciate their respecting your need to have the information you need to make an intelligent response.
9. DON'T attack the media. Ever. Neither directly, nor in communication with other audiences, because it will get back to them. The media can hurt you more than you can hurt them. Most media outlets LOVE being sued or threatened, it sells more papers or air time.
10. DON'T judge the impact of media coverage by the sensationalism of headlines or length of news coverage. Ask your important audiences, internal and external, how THEY are reacting to the coverage — in some cases, you'll find they don't believe it!

11. Do consider becoming your own publisher, using the Internet to post your perspective on issues of public concern — IF the general public is, in fact, an important audience for you. Or even on a password-protected Web site for selected audiences that are important to you.
12. Don't assume that you know how to talk to reporters about negative news just because you're skilled at "good news" interviews — get media trained.
13. Do establish both internal and external rumor control systems to short-circuit rumors early on, before they do too much damage.

INTERNAL CRISIS COMMUNICATIONS

All businesses are vulnerable to crises. You can't serve any population without being subjected to situations involving lawsuits, accusations of impropriety, sudden changes in company ownership or management, and other volatile situations on which your audiences — and the media that serves them — often focus. The cheapest way to turn experience into future profits is to learn from others' mistakes. To ensure that your crisis will flourish and grow, you should:

1. *Play Ostrich*: Hope that no one learns about it. Cater to whoever is advising you to say nothing, do nothing. Assume you'll have time to react when and if necessary, with little or no preparation time. And while you're playing ostrich, with your head buried firmly in the sand, don't think about the part that's still hanging out.
2. *Only Start*: This is closely related to item 1, of course. Even if you have decided you won't play ostrich, you can still foster your developing crisis by deciding not to do any advance preparation. Before the situation becomes public, you still have some proactive options available. You could, for example, thrash out and even test some planned key messages, but that would probably mean that you will communicate promptly and credibly when the crisis breaks publicly, and you don't want to do that, do you? So, in

order to allow your crisis to gain a strong foothold in the public's mind, make sure you address all issues from a defensive posture — something much easier to do when you don't plan ahead. Shoot from the hip, and give off the cuff, unrehearsed remarks.

3. *Treat the Media Like the Enemy*: By all means, tell a reporter that you think he/she has done such a bad job of reporting on you that you'll never talk to him/her again. Or badmouth him/her in a public forum. Send nasty faxes. Then sit back and have a good time while:

   — The reporter gets angry and directs that energy into Really going after your organization.

   — The reporter laughs at what he/she sees as validation that you're really up to no good in some way.

4. *Get Stuck in Reaction Mode Versus Getting Proactive*: A negative story suddenly breaks about your organization, quoting various sources. You respond with a statement. There's a follow-up story. You make another statement. Suddenly you have a public debate, a lose/lose situation. Good work! Instead of looking at methods that could turn the situation into one where you initiate activity that precipitates news coverage, putting you in the driver's seat and letting others react to what you say, you continue to look as if you're the guilty party defending yourself.

5. *Use Language Your Audience Doesn't Understand:* Jargon and arcane acronyms are but two of the ways you can be sure to confuse your audiences, a surefire way to make most crises worse.

6. *Assume That Truth Will Triumph over All*: You have the facts on your side, by golly, and you know the American public will eventually come around and realize that. Disregard the proven concept that perception is as damaging as reality — sometimes more so.

7 *Address Only Issues and Ignore Feelings*: The green goo which spilled on our property is absolutely harmless to

humans. The development plans are all in accordance with appropriate regulations. The lawsuit is totally without merit.

8. Make Only Written Statements: Face it, it's a lot easier to communicate via written statements only. No fear of looking or sounding foolish. Less chance of being misquoted. Sure, it's impersonal and some people think it means you're hiding and afraid, but you know they're wrong and that's what's important.

TEN STEPS OF CRISIS COMMUNICATION

All companies which provide goods or services to seniors are, routinely, faced with minimizing the impact of such crisis scenarios on their ongoing marketing programs. However, not all companies, unfortunately, are aware of the difference between marketing in routine versus crisis situations, namely:

— Marketing's routine function is to build the value of the business.

— Marketing's crisis communications function is to preserve the value of the business.

Preparation vs. Reaction

What are your chances of having to deal with such situations? Well, the bottom line is that there is no such thing as a business in which crises don't occur. Perception is as damaging as reality. If any of your external or internal audiences think or might think that there's a problem, then your communications program needs to address their concerns.

This leaves you with two choices: prepare for crises or just react to crises. The longer it takes to react effectively, the greater the potential for damage. This is increasingly true in our world of instant communication; a world where bad news is the favorite menu item of sensation-hungry media audiences. In fact, the most dangerous thing you can do is nothing, to go into paralysis. If anything, marketing and public relations becomes more important during a crisis. Very few crises are total surprises. Usually, key executives are privy to information which suggests the possibility or probability of crisis and this is the absolute latest point at which contingency planning should start.

Following are the ten steps of crisis communications:

1. Identify Your Crisis Communications Team

A small team of senior executives should be identified to serve as your company's crisis communications team. Ideally, the team will be led by the company CEO, with the firm's top public relations executive and legal counsel as his or her chief advisers. If your in-house PR executive does not have sufficient crisis communications expertise, he or she may choose to retain an agency or independent consultant with that specialty. Other team members should be the heads of major company divisions, to include finance, personnel and operations.

Often, during a crisis, a natural conflict arises between the recommendations of the company's legal counsel on the one hand, and those of the public relations counsel on the other. While it may be legally prudent not to say anything, this kind of reaction can land the company in public relations "hot water," which is, potentially, as damaging or even more damaging than any financial or legal ramification. Fortunately, more and more legal advisors are becoming aware of this fact and are working in close cooperation with public relations counsel. The importance of this understanding cannot be underestimated.

2. Identify Spokespersons

Within each team, there should be individuals who are the only ones authorized to speak for the company in times of crisis. The CEO should be one of those spokespersons, but not necessarily the primary spokesperson. The fact is that some chief executives are brilliant business people but not very effective in-person communicators.

This doesn't matter for written communications and may not matter for some audiences (see discussion of audiences below). Often, however, image communicates as strongly as facts, as politicians know well. Hence, communications skills are one of the primary criteria in choosing a spokesperson.

3. Spokesperson Training

Two typical quotes from well-intentioned company executives summarize the reason why your spokespersons should receive professional training in how to speak to the media:

— "I talked to that nice reporter for over an hour and he didn't report the most important news about my company."

— "I've done a lot of public speaking. I won't have any trouble talking to the press."

— Regarding the first example, there are a good number of Mike Wallace's "60 Minutes" victims who thought they knew how to talk to the press. In the second case, most executives being interviewed have not learned how to help ensure that "the most important news" gets across to the interviewer.

Also, analysts, institutional investors, individual stockholders and other key investment community audiences are just as capable of misunderstanding or misinterpreting information about your firm as the media and it's your responsibility to minimize the chance of that happening.

4. Establish Communications Protocols

Initial crisis-related news can be received at any level of a company. A janitor may be the first to know there is a problem, or someone in personnel, or notification could be in the form of a midnight phone call from an out-of-town executive. Who should be notified, and where do you reach them? An emergency communications "tree" should be established and distributed to all company employees, telling them precisely what to do and who to call if there appears to be a potential for or an actual crisis. In addition to appropriate supervisors, at least one member of the crisis communications team, plus an alternate member, should include their office and home phone numbers on the emergency contact list.

Some companies prefer not to use the term "crisis," thinking that this may cause panic. Frankly, using "potentially embarrassing situations" or similar phrases doesn't fool anyone. Particularly if you prepare in advance, your employees will learn that "crisis" doesn't even necessarily mean "bad news," but simply "very important to our company, act quickly."

5. Identify and Know Your Audiences

Who are the audiences that matter to your firm? Most firms care about the media, customers and prospects. Private investors may be involved. Publicly held companies have to comply with Securities and Exchange Commission and stock exchange information requirements. You may answer to local, state or federal regulatory agencies. For each audience, you need to have in advance complete mailing, fax an phone number lists to accommodate rapid communication in time of crisis. And you need to know what type of information each audience is seeking.

6. Anticipate Crises

If you're being proactive and preparing for crises, gather your crisis communications team for long brainstorming sessions on all the potential crises which can occur at your organization. There are two immediate benefits to this exercise: You may realize that some of the situations are preventable by simply modifying existing methods of operation; and you can begin to think about possible responses, about best case/worst case scenarios, etc. Better now than when under the pressure of an actual crisis. In some cases, of course, you know that a crisis will occur because you're planning to create it e.g., to lay off employees, or to make a major acquisition. Then, you can proceed with steps 7-10 below, even before the crisis occurs.

7. Assess the Crisis Situation

Reacting without adequate information is a classic "shoot first and ask questions afterwards" situation you could be the primary victim. But if you've done all of the above first, it's a simple matter of having the crisis communications team on the receiving end of information coming in from your communications "tree," ensuring that the right type of information is being provided so that you can proceed in determining your reaction.

Assessing the crisis situation is, therefore, the first crisis communications step you can't take in advance. But if you haven't prepared in advance, your reaction will be delayed by the time it takes your in-house staff or quickly-hired consultants to run through steps 1 to 6. Furthermore, a hastily created crisis communications strategy and team are never as efficient as those planned and rehearsed in advance.

8. Identify Key Messages

You already know what type of information, categorically, your audiences are looking for. Now, what do you want them to know about this crisis situation? Keep it simple have no more than three main messages for all audiences and, perhaps, a few messages targeted at specialty audiences. In a hypothetical "death under suspicious circumstances" scenario, a retirement facility's key messages might include:

We deeply regret this tragic los of life, and we are cooperating fully with the police department and coroner's office to confirm the cause of death. This organization has a superb safety record and meets all regulatory requirements for health and safety. We will provide the media with updated information as soon as it is available.

9. Decide on Communications Methods

There are many different ways to communicate about a crisis situation, internally or externally. Employees, clients, prospects and investors can be briefed in person, or sent letters, newsletters or faxed messages. The media can receive press releases and explanatory letters, or attend one-on-one briefings and press conferences. Each of these options and the many others available have a different type of impact and must be evaluated by a professional who thoroughly understands the pros and cons of these various methodologies as applied to each company's needs.

10. Riding Out the Storm

No matter what the nature of a crisis...no matter whether it's good news or bad...no matter how carefully you've prepared and responded...some of your audiences are not going to react the way you want them to. This can be immensely frustrating. What do you do?:

— Take a deep breath

— Take an objective look at the reaction(s) in question. Is it your fault, or their unique interpretation?

— Decide if another communication to that audience is likely to change that impression for the better.

— Decide if another communication to that audience could make that impression worse.

— Decide if making that additional communication is worth the effort.

— It Can't Happen To Me"

The Price of Complacency

Complacency, a self-satisfaction accompanied by unawareness of actual dangers or deficiencies. When terrorists killed thousands of Americans on September 11, we have no doubt they knew that they were also causing massive "collateral damage" to American businesses and other organizations. Overseas, anti-American speakers have crowed over the complacency of rich, fat Americans who thought they were invulnerable to such inhuman acts. Few organizations would logically plan to respond to a massive terrorist attack. But all organizations can and should have crisis communications plans that allow them to deal with scenarios such as:

— Service interruptions

— Events which traumatize employees

— Deaths of key employees

The most directly affected businesses, such as the two hijacked airlines, followed all of the important tenets of crisis communications. They were prompt, expressed concern and compassion, provided honest and accurate information, and gave customers and victims means for two-way communications. A small number of adequately prepared online retailers and other service providers expressing their regret that they can't ship orders as usual and what they plan to do about that.

Respond to Crises Before They Arise

There's a death or serious injury due to questionable circumstances. An employee is accused of impropriety. Your company is acquired by or is acquiring another. A natural disaster occurs. There's an investigation of your facility by a regulatory or law enforcement agency. By the definition given above, all of these are crisis scenarios such as those routinely faced by most organizations. In any field, there is no such thing as a business in which crises do not occur. Unfortunately, not all organizations are aware of the difference between marketing in routine situations versus marketing in crisis situations, namely:

— Marketing's routine function is to build the value of the business.

— Marketing's crisis communications function is to preserve the value of the business.

— Often, organizations are prepared to respond to the operational components of a crisis (e.g., for a fire: call the fire department, evacuate the building, etc.). However, there are many audiences potentially affected by any crisis, and each of these will want to know the facts as soon as possible; members of each audience will start to worry and/ or react inappropriately in the absence of such facts.

Typical audiences include clients/patients/customers, the media, employees, investors, community leaders, and regulatory agencies. Each of them requires a specific type of communication (e.g. phone call, fax, mail), and has differing information needs. If an organization is prepared, in advance, to respond to those needs promptly, confusion and damage is minimized.

Some of these situations, lacking proper response, could have resulted in significant damage to the firm's credibility and profitability. Fortunately, and very atypically, the organization had recently commissioned a crisis communications plan which provided them with a system for coordinated, prompt, honest, informative and concerned response to crises. This plan consisted not only of a manual with scenarios and instructions, but also involved a comprehensive audit of the organization's vulnerabilities that resulted in numerous recommendations for operational/system changes which, unchanged, created a potential for crises.

For example, the audit and subsequent analysis (conducted over a six-week period) revealed a lack of standard procedure on how to route media calls and who should handle the calls. Yet, particularly during a crisis, all employees need to know to whom a reporter should be referred or else a number of "loose cannons" are likely to be quoted instead of trained, authorized spokespersons.

Additionally, there were no fixed policies on some controversial issues such as the interaction of HIV-positive employees with patients nor was there a standard procedure for responding to needle sticks by medical personnel. This lack of policy could have resulted in significant criticism or worse, and the recommendations made during the crisis planning process ensured that the crisis would not happen.

In some cases, the board of directors or administrative staff were aware of system weaknesses but hadn't thought of the marketing communications/bottom-line impact of failure to quickly correct the problems. Prevention, then, versus reaction, is the ultimate key to successful crisis communications.

Media Training

Reporters come to any interview with an agenda based on the editorial demands of their employer and their own desire for high-level visibility. The newsroom is a very competitive place and if an interview with you can help propel the story to the front page or the lead of the 6 o'clock news, it's difficult for most journalists to retain complete objectivity. Media training teaches you to let your agenda direct an interview in a manner which still gives a reporter what he or she is looking for — newsworthy information — while reducing the chances of inaccurate facts and quotes being used.

The media training process typically includes education on how to prepare for an interview, what the "rules of the game" are, how to make sure your key messages get across no matter what's being asked, and very specific, personalized instruction on how you can be a better interview subject. The latter is accomplished by videotaping, replaying and critiquing a series of mock interviews during the course of the training session — and then giving you the tape to take home and study again. Many people who thought they were great interview subjects pre-training have been shocked at the initial results when viewed on tape — but then pleased with the positive changes evinced as training points are integrated into subsequent interviews.

7

Waste Management

All businesses look for ways to cut costs. Management seeks opportunities to streamline processes, improve systems, and maximize profit. They may call it efficiency, quality, or the search for excellence, but they are all looking for new ways to improve product or services while maintaining or lowering costs. In analyzing operations and procedures, many innovative companies have turned toward reducing their waste as an additional cost cutting method. Waste prevention is a reduction in the amount and/or toxicity of materials entering the waste stream prior to recycling, treatment, or disposal. It is a strategy, which calls for business consumers to think first before purchasing any material or service.

Evaluating practices and products not only on price and quality but also on durability, reusability, recyclability, and content. It may mean changing the way things are done or how a product is packaged. Waste prevention is a resource management technique that can save industry money while helping the environment. Waste management is a growing trend throughout the world.

The most effective way to reduce your company's waste is to generate less in the first place. Why pay for throwing away cardboard that can probably be sold to a recycling company? This looks like a pretty simple decision - but there is more to this equation than meets the eye. The process of analyzing the inputs, outputs, and individual processes can often enhance overall efficiency and productivity. Hotels can adopt one or more of following strategies to reduce waste:

— Eco-Purchasing

— Recycling

— Composting

There will always be some waste that will have to be disposed of. Planning is the first step in implementing a successful hotel waste reduction plan. The ultimate goal is to have waste reduction activities absorbed into every facet of the facilities operation. Waste reduction should become an integral part of the corporate culture of your business. Through careful strategic planning, waste reduction procedures can become an accepted part of the work environment. Management support of the waste reduction process is vital to ensure guidelines are understood, followed through upon, and that staff is supported in their efforts. There is no reason to reinvent the wheel. The following checklist should be helpful in getting started.

— Inform the hotel's owners and corporate management. Let them know what you are trying to achieve and ask for their support.

— Appoint a waste reduction coordinator to provide a central point for leadership of this initiative.

— Establish an accounting system that reflects monthly waste management costs. Formulate a monthly report for tracking waste disposal and reduction information.

— Learn about your waste. Research your waste disposal costs, options, and alternatives. Contact your local municipality and find out what is available in your area. Ask your hauler if there are any questions about how charges are billed.

— Set up a waste reduction committee made up of staff members from each operational area. Ensure that they understand their responsibilities and hold them accountable for follow through.

— Perform a waste evaluation, examining purchasing and disposal cost records. Take the committee on a site visit, ask questions, gather information, and formulate recommendations.

— Working with the committee, set goals and objectives, based on a realistic time line. Map out action plans to reach these goals and objectives and assign responsible parties.

— Establish a budget for supplies, educational/promotional materials, and project labor.

— Find a hotel of similar age and size to partner with. Florida has several environmentally award winning hotels, many of which are listed in the resource section of this workbook, that are willing to mentor other properties.

— Monitor, measure and report progress. Celebrate successes! Conducting routine waste evaluations are a critical part of planning your program. These evaluations generally consist of four phases.

During the first phase, an audit team gathers information and then sits down with the manager for each functional area, going over the operation and asking questions. Next, the team actually visits the site, making observations, reviewing purchasing and disposal records while asking more questions. In the third phase the team analyzes the information they have collected and forms a series of recommendations. The final stage consists of implementation of the recommendations, monitoring, and reporting. Documentation is also important.

ECO-PURCHASING

The purchasing function is the starting point. In reviewing the inputs to each operational area of the hotel we have found that the purchasing department or function is one of the most vital but often overlooked areas. Just think about the following questions for a minute. Are you are purchasing food in packaging that is not recyclable? Is your landscaper using mulch or compost made from someone else's yard waste? Are you buying only new laser printer cartridges when rebuilt cartridges are available at about half the price? How about those wooden picnic benches that must be replaced every couple of years? Is the copy paper or toilet tissue you purchase made from recycled paper? Are you buying rags for your housekeeping or maintenance areas from an outside firm? Does your hotel maintain a warehouse or inventory of varied supplies? Once you get started looking, it easy to see how critical the purchasing function is to the success of your program.

In recent years packaging has become more and more convenient. Plastic wrap and bags, aluminum and steel foils, and many products come in boxes inside designer boxes. We should begin to look at packaging from the standpoint of what do we really need to get the job done. Request that all vendors supply you with the simplest and most recyclable packaging. For example, one hotel manager tells the story of his beer purchases. In the process of setting up a recycling program, this manager looked at the items that were recyclable. He found that his hotel generated a great deal of beer bottles.

The local recycling program did not offer collection for brown or green bottles, but did take aluminum cans. So this manager met with his food and beverage staff and they worked together to install the capability to handle draft beer in the high volume bars. For the remaining areas and the room servi-bars, the manager talked to the beer supplier about switching to aluminum cans. The cans arrived in twelve pack boxes that were laid inside cardboard flats. The manager asked the vendor to deliver the beer loose in flats, the vendor could not comply but he could offer beer in plastic six pack rings, in cardboard flats.

In another area of the hotel, housekeeping was shorthanded and the head housekeeper spent a week helping in Laundry and stocking the maid's carts. She realized that each week they went through several plastic barrels of detergent and buckets of other cleaning chemicals, which the maids used to clean the rooms. These buckets were being tripled rinsed and thrown away because the local recycling program only accepted plastic beverage bottles. So the head of housekeeping sat down with the vendor to discuss alternative packaging and to ensure that they were maximizing their use of concentrates. The vendor was able to arrange to have the empty containers returned to the factory to be refilled when new product was delivered to the hotel.

In addition, the same vendor was able to introduce the hotel to a new more concentrated laundry detergent, which actually saved the hotel money on each wash load. Not only was the head housekeeper reducing plastic waste by over 150 pounds per week by utilizing refillable detergent containers, but also she was able to reduce costs for the laundry operation! Most vendors are only too willing to brainstorm and help out. Many salespeople have new products they would love to show, but are concerned about taking up too much time during a sales call. Partnering with vendors helps them serve your business better. Remember that they want your business. It is time to start looking around for an alternative source, if a vendor can't or won't help you reduce your waste stream. The following checklist offers additional considerations:

— Look for quality, a local supplier, simplicity, energy efficiency and minimal packaging. ¨ Select vendors carefully, choose vendors that have demonstrated a commitment to the environment.

— Purchase and maintain durable equipment and supplies.

— Consider the life cycle cost of products, replace disposables with reusuables (serving ware, napkins, buckets, rags, etc.)

— Buy in bulk or in concentrated form whenever feasible (condiments, single serving containers, beverages, etc.)

— Substitute nontoxic cleaning products and try alternative methods for pest control. ¨ Manage and minimize inventory levels (Just in Time, First in - First Out). Purchase only items that you need in quantities that you can use.

— Consider if packaging is recyclable in your area/program? If not, talk to your vendor about changing to a different type of packaging.

— Minimize nonrecyclable packaging - chicken, fish, and vegetables are often packaged in waxed cardboard, ask your vendor to pack in reusable or recyclable containers or crates.

— Avoid fresh produce that is packaged or has stickers on it. Let vendors know that stickers are wasteful and time consuming to remove.

— Monitor operations and talk with your staff, ensure supplies and materials are used efficiently.

— Buy recycled products manufactured with postconsumer materials whenever possible (toilet paper, paper towels, writing and computer paper, office supplies, playground equipment, picnic/park benches).

— Buy and use re-refined oil.

— Purchase and promote organically grown foods.

Minimize the Use of Hazardous Materials

"Environmentally friendly" substitutes for standard cleaning solvents and other materials used by maintenance departments are available, which are free of the hazardous ingredients. The benefits of reducing toxicity are two-fold. Often, natural nontoxic cleaners are less expensive to use and there is reduced liability because your staff is not using products, which if improperly handled can cause severe injury and even death. Ask suppliers to direct you toward reformulated products. In addition, many municipal programs offer standardized information on alternatives to common hazardous materials.

Inventory control is another important way to minimize hazardous waste. Just-in-Time inventory methods can reduce the need to store chemicals and other products. Find vendors which are willing to ship product when you need it. Also make sure that all stored materials are date stamped when they arrive and that the older product is always used first. The concept of "Life Cycle Costing" is new to many of us, but it is really very simple. The idea is to look at the total costs associated with a product. Remember you pay for products twice, once when you purchase them and again when you dispose of them. There are many products that you should consider life cycle costing when making purchasing decisions. For example: disposable napkins, cups, and servingware; paper towels, individually packaged condiment or amenity items, batteries, and laser toner cartridges.

RECYCLING

Recycling is the process by which materials, otherwise destined for disposal, are collected and used as raw materials for new products. Recycling prevents potentially useful materials from being landfilled or combusted, thus saving energy and natural resources. The common symbol for recycling is three chasing arrows, as seen above. The arrows represent recovery, remanufacture, and reuse. There are the three stages in recycling which make the process complete. To be recycled, a material must go through all three of these steps. This symbol is used to indicate either that a product is recyclable, or that it has been manufactured with recovered materials.

Again, the three steps in recycling are:

— Collecting or recovering the recyclable components of the waste stream

— Processing and manufacturing them into reusable forms or products

— Purchasing and using the goods made with reprocessed materials

The concept of a complete cycle is important and is known as "completing the loop." In order to decide what materials to target for recycling, it is best to contact your local municipality and find out what recyclables are collected and/or processed in your area. Local recycling coordinators often have lists of recyclers in the area. Contact local recyclers and find out if they have collection services and what types of materials they will accept. If they do not offer collection service, then call local waste hauling companies and find out if they offer recycling collection services. Since most haulers base charges on operational costs, they often require a minimum quantity of materials. This may or may not create storage issues, especially for properties with small service areas. Consider these challenges in making decisions on how and what materials to collect.

Below are sample questions that may help you in deciding on a hauler:

— What materials do you collect?

— Do you supply containers? If so, which containers and is there a charge? Who is responsible for cleaning and maintaining bins? How are the bins marked?

— Is there a minimum volume or weight required for collection?

— Where do you process recovered materials? Can we visit your facility?

— What do you charge for collection? Are there surcharges or penalties for contaminated materials?Can we get a rebate for clean materials?

— Do you provide employee training, educational, or promotional materials? What does this include?

— How do you collect materials, source separated or commingled?

— Can you provide us with feedback on the weight, volume, and quality of the materials?

— May we have a list and contact your other recycling customers?

Your local city or county recycling coordinator may already have some of this information which can save a great deal of time and telephone calls. Some communities even have handouts or pre-printed booklets that cover starting up a business or commercial recycling program. Once you get some idea of what materials can be recycled and determine what the costs associated with collection will be, then you can start to look at how you will recycle. Haulers typically collect from one central point, such as a service area or loading dock.

It is important to design an effective system to get the materials from the point of generation to the location in which they will be collected by the hauler. There are a wide variety of systems and containers that have been designed for this purpose. Many programs have successfully centralized garbage cans into one large common container for an area and have turned the small deskside trash cans into recycling receptacles simply by placing stickers on them. This is a big step for some folks and if you decide to do this, then monitor the process closely to ensure that garbage is kept out of the recyclables.

Other hotels use specially marked desktop recycling boxes or deskside bins for collection of office paper. These are usually emptied by the employee into an intermediate container. The intermediate container is then collected by housekeeping or stewarding and emptied into the final collection container in the service area. For materials other than office paper, the process usually consists of only the intermediate and final containers. Signage and stickers are very important and must be easy to read and understand. Many hotels are using pictograms either with or without words to get their message out.

In today's workplace more than one language is commonly spoken. Take this into consideration when designing signage. There is also a division about where the experts think signage should be placed. One group says that the location of the container should be marked, at eye level on the wall above the bin. Others feel it is important to mark the container. Color coding containers to differentiate them from trash cans is another good idea.

Some programs even have a different color bin for each type of recyclable: blue for aluminum, gray for newspaper, yellow of bottles, etc. If you are on a shoestring budget, then you may want to use clean excess trash cans that are marked properly. However, using extra trash cans will require even more stringent monitoring and extra employee education to ensure that they are not used for trash. In considering what to recycle in your hotel program, consider the following list of commonly recycled materials:

— Cardboard
— Building materials
— Office
— Magazines
— Florescent bulbs
— Batteries
— Aluminum cans
— Scrap metal
— Food waste
— Glass jars
— Landscape waste
— Steel containers
— Appliances
— Wood
— Plastic Bottles
— Cooking Grease
— Carpet
— Magazines
— Furniture
— Paint
— Motor Oil
— Antifreeze
— Freon
— Plastic buckets
— Telephone books

Composting

Some hotels have begun composting the organic portion of their waste stream. Some use the compost in their landscaped areas. Other properties give the excess compost away free to their employees. One hotel utilizes the compost they produce in their Chef's herb garden where they raise many of the herbs used in the kitchen. If properly planned and maintained, a compost project can benefit a hotel in many ways.

There are many good guides for composting available, but one of the best places to start is your local Cooperative Extension Service. These knowledgeable folks can assist in setting up a program and help troubleshoot if problems arise. The number for the closest office is in the blue pages in the front of your local telephone book. Composting is a process, which begins whenever you place moist organic materials together. The organics naturally begin to decompose into smaller materials and eventually you have compost. Keeping the materials covered and routinely turning while adding additional moisture can accelerate this ongoing process.

The optimal size for a small compost pile is about three feet by four feet. You may choose to utilize one of the many commercial composting bins but a simple enclosure can be constructed by securing the ends of a twelve foot length of 2"x4"x36" chicken wire fencing and covering with a tarp or board. You can also use old trash cans with lids if you cut one-inch air holes spaced about four inches apart all around the can.

Place the container in a location that is well ventilated and then simply add landscape waste (some may have to be cut to fit), kitchen scraps (excluding meat products), discarded paper napkins or paper towels and mix. The kitchen scraps and paper should be buried in the pile to reduce the possibility of pest problems. The bin will need to be monitored moisture added, and turned about once a week. If there is a problem with odor, the material should be turned more often and dry material should be added to increase the airflow. Your compost is ready when the materials have been transformed into a crumbly looking humus material.

An indication that the process is complete is when the compost is cool to the touch. You may choose to refine the material by sifting it through a screen, but this is not required for use. If you lack the space or decide composting is not for you, then you should still ensure that your landscape materials are disposed of in a responsible manner. Find out what your landscaper does with their cuttings and if they are using compost products where they come from. If these materials are being taken to a local landfill, find out if they are processed or just buried. If these valuable materials are buried then ask the Cooperative Extension and look around for other organic disposal opportunities in your community.

OTHER WASTE REDUCTION STRATEGIES

Even after you've prevented, recycled, and composted there is more that you can do. The following is a checklist of items that should be considered.

- — Use double sided copies whenever possible. Ensure that all new copiers purchased or leased have this important duplexing capability.
- — Reduce fax and report coversheets to a minimal size.
- — Print draft correspondence and reports on paper that has already been printed on one side.
- — Cut up scrap paper and staple together for notepads.
- — Donate excess furniture, building and office supplies to charity.
- — Procure battery chargers and use rechargeable batteries.
- — Repair rather than buy and rent rather than purchase, items that are rarely used.
- — Purchase and use solar powered items
- — Participate in a materials exchange program with other businesses to trade, sell, and donate goods that are no longer needed.
- — Close the loop with laser printer cartridges; have spent cartridges remanufactured, and purchase only remanufactured cartridges for replacement.

— Make rags out of damaged towels and linens.

— Contact a local pallet vendor about repairing, reusing, or recycling excess wooden shipping pallets.

— Set up a program to collect and recycle scrap metal.

— Ask your local dry cleaner to take excess hangers.

— Ask your vendor to take back empty two and a half, five, and thirty-gallon plastic containers. If they are unable, clean them out and use them or give them to employees.

— Collect partial toilet paper rolls and use in staff restrooms or donate to homeless shelters.

— Collect partially used soap bars and check with local charities for programs which melt them down for reuse by the homeless.

— Rotate, circulate, or post memos, reports, and magazines rather than distributing individual copies.

— Utilize e-mail whenever possible for correspondence.

— Donate unwanted books and magazines to doctors' offices, libraries, and schools

— Reformat reports, especially draft copies, so that more words will fit on a page by reducing fonts and margins.

— Encourage employees to bring their own coffee cups to work, eliminate disposables for employees.

— Donate unused (raw or prepared) food to a local food bank for distribution to charity.

— If consistent with your image, replace individual shampoo and conditioner bottles with refillable dispensing units.

— Save unused portions of shampoos, conditioners, lotions, etc. and donated them to a local mission or shelter.

— Survey the use of amenities and remove items that are rarely used like shower caps and sewing kits. Offer these items upon request only.

— Save and reuse packing materials or donate them to local Mailbox or Pack & Save businesses.

— Reuse manila and interoffice envelopes.

— Offer newspapers, shower caps, and shoeshine/sewing kits to guests only upon request.

— Return laundered clothes to guests in reusable garment bags or baskets.

— Offer guests the opportunity to decline delivery of daily newspapers or better yet make them available only on request.

— Offer unneeded bibles and other books to local missions or prisons.

— Change lighting from incandescent to fluorescent. Fluorescent bulbs last much longer, meaning that you have fewer bulbs to dispose of and spend less time changing them. The initial outlay will quickly pay for itself in reduce energy costs.

For a waste reduction program to be successful, it is imperative for the upper management in your hotel to offer continuous support. The general manager and the executive team must demonstrate this support with their own participation. Token efforts and words will not be enough. Employees watch their leaders to see if they buy into the program with actions as well as words. If you are having problems getting this support, then you will need to do your homework carefully and be able to accurately project the benefits. Most general managers will support programs, which can demonstrate positive economic benefits and guest support.

WATER CONSERVATION STRATEGIES

Equipment Replacement

Considerable water conservation opportunities were identified through replacing or substantially upgrading older equipment. After utility incentives are factored in, most of these upgrades could be made with a simple payback of two years or less. The most significant equipment measures include:

— *Guest Room Toilets:* Replace older 3.5 gpf toilets with more modern 1.6 gpf models. In addition to excessive flush volumes, individual floor metering revealed significant water loss attributed to leaking flappers.

— *Guest Showers:* Replace older 3.5 gpm showerheads with models using 2.5 gpm or less. The Westin Hotel tested 1.75 gpm models on one floor with excellent results.

— *Faucet Flow Restrictors:* Replace existing 2.5 gpm & 3.0 gpm faucet aerators with 1.5 gpm or lower aerators. These lower flow aerators also result in less splashing and associated cleanup, with no discernable difference to the guest. Install 2.5 gpm in-line flow restrictors in kitchen prep sinks commonly used for thawing and rice washing.

— *Single Pass Water-Cooled Ice Machines:* Replace existing water-cooled ice machines or connect to an existing cooling water recirculation system.

— *Laundry:* Install ozone systems and/or rinse water recycle system to reduce laundry water and associated water heating and chemical use.

— *Dishwashers:* Replace inefficient dishwashers with water conserving models. This measure may only be cost effective for dishwashers which are already nearing the end of their expected life.

Behavioral Measures

In addition to equipment replacement, a number of measures were identified relating to maintenance and other behavioral changes. The most significant behavioral measures include:

— *Toilet leaks:* Significant sources of leakage were discovered related to deteriorated toilet · flappers. Implement a regular toilet flapper replacement schedule.

— *Steam Heat Exchangers:* Install sub-meters on cold water feed lines to all heat exchangers.

Regularly log readings and make repairs to heat exchangers as necessary. Other Sub-metering: Install sub-meters for other significant water consuming operations including dishwashers, pools and spas, laundry, irrigation, and kitchens. Log usage and perform maintenance as necessary to reduce waste.

— *Cooling towers:* Cooling towers were not being operated at optimum levels. Conductivity readings should be recorded at least weekly. Cooling tower controls should be upgraded as necessary and set to maintain cycles of concentration near 10. Cooling tower maintenance contracts should be amended to ensure the water treatment service provider maintains the target cycles of concentration.

— *Food and beverage:* Significant excess use was observed in kitchens where continuously running water, often for hours at a time, was used for thawing frozen food and washing rice. Educate kitchen staff regarding correct methods for thawing frozen food and rinsing rice. Frozen food may be thawed in a refrigeration unit and sushi rice should be agitated in a colander. Additionally, sub-metering of kitchen use and back charging costs to the kitchens could help raise awareness among kitchen managers of wasteful practices.

— *Housekeeping:* Publicize towel-linen programs. Educate custodial staff to reduce number of times toilet is flushed during room cleaning.

Benefits of Conservation

Since water is a shared resource between individuals, businesses, industry, farmers and wildlife, conservation assists in the development of sustainable communities, including a sound economic base from which to responsibly manage growth in the region.

Reliability: Water efficiency, the same concept as water conservation, extends water resources and provides a measure of reliability for water resources. The time of year in which water demand is highest happens to coincide with the region's dry period. Conservation measures will make less likely severe water restrictions.

— Postpone Rate Increases
— Decrease water costs by decreasing use
— Ensure habitats for animals and ecosystems are maintained
— Guests are paying attention to the manner in which the hotel uses water
— It is a fundamental platform of sustainable tourism
— Future generations depend on our intelligent use of water

Water Management Principles

Water management applies not only to the equipment and physical processes that use water, but also the human and corporate influences on water use. Water management can be categorized as:

1. Loss reduction (leak detection in faucets and pipes)
2. Equipment and process water reduction
3. Water reuse (closed loop systems)
4. Demand reduction (through programs and incentives)

Reduction in water demand and use correlates to savings in chemical use, energy, treatment costs (wastewater), cooling and boiler use, and pretreatment. Set forth specific goals that can be achieved within a discrete period of time. For instance, set department level reductions, expressed in gallons per day, gallons per minute and gallons per function (e.g.; cleaning, dishwashing, guest watering). Establish dates to achieve the goals and set priorities such that the easiest, referred to as "low hanging fruit," are accomplished first. Performance measures are the measures the hotel would establish to gauge whether its programs and conservation efforts are actually reducing net water use. Linking them with goals and priorities that are mutually developed can optimize their effectiveness.

General managers, regional managers and the Chief Executive Officer (CEO) of the parent corporation must make a demonstrable commitment to water conservation and sustainability to ensure a water management plan works over the life of the hotel. This commitment needs to be more than just a generalized notion but ideally should be in writing, with goals, incentives and enveloped in a more comprehensive sustainability plan or EMS.

Environmental Management Plan

Water conservation or efficiency is part of an overall environmental management plan for improving efficiency, reducing operating costs and natural resource impacts, thereby giving the hotel a central point around which to secure loyalty by both managers, staff and returning guests.

Collect all facility information, paying particular attention to meters, submeters, data logger results and review the hotel's facility operating schedules.

Conduct a Facility Survey: Conduct a walk-through of the hotel and:

- List all equipment and processes that use water
- Identify staff functions that use water
- Log consumption for each device and adjust flow rates for fixtures such as faucets to an average or typical flow rate
- Meter large equipment
- Record hours of operation for fixtures, processes and staff related functions (cleaning, thawing)
- From the project data in combination with your own, determine a daily facility consumption rate
- Note issues having an impact on water consumption such as leaks, policies, single-pass cooling flows, outdated equipment. Record these.

Water Management Options

Evaluate options: Options may include simple changes such as adopting a vigorous leak detection program, replacing toilet flappers, or changing the frequency in which guests are provided drinking water, or may be more involved, such as closing single pass systems and replacing equipment.

Perform economic analysis: You may consider extending your payback period for those management options that will yield longer term value, such as installing an ozone laundry system or replacing inefficient equipment that has a particularly high number of units, such as ice machines.

Estimate total cost of water: Calculate the water, wastewater and sewer charges, seasonal costs, heating and cooling, chemical and other treatment costs should be calculated using current prices. However, energy related expenses such as pumping and heating may need to be converted into unit costs.

Implementing the Plan

Develop a water management plan and schedule: Establish priorities for your water management options and develop a work schedule that accounts for budgeting, delays, and seasonal impacts on ability to carry out the action.

Communicating the plan: Ideally, a letter of support from both the corporate CEO and the property's General Manager, should be distributed to all managers and staff, including the company's Board of Directors. This letter could set forth the priority of water conservation as a cornerstone of the company's environmental policies. Both hotels in the pilot have already adopted a wide range of environmental options, including lighting retrofits, energy management, proposed ozone laundry, changes in providing guests unsolicited drinking water, food donation and recycling. Given this progress, it is not a substantial step to encapsulate this progress and fold it into a broader policy that highlights water conservation.

For instance, Fairmont Hotels developed its comprehensive environmental program by asking staff throughout the chain their opinions about the corporation adopting an environmental policy and programs. They overwhelmingly supported program adoption and have been instrumental in refining its policies and implementation over the last ten years.

— Post signs in the back of the house.

— Establish department "green teams" that can engage in friendly competition to reduce water and other natural resource use. Make sure managers are involved, set clearly defined goals and communicate with sales and marketing so they are both engaged and informed about progress.

— Goals should be specific, measurable and achievable.

— Provide incentives to inspire cooperation. These incentives may vary from person to person and could include compensation time, time off, flex time, cash bonuses, gifts, public recognition, or increased control over work.

— Communicate about your progress through staff newsletters, bulletin boards, through paycheck inserts, special events and staff meetings.

— The Grand Coaster. In its most recent issue, it highlighted the region's water and energy crisis, giving tips for reducing impacts.

— *Implement the water management plan:* Ensure that everyone knows what their role is with respect to the water management plan so responsibility is not shifted to other associates and managers. Everyone in the hotel must have some role in the plan's implementation and success.

— *Monitor the water management plan:* Once the plan has been initiated, monitor reduction in water use by:

(a) equipment;

(b) process;

(c) time of day;

(d) function and

(e) department.

Promotion of Sustainable Tourism

Water conservation measures adopted by lodgings, which include hotels, motels, B & Bs/country inns, bungalows and cottages, are often undertaken coincident with a more comprehensive environmental management program. Agenda 21 for sustainable tourism was born in the wake of the 1992 Rio Earth Summit, occasioned in part by the growing realization that tourism had profound, and incontrovertible, effects on natural resources and economic growth. Agenda 21 was designed and implemented by the World Travel & Tourism Council (WTTC), the World Travel Organization (WTO) and the Earth Council. Shortly after Agenda 21 became effective, Inter-Continental Hotels approached the Prince of Wales Business Leaders Forum in London to promote its recently adopted environmental initiative and urged the Forum to create a standing body to address environmental issues within the lodging industry.

It is now known as the International Hotels Environment Initiative and is supported by the largest hoteliers in the world, including Marriott Corporation, Hilton, Holiday Inn, Inter-Continental, ITT Sheraton, Starwood Lodging and American Express as its first corporate sponsor. IHEI fosters the development and practical implementation of sustainable tourism practices and enjoys a growing membership. Many of the domestic examples of environmental management or sustainable tourism practices, are the product of IHEI affiliation and/or the exploding market for ecotourism. The monikers "eco-tourism," "green tourism," "adventure tourism," "responsible tourism," "sustainable tourism" and "green travel" are frequently used interchangeably. Most of the early models of sustainable tourism development were spurred by desires for foreign exchange as well as to capitalize on the ecotourist market. In many of these developing countries, natural capital is the primary economic base upon which earnings are predicated.

Domestically, largely economic considerations and gentle pressure from federal and state authorities motivate hotel environmental management programs. EPA's Office of Wastewater Management developed Water Alliances for Voluntary Efficiency, or WAVE, to engage hoteliers in water conservation measures. The Department of Energy sponsors the Hospitality Industry Forum on Energy Conservation (HIFEC), administered by Battelle and aimed at introducing energy efficient and effective lighting, equipment and other measures to the lodging industry. It was responsible for financing one-third of the microfiltration system for water re-use by Red Lion Central Laundry in Portland, Oregon.

More recent developments include EPA' Sustainable Travel and Tourism Program, Resources for the Future's report on the environmental impacts of tourism, The Conference Board's development of Business Enterprises for Sustainable Travel, 5 and the Seattle/King County Convention and Visitor Bureau program on tourism and the environment. In several states, solid waste utilities have developed programs directed at lodgings for solid waste reduction and recycling.

Solid waste reduction taken in isolation is not enough to ensure successful programs. The more successful Asian, Canadian, Caribbean, and European models for sustainable tourism incorporate elements such as pollution prevention, supplier relationships, packaging reduction, energy efficiency, water conservation, materials use and reuse, composting and community relationships. These programs place the lodging in a pivotal role vis-a-vis the cultural and environmental milieu and give us a context through which to implement the hotel education demonstration project.

Placing Water Conservation in Context

Accordingly, hotel water conservation can be viewed as the first step towards introducing responsible tourism to the tourist, and incorporating the principles of ecotourism into all travel venues. "Tourist" is broadly defined as any person who is experiencing a new sensation, experience or destination outside of their physical home and routine. In Washington State, most hotel guests actually reside in the State and may therefore be more amenable to linking personal behavior and value-based purchasing with travel.

"Value-based purchasing," means the purchase of goods and services by individuals or groups, which reflects the personal value system, beliefs, and morals of the consumer. For those people unable or unwilling to invest publicly in companies, it is often the only means by which to direct personal destiny, speak through dollars and help to shape business behavior and outcomes. It is a very powerful tool that underscores the proliferation of socially responsible investing and green marketing. Water conservation ideally must be viewed within the larger context of urban green tourism, or responsible tourism, whereby both the guest and the lodging can play an active, positive role in improving the local environment and reducing tourism impacts.

Defining sustainable tourism and travel

Planning, development and activities, including purchased products, that will ensure future generations they can meet their own needs:

— Requires long term planning and defining a vision
— Involves every person in an organization
— Extends to every facet of the tourism industry, including hotels

Involving tourism and travel sectors in sustainability

The sector is represented everywhere: lodging, food, recreation, national parks, culture, natural areas, interpreters, retail, transportation, banking and insurance

— It is universally connected to the physical and cultural environment
— Growth patterns are creating pressure on sensitive areas
— Balanced planning ensures long term economic stability and healthy communities
— Growing public demand for accountable, responsible business practices
— Can promote best practices and loyal customer base

Drivers of sustainability

- Enhanced public perception
- Customer appeal in that they can reward those businesses providing environmentally preferable services
- Avoids regulatory pressure if adopted voluntarily
- Individual control over local use of resources
- Economic incentives: green is lean and clean
- Diversifies tourism experience by meeting demand for greater educational experiences
- Public pressure and growing market demand

Lack of interest in touring "devastated landscapes" and promoting competition and open markets. WTTC partners with a related organization known as Green Globe, the environmental management program for travel and tourism companies. It was developed in 1994 by WTTC and has the support of over 20 international industry associations, representing thousands of businesses worldwide, the WTO, the United Nations Environment Programme and the Earth Council. WTO, an intergovernmental organization, promotes tourism as a significant means towards peace and understanding, fostering international economic development and international trade. Its environmental section works to ensure that new tourism development is properly planned and managed to protect natural and cultural environments. The Earth Council is a non-profit developed to advance the implementation of the Earth Summit agreements. It enjoys support from international members drawn from business, politics, the sciences and non-governmental organizations.

Using behavioral change to create a conservation culture

Creating a conservation culture

Conservation behavior is a learned, shared norm that is developed with the guidance, direction and support of the corporate office and other associates. Although it is fair to say that some unspecified number of people are interested in water resources, that generalized sense does not necessarily translate into direct conservation behavior, particularly at work, unless directly supported and encouraged by the employer.

In addition, piecemeal approaches to conservation can be confusing and reactive, such as when businesses adopt projects and temporary pilots in the absence of an overarching policy, mission, goals and measurable targets. For this reason, an ideal approach is to develop a facility wide conservation and sustainable tourism policy within which water conservation goals are easy to understand, incentivized and supported by the corporate office. To facilitate a conservation culture, one must reach beyond traditional engineering approaches to natural resource issues and evaluate the underpinnings of behavioral change.

Traditional methods of environmental education, outreach and program activity predicate change based on providing information. The overwhelming body of behavioral science research suggests that information alone is rarely enough to change entrenched habits that have environmental impacts. The following basic guidelines should be used in developing water conservation projects:

1. Identify both internal and external barriers to change and remove or minimize them.
2. Give people and the organizations they work in the tools to change: what's the issue, who to call, what to do. It can be as simple as giving out phone numbers and the authority to make change in each department, for each person's position.
3. Information must come from a credible source the receiving audience will listen to. Based on staff meetings, this might be the chief engineer, their peers, or the hotel magazines and periodicals read for current trends. Despite the trend in antigovernmental sentiment, local government is still considered a good source because it is relatively impartial and objective.

4. Use champions from the same industry. For the hotel sector, hotels will be more interested in what other lodging companies are doing.
5. Tailor information specifically to the sector and use the types of persons characteristic of that industry in collateral development.
6. Provide immediate and regular feedback to support the desired behavior. Remote feedback is less effective.
7. The message should be frequent, positive and the action framed such that the receiving audience believes it is losing something, as opposed to gaining something, as the result of not taking certain action.
8. Use focus groups to ascertain whether "conservation" and "efficiency" impart the same meaning. Even though they are essentially the same, research findings suggest that the word "conservation" is viewed as having to sacrifice something of value, and therefore people are resistant to the notion.
9. Design methods and tools in such a manner that persons and the organizations they work in can "pay attention" to water efficiency and water demands in the context of their daily experience.
10. Gently permit people to recognize their own internal barriers to change and help create well-designed social pressures and social norms that favor water efficiency behavior, attitudes and practice.
11. Understand the audience's unique perspective and barriers to change.
12. Use existing social networks to diffuse information and use effective opinion leaders in the same organization and industry.

Communicate expansively

Water conservation goals cannot be achieved unless each and every associate and manager is aware of what these goals and objectives are. Consider the informal pathways by which associates and managers communicate-it may be word of mouth, lunchroom conversation, journals, meetings, or outside socializing.

1. Establish a written water conservation policy, goals and objectives
2. Distribute to all associates and managers
3. Convene a meeting that focuses specifically on water and energy issues
4. Ask associates for their opinions and whether they support the project
5. Establish green teams, and interdepartmental water wizard teams to help inspire, create, and enable associates to own the project and derive benefits directly when the goals are achieved
6. Ensure that associates, corporate offices and your guests understand what you are doing, why and what the results are
7. Communicate with investors and learn more about how the socially responsible investing community can affect your business and respond to what you are doing

The hotel's water conservation plan should be introduced in a formal roll-out or launch. Conduct a classic SWOT analysis; strengths, weaknesses, opportunities and threats.

Index

Alcohol-based products 36

Barometric Installation 229
Blood Borne Pathogens (BBP) 147
Businss Travel Programs 43

Chemical Hazard Communication Program 93
Chief Executive Officer (CEO) 293
Counter-mounted equipment 209
Cubic Feet per Minute (CFM) 237

Do Not Disturb (DND) 97
Dual bucket systems 39
Duct Location 242

Eco-Purchasing 279
Electrical cords 89
Entry-level housekeeping positions 87
Entry-level position 86
Environmental contamination 39
Environmental Protection Agency (EPA) 94
Equipment Replacement 290
Evacuation equipment 89
Executive housekeeper 39

Food Safety Management 247
Furniture, Fixture and Equipment (FFE) 136

Guest feedback 251
Guestroom items 41

Hand Washing 206
Hazardous materials 39
Heating, Ventilation, and Air Conditioning (HVAC) 238
House Cleaning Services 142
Houskeeping Operations 88

Installation Requirements 210

Locker Rooms 246
Lodging companies 41
Lodging industry 88

Management functions 87
Material Safety Data Sheets (MSDS) 94
Mechanical Backflow Assemblies 230
Metal cleaners, 36
Mop Cleaning Facility 244

Occupational Definitions 86
Occupational Safety and Health Administration (OSHA) 39, 93

Operational budget 87

Performace Skills 88
Performance Assessment Criteria 107, 152
Person Protective Equipment (PPE) 94, 109
Physical Backflow Prevention Methods 228
Piecemeal approaches 301
Portable Equipment 210
Potable water system 223
Preventative Maintenance (PM) 103
Preventative Maintenance Order (PMO) 149
Profitable Food Service 248

Quality of lodging establishments 41

Refrigeration Facilities 200
Reheating Facilities 203
Room block 39

Sneeze Guard Installation 219
Stock Housekeeping Cart 104
Sustainable Tourism 296

Wall Attachment 217
Waste prevention 277
Waste Reduction Strategies 288
Waste-baskets, 41
Water Conservation Strategies 290
Water-using operations 207
Women's hangers 41
World Travel & Tourism Council (WTTC) 297
World Travel Organization (WTO) 297
Written Preventative Maintenance (PM) 149